NATIONAL ASSOCIATION OF INDEPENDENT SCHOOLS

[THE Inclusive SCHOOL]

A Selection of Writing
on Diversity Issues
in Independent Schools

Edited by Michael Brosnan

ISBN: 1-893021-94-7
Printed in the United States of America.

National Association
of Independent Schools

1129 20th Street, NW, Suite 800
Washington, DC 20036-3425

The National Association of Independent Schools provides services to more than 1,700 schools and associations of schools in the United States and abroad, including 1,400 nonprofit, private K-12 schools in the U.S. that are self-determining in mission and program and are governed by independent boards. For more information, visit *www.nais.org*.

Editors: Sarah Hardesty-Bray, Nancy Raley
Designer: Fletcher Design, Inc./Washington, DC

Contents

If there is no struggle,
there is no progress.
— Frederick Douglass

Foreword

Roosevelt Thomas, well-known corporate diversity expert, posits that diversity efforts have gone from a focus on simple representation of people identified as underrepresented in the 1960s through the mid-1970s, to building relationships with the underrepresented from the mid-1970s through the mid-1980s, to full engagement and empowerment of the underrepresented from the mid-1980s to the present day. The same progression can arguably be applied to the continuum of diversity efforts — historical to present — in independent schools in the United States, as well as a number of independent schools in other countries, that have enacted mission-driven, strategic initiatives to build and sustain diverse, inclusive, and equitable communities.

This collection of articles — first appearing in *Independent School* beginning in 1999 and continuing through the first decade of the 21st century — represents a wide-ranging lens through which independent schools can view both the opportunities and complexities of what we often simply call "the work": diversity work. Just as with Thomas's view, some articles in this collection focus on representation, others on building relationships, and still others on full engagement and empowerment. What pulls these 30 articles together in such a compelling and significant way are the passion and expertise of both the authors and editor Michael Brosnan in sharing best practices and challenges to "the work."

As we enter the second decade of the 21st century, the concepts, opportunities, possibilities, and challenges of diversity work in independent schools are becoming more complex. Diversity professionals will need more support and authority, and all constituent groups in independent schools will need opportunities to become cross-culturally competent. This collection of articles from *Independent School* serves as an exemplar of what has been accomplished, but even more important, what still needs our attention as we continue to strive for the full engagement and empowerment of all in independent schools.

Gene Batiste, Vice President, NAIS
School Consultancy Services and Equity and Justice Initiatives

Over the past 15-plus years … I've observed a significant and impressive cultural shift in independent schools towards greater inclusivity on all levels.

Introduction

During the mid-2011 debate in Washington, DC, over the federal debt, the debt ceiling, and taxation (often referred to hyperbolically as the "debt crisis debate"), *The New York Times* ran an article on a study by the Pew Research Center on inequities in wealth, based on recent U.S. Census Bureau data. Here's the second paragraph in its entirety:

> The study, which used data collected by the Census Bureau, found that the median wealth of Hispanic households fell by 66 percent from 2005 to 2009. By contrast, the median wealth of whites fell by just 16 percent over the same period. African Americans saw their wealth drop by 53 percent. Asians also saw a big decline, with household wealth dropping 54 percent.

The title of the article tells it straight: "Recession Study Finds Hispanics Hit the Hardest." To make the point more striking, the *Times* notes that the average wealth of whites is 20 times that of African Americans and 18 times that of Latinos. So, for every $100 a white family has, on average, an African-American family has $5.

I mention the *Times* article, rather than highlight the Pew report directly, because I think the news coverage of the report on the Census Bureau data is as important as the report itself. The *Times* article attributes the losses in wealth to the recession — as if it's simply a matter of bad luck that Latinos, African Americans, and Asian Americans were hit harder than whites. The story lets us know that Latinos tend to live on the economic margins of this nation, in areas hardest hit by the recession, and have little savings. But it does not delve into the why of it all. It doesn't touch the topic of racial inequities — why there is such a disparity in wealth based on race. It doesn't ask any expert on race to speak to these inequities. While highlighting the Pew Research findings, the *Times* reporter makes no effort to dig deeper — as if believing it's not important for the story. Or perhaps an editor considered the topic too politically charged. In any event, the article asks and answers no hard questions about what is, to me, the underlying issue: persistently broad institutional inequity.

Indeed, the desire not to look carefully at racial inequities seems to be an unspoken agreement among the mainstream media and most politicians — and, thus, in the broader culture. And this silence has a troubling effect.

Racial inequities are unconscionably large in our nation, worse then they were a decade ago — the worst, in fact, that they have been in the 25 years the Census Bureau has been keeping such statistics. It *should* be impossible not to be outraged — or at least alarmed — by these clear and growing inequities in our democratic nation. However, there are, as yet, few public signs of deep concern — with the exception of the Occupy Wall Street movement, which, as of this writing, is a young, but growing movement without a clear focus beyond a deep frustration with broad financial inequities and the excessive political power of the wealthy.

A week or so after the *Times* story came out, I read another article in the *Washington Post* about the growing number of students getting arrested in public schools for what should be routine disciplinary matters. The article highlights the degree to which school officials would rather bounce discipline problems to the courts than deal with them directly. But it also underscored the level of racism in these efforts: "In Dallas, where 30 percent of students are African American, 62 percent of those ticketed [by police for school infractions] are black…. In the Houston area [lawyer Yvonne Q.] Taylor said, 'I rarely see a white face in the court room.'"

In arguing for more well-functioning, diverse public schools, a recent report by the National School Boards Association, "Achieving Educational Excellence for All: A Guide to Diversity-Related Strategies for School Districts," includes this fact: "More than 80 percent of segregated black and Latino schools are poverty-concentrated, while only 5 percent of segregated white schools are."

I don't think I'm highlighting anything new here. What these statistics and news stories underscore, however, is that those of us who want to reverse these trends, those who prefer a nation truly based on equity and justice, have to figure out a way to work harder — to push harder against the cultural forces that, left alone, seem to increase inequities.

And this is where educators come in.

Of course, diversity issues in society and in schools run deeper than race. I tend to focus on race simply because I think it is currently the most difficult area of "diversity work" to get right. While we seem to be able to talk openly — or at least more openly

— about gender, religion, sexual orientation, and learning differences, race is still a difficult conversation in our culture. So, it seems to me, it's worth doubling our efforts in this area. If we can get race right — if we can dream of the day, say, when there is no statistical difference between whites and other racial groups in median family wealth — we can make great cultural strides in all areas.

I am also aware, of course, of the growing income gap between the rich and poor in this nation. Socioeconomic divides are getting worse. According to the 2009 census, the United States has the largest income gap of any nation in the northern hemisphere — and the largest gap in our country's history. As novelist Erik Reece points out in his 2011 *Orion* article, "The Schools We Need," this income disparity is not just a problem in and of itself. It's at the heart of *all* of our societal problems. "As a result," he writes, "the U.S. has higher levels of mental illness, infant mortality, obesity, violence, incarceration, and substance abuse than any other country north of the equator."

What Reece argues for — in the field of education, at any rate — are schools that connect education to what he calls "individual self-invention," and that create a space "where that individual takes on the role of the social citizen." In my mind, the best way to do this in schools is, first, to acknowledge and face these truths so that our school communities look more like the communities we want for our children, and, second, to help students develop the "habits of mind," as Deborah Meier puts it, that will allow them to grow up to become engaged citizens who will manage this democracy better than our generation does. Focusing solely on test-prep, the next level of schooling, and job preparation is not good enough.

Over the past 15-plus years as editor of *Independent School*, I've observed a significant and impressive cultural shift in independent schools towards greater inclusivity on all levels. I've listened in to the conversation and have had the privilege of working with great writers and educators who want our schools to be moral institutions of the highest order, to be educational communities that understand that "academic excellence" — a hallmark of independent schools — requires a sophisticated understanding not only of subject matter but also of cultural issues. All across America, independent schools have pushed hard to deepen their knowledge and work for change, unflinchingly. As a result, there is greater diversity among students and teachers, more nuanced curricula, a push for greater social responsibility and community engagement, and a growing acceptance of the value of a multicultural education for all. Indeed, if schools are to prepare students well for the rest of this volatile and promising century — both as citizens and professionals in whatever field — they know they must strive constantly for greater inclusivity and equity all around.

But clearly more work must be done. Developing diverse, inclusive communities in schools requires constant attention, good will, and continuing dialogue — which is why we've decided to reprint key articles from *Independent School* that we believe have particular relevance to this work, articles that are worth revisiting, sharing widely, discussing, and acting upon. As Dwight Wilson, head of Friends School in Detroit (Michigan), writes, "What independent schools and our constituencies do with the thimble full of power entrusted to us has the possibility of changing generations, breaking cycles of lost opportunity, and redirecting the energy of a nation towards its democratic vision."

Think of this book — the voices of thoughtful independent school educators who have dedicated their working lives to the idea of a better education, better schools, better democracy — as part of our thimble.

The book is arranged, not chronologically, but from the general to the specific — starting with articles that look broadly at diversity in schools and moving toward specific areas of diversity. It is not intended to be comprehensive. Rather, the articles here focus on areas of diversity that, for whatever reason, have been most challenging to schools and, thus, command our attention.

A quality school in the 21st century, in order to educate the next generation of enlightened leaders and engaged citizens, requires a deep understanding of diversity issues in this nation and how schools can work against some of the larger cultural confusion about diversity in America. And it requires that educators figure out how to institutionalize this commitment. As Illana Kaufman, head of Windrush School (California), writes in her article on directing diversity, "As I see it, the systems that keep individuals and groups from experiencing schools in ways that are equitable are simply that, systems. With enough key people in place who can decode the systems and translate them for others, it is more likely that those who have been traditionally marginalized will be able to skillfully negotiate their way to the metaphoric table — to move gracefully and deliberately from margin to center."

Maybe then the Census Bureau will start reporting statistics that make us proud.

Michael Brosnan
Editor, *Independent School*
January 2012

Life is not about the individual.

Beyond Black and White

What the Eye of the Hurricane Revealed

::

BY DWIGHT L. WILSON

What independent schools and our constituencies do with the thimble full of power entrusted to us has the possibility of changing generations, breaking cycles of lost opportunity, and redirecting the energy of a nation towards its democratic vision. Either we will take ourselves seriously in this endeavor — understanding that we are not just about high academics, but also about educating citizens for intellectual and moral leadership — or our lives and our work will become a joke.

If you have any doubts that we still live in a highly divided nation, the impact of Hurricane Katrina should erase them. Yes, the hurricane itself was indiscriminant, hitting the wealthy and middle class as well as the poor without regard for status. But it is the poor who suffered the most, not having the means to easily evacuate New Orleans and other areas in the hurricane's path and living in neighborhoods most susceptible to damage.

People of color have been decrying the gap between the haves and have-nots for years, but it took scores of television scenes and newspaper photos to validate what has never been hidden. Class and socioeconomic distinctions are, literally speaking, deadly.

In a moment of facetiousness, novelist Toni Morrison said, "There is no world outside my door." If independent schools ever believed this, most understand today that they are called to be institutions of vision. We do not have the right to indulge in myopia. Because "we become what we see of ourselves," as novelist V.S. Naipaul put it, we are called to lead, not to join the educational herd. We are called to be countercultural in the desire to build a better culture.

In 1995, I addressed a Secondary School Admission Test Board assembly in Toronto. The topic was, "What Do Black Parents Really Want?" What I said, in brief, is that blacks want assurance that, in sending their children to independent schools, they will not spiritually lose them. They do not want their children to lose a sense of identity with those slaves who served 250 years in bondage. They do not want their children ashamed of or afraid to come back to either their present neighborhood or those of their grandparents. They do not want their children forgetting that blacks have not yet overcome. With the success of Condoleezza Rice, Kenny Chenault, Oprah Winfrey, Toni Morrison, Marian Wright Edelman, and Tiger Woods, how dare I suggest that we have not overcome? As long as significant numbers of blacks remain on the outside looking in, my personal comfort is more than misshapen. Life is not about the individual. It is about the "common-unity," and if America is ever to become AMERICA — an indivisible nation with liberty and justice for all — it will be about what Jamaican reggae singer Peter Tosh called, "Equal Rights and Justice." Currently, there is so much in our culture that indicates that, while we readily talk about equal rights and justice, we have not achieved them.

While saying this, I think it's also important to remember that — in the name of equal rights and justice — we need to do more than look at race and gender and sexual orientation and faith. We need to hold all these categories in our minds, but also look inside ourselves. When we search beyond black and white, we find a clearing where the sun shines on all. Marian Wright Edelman, founder and CEO of the Children's Defense Fund, says, "Race and gender are shadows…; character, self-discipline, determination, attitude, and service are the substance of life." I like to rephrase her comment this way: People of good character have the self-discipline to determine that the proper attitude serves all races, genders, religions, and sexual preferences. The attitude of which I speak does not extol tolerance — a misguided world view that places in the superior position one who pompously suffers the presence of another. Certainly tolerance is better than active persecution or even benign hatred, but those outside the mainstream prefer respect. Truth be told, those who walk the margins could even do with a little old fashioned L-O-V-E.

Beyond black and white, beyond diversity, is multicultural education. Diversity is the statistician's invention, concerning itself with numbers. But what matters lies far beyond numbers. When cultures come together, if the subordinate culture is expected to forfeit itself for the comfort of a dominant culture, the name for it is "assimilation": three times a four-letter word. If it costs a dominant culture nothing, it is not about love or even respect. The dominant culture receives what theologian Dietrich Bonhoeffer referred to as "cheap grace." It is cheap because there is little or no psychic expenditure. It is grace because people of color bring enriching gifts. These gifts may be in ways of learning or in music. They may be in style and language usage. They are certainly in perspective. One cannot be descended from those who have spent centuries on the bottom and get past the gatekeepers without understanding how to survive in more than one world.

When poet Maya Angelou said, "Living life as art requires a readiness to forgive," she was not merely speaking of Zulus and Xhosas emerging from South African apartheid, but also of the marginal in this country. "All misery," whispered novelist Isabel Allende, "has a common thread." That thread is unrequited hope. A refugee in the Sudan, one in Indonesia, and a third in the Superdome in New Orleans each recognizes common humanity. The long disenfranchised can forgive, embrace the ones who came to rescue, those who with foresight might have prevented tragedy. What about those of us of all colors who may have enjoyed privilege brought about through class or position if not race? Can we forgive those who have taught "white is right"? Can we open our doors to the spectrum? Can we disassociate ourselves from surfeit in the midst of drowning insufficiency?

People of color are ready to come out of the ghettos, barrios, reservations, and other bottoms. They are also ready to come from the suburbs, gated subdivisions, and exclusive residential districts. Independent schools have the power to make certain that this expansion does not stop with students and parents. We can hire and retain teachers and administrators, recommend trustees and committee members. To boast that we have 20 percent students of color while having 5 percent teachers of color and an even lower percentage of administrators and trustees of color is to admit that we have a long way to go. My sister Quaker, Elizabeth Fry, admitted in the 18th century, "I do not know the course I am to run, all is hid in mystery, but I try to do right in everything." "Do the right thing" is such a simple command, and yet if it becomes a commitment, we are assured of a better school.

Not quite certain of the course, we should be able to agree that inclusion is the American way and that trends seem to indicate that, by 2050, people of color will become the majority. Among school-age persons, people of color already are the majority in seven states and Washington, DC. Refusing to reach out will find us sewing the seeds of their schools' demise.

Please forget about being nervous because we do not understand every culture. Remember, instead, that sincere, welcoming, open-armed greeting. It can cover a multitude of shortcomings. If we are half as bright as we tell our public school colleagues we are, we can teach ourselves to smile as warmly at the stranger as at the friend, to be as nice to the new hire as to the millionaire prospective parent. "May I help you," should not be relegated to the trick-speech of the car salesman. It should be embodied in the very way an independent school community moves. If we learn these things, our school communities can be as easy with Kwanzaa and Cinco de Mayo as we are with Christmas and Rosh Hashanah. By embracing multicultural education, we can improve the quality of our schools, improve the richness of our communities, and help educate students who, in turn, can help make a difference in the world by embodying and passing along the qualities that matter.

Dwight L. Wilson is headmaster of Friends School in Detroit (Michigan). This article first appeared in the Winter 2006 issue of *Independent School*.

If the house is to be set in order, one cannot begin with the present; he [or she] must begin with the past.

—John Hope Franklin

From Assimilation to Inclusion
Starting the Dialogue

BY MICHAEL BROSNAN

Let's start with the obvious. The only way to sustain dialogue on diversity in schools is to establish absolute clarity on why the work is worth the effort, and then make sure everyone in the school is involved.

The board of trustees must be firmly behind diversity initiatives — put its commitment in writing in the school's mission statement and then help shepherd the school in its evolution into the sort of inclusive school it envisions. As one head of school puts it, this work should also be part of everyone's job description, and everyone from the head on down should be evaluated on how well he or she is doing in supporting and encouraging inclusivity.

But where does the clarity of vision come from?

There are numerous ways to answer this.[1] For one, there is the clear business motive. The nation's diversity is increasing every year. By midcentury, white people will likely no longer be in the majority. As Peter Braverman, now head of the middle school at Green Acres School (Maryland), and Scott Looney, head of Hawken School (Ohio), put it in an article for *Independent School*, demography is destiny. "Schools [that]

---

[1] See "The AISNE Guide to Hiring and Retaining Teachers of Color," available at *www.aisne.org*. It includes an overview on the practical and moral reasons for schools to make the shift from predominantly white schools to inclusive learning communities with both student and adult populations that mirror the larger community.

take assertive positive action to attract and retain a wider array of students and families will find the marketplace of the early 21st century more hospitable." In order to make a school highly attractive to a diverse group of families, of course, a school needs a diverse faculty skilled in running multicultural classrooms, a diverse administration adept at developing and managing an inclusive environment, a percentage of students of color that closely matches the region's demographics, and families of all races who feel comfortable on campus and speak favorably of the school's culture and climate.

Most schools that have embraced diversity also zero in on the ethical question of what is right. If the goal of the United States is to be a well-functioning pluralistic society, then the goal of schools should be to prepare students to be well-functioning members of that pluralistic society. If we want a percentage of our students to be future leaders of this society, we need them to live and learn in diverse environments and understand from experience the value of cross-cultural dialogue. We don't just want to expose the majority white students to some students of color so that the white students will be more comfortable in the world when they graduate. We want students of color and white students to be leaders in the school and, eventually, in the nation and world. Schools need to believe that the cross-fertilization of ideas makes for, as one teacher puts it, "the maximum opportunity for learning." "We want our students to be engaged in their communities and help move this democracy towards its ideal," says a diversity director. "They can't do this in a monoculture. They need a diverse school community and a multicultural curriculum." As another diversity director notes, when schools open up discussion on what a world-class education looks like today, "they will inevitably conclude that it includes diversity."

The bottom line: For a variety of reasons, you can't call your school an excellent school unless you embrace diversity and put in a concerted effort to ensure a well-functioning inclusive community. This is not to say that there aren't other important factors in excellent schools; it simply means you can't ignore diversity these days and be a top-notch school.

This new model for a quality independent school — being an attractive option to a diverse group of students and their families, while focusing on educating all students to live and work in a multicultural world — has begun to emerge in every region of the country. But the process has been what one educator described as a "slow awakening" — beginning in the 1960s, in parallel to the Civil Rights Movement, and gaining momentum ever since. Yet, it wasn't until the turn of this new century that independent schools reached something close to a consensus on the importance of this work, even as they continue to wrestle to get it right.

The Inclusive School
A Selection of Writing on Diversity Issues in Independent Schools

SEEING HISTORY

The imperative for diversity is driven, in part, by the clear moral argument embedded in our Constitution and other founding documents for equity and justice in society, as well as in tenets that underlie every religion. But as we start down the path of this new century, there seems to be an increasing restlessness to get it right now. In other words, schools are looking not only at the historical inequities in the United States, but also at the continuing inequities, and they are saying clearly that they don't want to be part of them anymore.

Although the racial brutality exhibited in the founding of our nation and in the political and cultural systems of inequity leading up to recent times — that is, in all the years of our nation's existence — is not accurately highlighted in most textbooks, educated Americans know the problem well enough. The United States was not so much discovered as conquered. When Columbus landed in the Bahamas, the Arawak people couldn't have been more open and gracious. Columbus repaid their generosity by enslaving many of the natives (here and elsewhere), taking their land, destroying their culture, and working many of them to death in the pursuit of gold. When the colonists started to "settle" the mainland, they offered the Native Americans, among other things, a handshake and blankets riddled with small pox. Then they kicked the remaining Native Americans off their land.

The racism was most obviously exhibited with the use of slaves in the colonies, a practice that continued even with the establishment of the United States as an independent democracy. All the work in Philadelphia on the U.S. Constitution couldn't quite measure up to the egalitarian ideal of a true democracy. Right from the start, blacks were considered lesser than whites (in the bizarre language of political compromise, one black person counted as three-fifths of a person). "If one had to identify a single theme in the discussions leading up to the Constitution," Judge A. Leon Higginbotham of the U.S. Court of Appeals for the Third Circuit, said, "it was that slaves should be viewed as property, as subhuman."

Tim Wise, author of *White Like Me: Reflections on Race from a Privileged Son*, writes that "the history of this nation for folks of color was, for generations, nothing less than an intergenerational hate crime, one in which 9/11s were woven into the fabric of everyday life: hundreds of thousands of the enslaved who died from the conditions of their bondage; thousands more who were lynched (as many as 10,000 in the first few years after the Civil War, according to testimony in the Congressional Record at the time); millions of indigenous persons wiped off the face of the Earth."

Although the Civil War ended the official practice of slavery, "freed" black people were brutalized for another 100 years with Jim Crow segregation laws. Looking back on the worst days of post-emancipation discrimination in the 1890s, historian Lerone Bennett describes the shackled spirit of African Americans from years of cultural and systemic brutality:

> To work from sunup to sundown for a whole year and to end up owing "the man" for the privilege of working; to do this year after year and to sink deeper and deeper into debt; to be chained to the land by violence and bills at the plantation store; to be conditioned by dirt and fear and shame and signs; to become a part of these signs and to feel them in the deepest recess of the spirit; to be powerless and to curse one's self for cowardice; to be knocked down in the streets for failing to call a shiftless hillbilly "mister"; to be a plaything of judges and courts and policemen; to be black in a white fire and to believe finally in one's own unworthiness; to be without books and words and pretty pictures, without newspapers and radios; to be without understanding, without the rationalizations of psychology and sociology, without Freud and E. Franklin Frazier and *Jet*; to give in finally; to bow, to scrape, to grin; and to hate one's self for one's servility and weakness and blackness — all this was a Kafkaesque nightmare that continued for days and nights and years.

Discrimination in this nation, of course, was not just reserved for African Americans. At various times, our history includes the abuse of Chinese immigrants, the expulsion of Mexican Americans, and the internment of Japanese Americans. Even particular European Americans were at times victims of intense discrimination until they managed to find their way into the white fold. In short, just about every minority group was, at some point, subject to repression and abuse by the majority.

Restrictive covenants, developed in the 1890s in California and approved by the Supreme Court in 1926, allowed for nearly a half-century of officially sanctioned racial discrimination in housing. Schools were also legally segregated by race for decades.

THE POST-CIVIL-RIGHTS ERA

In many ways, it's difficult for the average white person to grasp the continuing racial discrimination in our nation. It's not highlighted in schools. It's rarely mentioned in mainstream media except in times of crisis. If you live in a predominantly white neighborhood, in fact, it's pretty easy to think that we've finally reached an era of equity in which each and every one of us can be measured by his or her own merits. But statistical evidence tells us otherwise.

"The United States," writes Adam Howard, professor of education at Colby College and author of *Learning Privilege: Lessons of Power and Identity in Affluent Schooling*, "is the most highly stratified society in the industrialized world." It's sad enough to have such stratification in a democracy; sadder still when it is closely aligned with race.

To many Americans, this may seem like an exaggeration, or some sort of manipulation of the truth. Our official line is that ours is the wealthiest nation in the world and that our democracy is functioning as well as any democracy can function. America is great. America is the land of opportunity. America is a model for the rest of the world. And so on.

But, despite any virtues one might attribute to this nation, America is also a nation in which more than 30 million people currently live in poverty[2]. America is a place where the top 1 percent of the population now has more wealth than the entire bottom 95 percent. According to the U.S. Census Bureau, the share of income of the poorest one-fifth of U.S. households dropped in the past decade from 4.2 percent to 3.5 percent. In other words, the gap is widening.

In a *New York Times* poll, 75 percent of Americans reported that they believe that their chances of moving up from one social class to another has risen in recent years, when, in fact, social class has played a greater, not lesser, role in shaping everyday realities of Americans. Michael Holzman, researcher for the Schott Foundation for Public Education, notes that "more than half — 53 percent — of African-American males did not receive diplomas with their cohort in 2005–2006 school year." The U.S. Census Bureau also informs us that African Americans are twice as likely to be unemployed as white Americans, and that "African Americans and Latinos have the lowest home-ownership rates in the nation — under 50 percent, compared to 76 percent for whites."

According to the Survey of Consumer Finances, in 2004 the median net worth of African-American families was $20,400 and $27,100 for Latino families, as compared with $140,700 for white families. Put another way, white families, on average, have a net worth that is almost seven times that of African-American families — a 700 percent difference. It also reports on U.S. Census data that tells us that the 2005 median income was $30,858 for African Americans and $35,967 for Latinos, while for white Americans it was $50,784.[3] In addition, we know that the recent subprime loan crisis has had the greatest impact on African-American and Latino communities. As Delvin Davis, a research associate at the Center for Responsible Lending, points out in *Poverty and Race* (May/June 2007), discrimination in the home loan industry is for real today. "Data from the Home Mortgage Disclosure Act (HMDA) indicate that African Americans are three times as likely as whites to receive a subprime loan, and four times as likely to refinance from a subprime loan.... Even when controlling for factors of creditworthiness,

---

[2] The number of Americans living in poverty jumped to near 45 million in 2011.

[3] In the few years since this article was written, all the indicators of income disparity by class and race have widened.

both African Americans and Latinos are more likely to have a higher rate loan with pre-payment penalties than white borrowers." Consequently, they are more likely to default on their loan and lose their homes. Davis underscores this grim news, noting, "Without a healthy, fair, and affordable mortgage market, the gains of homeownership for people of color will drain away through foreclosure and equity-stripping."

These are basic equity issues, and it's hard to read these facts without acknowledging how much needs to change if America wants to come close to living up to its democratic principles. And, yet, you have to search out this sort of information. You have to remind people — especially those who argue that the playing field is now level — that large-scale discrimination is not yet a thing of the past.

Perhaps the most troubling aspect of this discrimination is that it's not front and center in the media. Garret Keizer writes in *Harper's* about his frustrations with the way we seem to deliberately (and perhaps unconsciously) suppress race and class issues. What sets him off, he says, is how quickly we've turned our collective attention to global warming. Not that global warming isn't worth addressing, but Keizer feels we should express similar urgency about the class and racial divides in this country. "I am also aware, thanks to book after book by Jonathan Kozol," he writes, "that children are drowning in our inner-city schools and have been drowning there year after year and decade after decade, but I do not recall anything like the universal lament that has met the drowning scene in *An Inconvenient Truth*." As he puts it, our official take on race and class is "a blind spot as large as any hole in the ozone."

As it turns out, many educators agree with Keizer — which accounts for the diversity statements in many schools. The concern now, however, is making inclusive schools a reality in a culture that appears to be, at best, fuzzy on the issue, and, at worst, hostile to the idea that schools need to act in an equitable and just manner.

In voicing his dissent in the pivotal 1978 *University of California Regents v. Bakke* decision (in which the Supreme Court ruled against affirmative action quotas in college admissions, while still allowing that race can be a factor as long as it was not the sole factor), Justice Thurgood Marshall wrote, "In light of the sorry history of discrimination and its devastating impact on the lives of Negroes, bringing the Negro into the mainstream of American life should be a state interest of the highest order. To fail to do so is to ensure that America will forever remain a divided society."

But racial equality has not been a state interest of the highest order, nor a national interest of the highest order. Since the late 1960s, there seems to have been a concerted effort not to talk about it, or, if we talk about it, to gloss over it and move on to other seemingly more pressing topics. Of course, many people have dedicated their lives to righting this injustice, but the mainstream culture (read "white culture") seems to treat it mainly as a distraction. To their credit, schools have pressed the issue. But the weirdness in the culture can't help but impact the efforts in schools, all of which means that schools need to be far more deliberate in how they proceed.

Beverly Daniel Tatum, president of Spelman College, addresses this general discomfort in her book, *Can We Talk About Race?* For one thing, she notes, we live "in a unique moment of legal history in which the notion of considering race (talking about race) in school admissions is being challenged at the K–12 level as well as in higher education." But she is also concerned that we have trouble even knowing how to talk about race in a constructive way. "Can we get beyond our fear, our sweaty palms, our anxiety about saying the wrong things or using the wrong words," she writes, "and have an honest conversation about racial issues?"

The answer, of course, is yes. But it takes concerted effort. "It's never going to be easy," says one diversity director. "It's never all *kumbaya*. There's always going to be resistance and pushback. And you're going to make mistakes, and feelings are going to get hurt. But if you set up the process right, you can make significant progress."

In School Leadership for the Future, Thomas Hoerr, head of New City School (Missouri), argues that, when it comes to diversity, a little cultural dissonance is a good thing. It represents the necessary tension needed to shift a school's culture from a place where students and faculty of color feel like guests in the school to a place where a multicultural norm dominates. Hoerr points to an interesting study in 1998 by the Friends Council of Education, "Embracing the Tension," in which schools with the least amount of diversity reported the highest level of tolerance. This unexpected finding suggests a certain degree of self-satisfaction. But the schools that reported greater tension were also schools with greater diversity. The tension, he notes, is a clear sign of a cultural shift toward something better and stronger. But it takes work. "Any advance takes time and energy and extracts a cost, and the quest for diversity is no different," Hoerr writes. He then goes on to describe the tenacity needed to move through this process. In a nutshell, Hoerr argues, "This issue is too important to be left to chance, to assume that it will just happen because everyone is well-intentioned. School leaders need to take the lead in making their schools places in which all kinds of people can thrive."

Michael Brosnan is the editor of *Independent School*, published by the National Association of Independent Schools. He has written three diversity monographs for the Association of Independent Schools of New England, all of which are available at *www.aisne.org*. This excerpt from "From Assimilation to Inclusion: How White Educators and Educators of Color Can Make Diversity Work" appeared in the online edition of the Fall 2010 issue of *Independent School*.

Repeated hurtful experiences can have a long-term psychological impact.

The Psychological Experience of Students of Color

BY MICHAEL THOMPSON AND KATHY SCHULTZ

In the last 20 years, independent schools have collectively taken many meaningful steps to become more diverse and more socially equitable places. Almost every school has undergone — or is undergoing — a significant evolution in its thinking about racial diversity.

These schools have admitted more and more students of color, administrators have made determined efforts to recruit faculty of color, and heads and boards of trustees have made a moral commitment to using the school's resources to increase diversity. Although there are miles to go in this journey, independent schools have achieved a great deal in the area over the past two decades.

I (Michael Thompson) am particularly proud of the gains at the school where I serve as a psychologist and at many of the schools with whom I've consulted over the years. In spite of my pride in what has been accomplished, when I listen to a lonely student of color describe his life, I sometimes have a dramatically different view. For the individual students on the frontline of change, the psychological price for being a minority student in a majority-white school is often heavy. I frequently come close to asking, "Is this worth it for you? I know this is a great education, and I know your parents think this is the most important thing you can do with your life, but can you bear it?"

In pursuing the issue of social isolation and the psychological challenges that students of color experience in independent schools, I became involved with a group composed of heads of school, trustees, and educators who specialize in diversity work. They had been invited by the New England Association of Schools and Colleges to explore the issue of equity in the educational experience for students of color and to determine how to effect change in schools, beginning with the top decision-making bodies. There I met Kathy Schultz, director of graduate support for Nativity Preparatory School in the Boston area.

Nativity Prep is a Jesuit-run middle school for boys in grades five through eight that takes disadvantaged boys — primarily black, Hispanic, and immigrant boys from poor families — and prepares them to go on to independent schools and public high schools. Kathy's job is to follow these young men after they leave Nativity through their high school and college years. Nativity encourages and supports its graduates emotionally — and financially when needed — so they do not get thrown off track due to lack of familiarity with the world of secondary and higher education.

Kathy knows intimately the psychological pressures that students of color face in many different independent schools, and she shared the experiences of her graduates with the group. It became clear that we both responded to these issues in the same way and wanted to share our thoughts with a wider audience. Based on our experiences in supporting students of color in independent schools, we would like to suggest that there are six particularly difficult psychological experiences which most — not all — of these students are likely to face: (1) social loneliness, (2) racial visibility and social invisibility, (3) class and cultural discomfort among white parents and administrators, (4) the burden of explaining oneself to white people, (5) the challenge of completing studies at a demanding school with minimal parent participation, and (6) the burden of having to feel grateful all the time.

Some other writers, with a more political or sociological point of view, would rightly describe all of these experiences as aspects of racism. Because we are counselors and not sociologists, because we work with individuals and not societies, we remain content to call them psychological burdens. When students talk to us, they don't experience these stresses as something cultural or societal. In the moment, what a child experiences always feels unique and personal. It is only with experience and detachment that a student can come to see that what is happening to him or her is a result of being a "student of color." As they grow older, they may come to recognize and label behaviors as "racist." The label may help take the sting out of those behaviors and enable a student to maintain some emotional distance. However, that emotional distance, to the extent that it can ever be achieved, is an achievement of maturity that only begins developing in middle school and high school.

In many ways, what we want to say boils down to this: Repeated hurtful experiences can have a long-term psychological impact. They are painful and depressing and can make a child feel lonely and defective. They may drive a child into a state of psychological distress, which he or she may be reluctant to share with administrators, teachers, and even with his or her own parents. As obvious as it may be, however, there seems a certain reluctance in independent schools to acknowledge the basic fact that schools with a white majority — even those schools strongly committed to diversity — often are psychologically complicated and painful places for students of color in ways these schools are not for white students. This is true regardless of class, but it's particularly true for students of color from poor, urban environments. We encourage schools to consider such psychological burdens and what they can do to reduce them — and, thus, better fulfill their promises to these students.

SOCIAL LONELINESS

Three psychological difficulties contribute to the loneliness of a child of color in a majority-white school. First, in a school where you are in the minority, you may not feel as if you have — indeed, you do not have — the same social pool available to you as white kids do. That is because all children tend to connect with others who are "like them," and all children's social groups seek homogeneity as a first goal. Being the only child of color in a class, or one of a few students of color, is enough to make some children feel unbearably lonely.

Second, a child who previously attended a school with a majority of students of color may have no experience in having white friends or approaching an all-white social group; as a result, he or she may withdraw socially.

Third, white kids may not have any experience in having children of color in their group and don't know how to extend an invitation, or may not want to extend an invitation, for social engagement. Students of color often report that they are not invited to join informal social groups, and they don't feel comfortable approaching those groups. The result is a social standoff. For white students, this isn't particularly problematic, since they have a large social circle of other white students. But for students of color with few students to befriend, the psychological impact is immense.

RACIAL INVISIBILITY AND SOCIAL INVISIBILITY

Everyone in the white community is keenly aware of who the "kids of color" are, but a significant number of people in the school, both faculty and parents, are interested in these children only insofar as they participate in, or have meaning for, the white community. Many whites are not, for a variety of reasons, interested in knowing about the complete life of a child of color. They cannot visualize where these kids live, what they have to do to get to Sunnybrook-by-the-Sea School, what their parents' background is like. The paradox is that while the kids become important to the community as symbols — "We're diverse!" — they often feel personally neglected and devalued. Schools continuously demand that students of color respect the values of the school, but the schools don't have much interest in respecting the values of the culture from which the student comes.

Aaron, an African-American boy we know, is familiar with this scenario. When he arrived at his day school, he said he was assigned a host family. The family was most kind. They invited him into their home and their life, and, on one occasion, invited his parents for dinner. Aaron's family reciprocated by extending an invitation to the host family several times, but the white family apparently felt uncomfortable visiting his home in the inner city and never accepted. Because he was so hurt by the imbalance, Aaron stopped visiting the home of his host family.

CLASS AND CULTURAL DISCOMFORT AMONG WHITE PARENTS AND ADMINISTRATORS

At a parent meeting, one father at an elementary school waved his hand in a sweeping, inclusive gesture and declared, "This has always been a neighborhood school." He was referring to a neighborhood where the average housing price is above $2 million. Actually, because of the commitment of the head and the board to diversity, this man's school was rapidly becoming racially diverse, but it was comforting to him at many levels to think of the school as being filled with people like his neighbors. It no longer was, not only because children of color attended his school, but because poor children of color did. These students had the kind of parents, as one African-American mother pointed out, who might well have worked as maids in this man's home.

Affluent school populations have little idea about the realities of the day-to-day life of the less affluent, even what it takes to get their child to school. An African-American mother of three children, each of whom attend different independent schools in the Boston area, could no longer take her youngest son to school on the subway and hold onto her job. She agonized about the decision, but finally, when the City of Boston provided him with a bus pass at age 10, she allowed him to take the subway to school on his own. She used their regular trips as practice runs. She quizzed him on the stops; she prepared him in every way and nervously sent him off on the subway with a cell phone in his pocket. When he started arriving at school on his own, many white parents in the school reacted with anxiety or began remarking unfavorably on his mother.

Senior girls in schools in Manhattan often comment on the length of their trips and the commitment of time they make to come to school from their homes in Queens and Brooklyn. The trips can take over an hour each way, with a long walk to the station. It is only recently that private schools have started to arrange for shuttles from their nearest public transportation stops. These older girls say that many people do not want to know what they have to go through to get to the schools they attend. We believe the fundamental discomfort here is with the discrepancy in wealth that makes the well-to-do majority uncomfortable. Such matters, however, always cut both ways.

Jeannine, a senior from a school in New York who had an extraordinarily successful career in her school from almost every point of view, admitted that she feels envious part of every day of the week. She thrived academically at her school, will have her choice of colleges, is considered a leader, and has made friends both among students of color and white students. She has one particularly close friend, Amanda, who is wealthy and white. As close as they are, there are some topics she cannot talk about with Amanda: her lack of money and her friend's extraordinary wealth. Why? "Because I feel as though she'd change the way she looks at me…. In our society, money equals success…. I'd be lying to you if I said that it didn't matter."

THE BURDEN OF EXPLAINING ONESELF TO WHITE PEOPLE

We had an African-American boy at Belmont Hill who was a powerful leader in the community, the president of his class, captain of the wrestling team, and the informal leader of every student of color on campus. To the astonishment of many people, he chose to go to Howard University. He was the first and only graduate ever to attend a historically black college. When, as a senior, he was asked why, he said, "I'm tired of educating white people." He also noted reasons why Howard was the right university for him, but the initial comment speaks volumes about the difficult weight of explaining oneself — sometimes justifying oneself — to others.

Students of color are often asked to educate white students. They are asked to be representatives for their race and culture. They also carry the added burden of explaining to white students and adults the importance of race consciousness in this country. They are often asked to take the lead while white students can sit back or join in as they wish. It shouldn't be surprising that bright students of color get tired of this and seek out college communities where they can simply be themselves.

Perhaps equally tiring to students of color is the degree to which they have to switch "selves" — in essence, maintain two identities. Sometimes students of color try to hold onto pieces of their former personal identity while trying to acclimate to the culture of the new school. One girl described it as "talking white and talking black."

COMPLETING STUDIES AT A DEMANDING SCHOOL WITH MINIMAL PARENT PARTICIPATION

Most independent schools are difficult to survive with your parents' help. To do it without your parents is very tough. Many parents know how to navigate the waters of a school culture simply because they have been through it themselves. If a student runs up against a problem, the parent usually has a sense of where to go for a solution. But parents who did not attend a private school, or have access to higher education in any form, do not have the same ability to help their children. This is especially true among certain immigrant groups. They not only don't know where to turn, they barely recognize the problem, except that it is damaging their child. Students are left turning to school advisors and mentors, who rarely realize the depth of this need.

One of the advantages of white privilege is having your parents feel comfortable at your school. For reasons of education, class, and culture, many parents of color never come to the school. We know a Nigerian woman, a cabdriver, who drives up to the school, parks her cab, and goes to parent events in the red-and-white checked flannel shirt she wears when she's at work. She is spectacularly proud and totally at her ease. She is also the exception to the rule.

One parent, who runs groups for parents of color at her children's school, says that many parents of color don't come to school because they don't want to experience the subtle turning of the backs that happens to many black parents.

THE BURDEN OF BEING GRATEFUL FOR THE OPPORTUNITY

No one likes to feel grateful all the time. Students of color may find it painful to be reminded constantly of "what an opportunity this is" when they are feeling lonely or misunderstood in the setting. It is true that many independent schools invest substantial amounts of money in scholarships for minority students (as well as for many white students). In return, they get a student body that better reflects the reality of our nation and creates a far greater learning environment than one would find in a homogeneous school community. At the very least, schools should see the myriad ways in which the white-majority community unconsciously expects gratitude from students of color — and how this makes students of color feel.

Schools need to acknowledge what a risk the child took to come to the school and show some gratitude for the student's willingness to stick it out. Schools know that they have to provide support on the academic side for kids (white students and students of color) who enter with inadequate preparation, and they are prepared to do so. But it's clear that they also need to look more fully at the lives of students of color — consider how the experience of an independent school will be different for them than for white students in a variety of ways. Even as schools educate, identify, and treat the anxiety, stress-related disorders, substance abuse problems, and eating disorders of the white majority (the dark side of upper-middle-class life), they often don't take the time to familiarize themselves with the psychological needs of students of color, especially poor children, and therefore they are often ill-equipped to address them.

There are, of course, many systemic things schools can do to alleviate the psychological barriers to success of students of color. Simply achieving a critical mass of students of color, hiring more teachers and administrators of color, and appointing trustees of color will help tremendously. Schools should also examine their curriculum, openly discuss white privilege, develop support mechanisms for students of color, and recognize the value of formal and informal affinity groups.

For some students of color, the psychological stresses of attending majority-white schools are too much, and they need to leave for their own mental health. Most students remain and thrive, though they may struggle psychologically. What makes their psychological pain bearable? It is to have it heard and acknowledged by others, and to have others help bear that pain. When boys and young men flock back to Nativity Prep from their various schools for the annual Christmas party, they have a chance to do exactly that: to share their stories with their old teachers and bear the difficulties together. Their reunion helps them renew their commitments to the sometimes difficult environments they find at their schools.

A few years back, Richard Melvoin, the headmaster of Belmont Hill, invited four alumni to the school (two African-American, one Asian-American, and a white student who had been on financial aid) to come back from college and describe their high school experiences to their old faculty — experiences not just on campus, but also in the broader community. The teachers were spellbound by the honest, articulate testimony they heard from their former students about their years at the school. However, the young men held up a mirror to the community, and it was at times uncomfortable.

At moments, many in the room must have thought, "This is too painful. It cannot have been worth it for these boys to come to school here."

At one point, however, one of the students, after making some powerfully critical remarks, looked around the room at the faculty and said, "You know, eight of the most important people in my life are in this room. My life was changed for the better because I came here."

At the end of the meeting, the faculty must have looked stunned and quite serious, because he added, "Don't worry, we talk like this at Brown all the time." If students talk like this in college, we can encourage them to speak of their experiences while they are in our care — so that we, too, may learn and grow and challenge both ourselves and the broader culture in which we work and live.

CONNECTING AND EMPOWERING STUDENTS OF COLOR

While schools work to increase diversity among students, faculty, administrators, and boards — and evolve culturally to embrace the new community dynamics — they also need to consciously support current students of color, who clearly wrestle with the feelings of otherness and isolation. For the psychological health of these students, we encourage schools to, among other things, connect students of color across schools — through student diversity conferences and leadership programs aimed at students of color.

Why do students of color need their own conference? One of Nativity Prep's students sent to the Student Diversity Leadership Conference, part of the larger NAIS People of Color Conference, stood up in front of his school and explained why. He and three other delegates had come back ecstatic to have learned that they had a forum to air and discuss issues of diversity as well as simply to have discovered they were not alone. "It was like you belonged there... it felt good to know that there were other kids like you... and you weren't alone.... No, because we were all there trying to put an end to the cultural injustices in our schools [and] in the world. We all await the day when such conferences will only be used for socializing... instead of for... issues regarding race." The boys had strengthened their own peer group and also established themselves as part of something bigger. The unstated fact that their school valued them enough to send them to the conference was also apparent.

Taking on leadership roles in their schools and community strengthens students of color in myriad ways. Students can do this partly through the Student Diversity Leadership Conference. At Nativity Prep, we also found that a program called Anytown, run by the National Conference for Community and Justice — an organization "dedicated to fighting bias, bigotry, and racism in America" — is effective. At Anytown, a group of students heads off for a week of workshops, skill-building exercises, and informal interaction with peers from a wide range of racial, cultural, ethnic, religious, and economic backgrounds. They come back with a better understanding of their own perceptions and stereotypes, as well as with an intensified respect for people whose backgrounds may differ from their own. They have gained a vocabulary to talk about these issues and have learned how to put their personal experiences in a broader social context. They have also gained techniques and tools to use to address these issues.

There are many other programs, each with its own special focus. Summer Search is a two-year program that matches students with scholarships for experiential learning opportunities during the summer of the last two years in high school. It focuses on organizational skills, independence building, and public presentation and speaking. The Food Project takes students from diverse backgrounds to work together to produce food, provide leadership opportunities, and inspire and support others to create change in their own communities.

We have noticed that Nativity Prep students involved in these programs often take on leadership roles in the schools they go on to attend. This year, 18 boys from Nativity will graduate from 14 different high schools. Two are co-presidents of their senior class; one is a student representative to the board of trustees of his school; one is president of the black students' organization; and several have leadership positions in their sports teams, dance clubs, and drama clubs. Students of color may come to independent schools to develop their academic skills and prepare for college, but schools can also help them better understand their cultural and political environment — and develop the leadership tools necessary to work within that environment. This will not only help support the psychological health of students of color, but also empower all students to help reshape school culture — and the greater society — for the better.

Michael Thompson is a school psychologist and coauthor of numerous books on the social and emotional life of children, including *Best Friends, Worst Enemies: Understanding the Social Lives of Children*. At the time of this writing, **Kathy Schultz** was director of graduate support at Nativity Preparatory School in Boston. She is now retired. This article first appeared in the Summer 2003 issue of *Independent School*.

…to rush forward with diversity initiatives without gauging the school community's **specific needs** for the work is a quick way to fail.

Things That Make You Say, "Hmmm..."

On Institutional Change and Diversity

BY ABE WEHMILLER AND ANDRÉ WITHERS

Although many schools have made an institutional commitment to develop and sustain an inclusive community — and to support the broad notions of equity and justice within the school and beyond — there is often significant distance between their stated goals and reality. The reasons for the gap vary from school to school, although the overarching challenge may simply be that diversity work is hard work and ever evolving.

It's a challenge in the nation at large, so there's no reason to expect it to be easy in schools. In the public sector, despite all the efforts at racial integration in education in the 1960s and 1970s, our public schools are more segregated today than ever. For independent schools, especially those that have traditionally served the upper-middle class and primarily white families, the transition to a well-functioning inclusive community can be slow and difficult on various fronts.

We have presented a number of workshops aimed at helping schools and people within them better align their missions and actions when it comes to diversity in all its dimensions. Here, we'd like to focus on the institutional issues. In particular, we will examine the organizational system within a school — the way decisions are made, as well as the operational culture of the school. It is our firm belief that one of the key reasons that a diversity initiative doesn't survive beyond the early efforts of committed, short-tenured people, or that it is defined by a short-term response to some unfortunate incident, is because schools fail to focus on the organizational systems that give rise to and sustain diversity initiatives.

We approach these issues here through a series of key questions — those we've heard echoed in many schools. Our approach is based on the belief that, if schools can identify the key institutional-level questions — the things that make you say, "Hmmm…" — and develop a framework for answering these questions in a way that is best for each institution, they can and will move the conversation forward in beneficial ways. An approach we've intentionally avoided is to provide specific examples of how other schools have responded to these questions, because we believe that no single answer fits all schools. We encourage you to use the following frameworks as you come across the important questions in your own work.

SELF-ASSESSMENT

A key question we hear often is, "How do we accurately evaluate our current school climate and the need and desire for change with regard to issues of diversity, multiculturalism, equity, and justice?"

Our answer to this question starts with an affirmation of the value of the question. It is important to accurately evaluate a school's climate and both the need for and desire to change; otherwise, it's hard to know how to proceed. And to rush forward with diversity initiatives without gauging the school community's specific needs for the work is a quick way to fail.

In order to evaluate the climate with regards to diversity, multiculturalism, equity, and justice (DMEJ), we believe it's best to start with the school's overall reaccreditation process. Why here? First, because this process is familiar. Schools often mistakenly look upon diversity issues as being adjunct to their core educational concerns, and therefore they attempt to address these issues using processes that lie outside their standard operating procedures. "This is a new focus for the school," the logic goes, "so we need a new assessment tool." While such tools are available, a potentially more successful approach is to examine diversity issues in the context of the overall mission and goals of the school as a whole. That brings us to the second advantage of the reaccreditation process: It is holistic in nature, and thus it allows all constituents to see diversity as part of the school's overall health and well-being.

Of course, if the reaccreditation process turns up a need for a closer and more specified look at issues of diversity in the school community, more tailored measures are appropriate. The Assessment of Inclusivity and Multiculturalism (AIM) — a tool developed by the National Association of Independent Schools (NAIS) that builds upon the work of its earlier Multicultural Assessment Plan (MAP) — can be effective for three key reasons. It packages all the elements a school needs for assessment (training of internal leadership, data-collection methods, and data analysis); it has been beta-tested and used formally in a variety of schools with successful early returns[1]; and it is administered by an organization that works specifically with independent schools. Outside consultants can be helpful as well, although we always caution schools against consultants who tend towards a one-size-fits-all approach. A good consultant will spend time getting to know a particular school on the front end of his or her work, and spend time following the school's progress through the stages of development.

READINESS FOR CHANGE

These self-assessment tools tell us where we are in DMEJ work in our schools. What remains to be determined — sometimes in less formal ways — is whether or not our schools are actually ready for the work that follows such an assessment. Along those lines, a useful question to ask is, "What are the benchmarks to gauge the readiness for change in each of the school's constituencies?"

Time is a precious commodity in all schools, so it's not unusual to hear some educators claim that there isn't enough time for diversity work, especially when everyone is already feeling overwhelmed with everything else that needs to be attended to. We've also heard the complaint that taking the time required to become astute with diversity work means taking precious time away from a school's effort to adequately prepare children for an increasingly complex global society.

Both these perceptions strike us as forms of resistance to diversity work, and we read such comments as clear signs that key constituents within these schools just aren't ready to properly embrace a diversity initiative. This is not to say that global issues aren't important or that time isn't a real factor to consider in all schoolwork. But steering the

---

[1] In the years since it was first developed around the time of this article, the Assessment of Inclusivity and Multiculturalism (MAP) has been used in more than 80 schools in the United States, Canada, and Bermuda with great success. See the NAIS website, *www.nais.org*, for more details about this assessment tool.

discussion of diversity in this direction does raise questions about readiness — or, rather, the lack of readiness — to move forward with any sort of DMEJ-based initiative.

Readiness must be defined as the state of the school in which all constituencies are ready to learn more about, and actively use the merits of, what it means to be a diverse school or to undertake a diversity initiative. Now, let's not confuse this with being ready to "sign off" on a diversity initiative. Our point is that "readiness" — a general communal desire to learn more — is essential in order for a school to explore the process of being an inclusive community. To meet with any lasting success down the road, a core readiness matters at the start. When all constituencies come to the table for something common, both to take and to give, they are more apt to band together to ensure that they are successful — in whatever endeavor. A sense of urgency at the leadership level for diversity initiatives also needs a sense of readiness on the part of the community.

For various constituencies within the school, here's what "readiness" might look like:

Parents Association: The parents association sees itself as a partner with the school in learning about the same diversity-related concepts and principles that teachers are pursuing in their classrooms.

Board of Trustees: The board sees the strategic and pedagogical value in pursuing diversity-related goals.

Alumni: Alumni understand that diversity does not mean that the current school administration wants to change the school they remember, but that the administration wants to ensure fond memories, a quality education, and a lifelong connection to the school for each and every student, regardless of cultural background.

Administration: The administration is clear about how to both lead and help manage the implementation of the diversity initiative while connecting the effort to mission, core values, professional-development dollars, and teacher evaluation.

Faculty: Teachers are clear about how diversity is an integrated instructional piece of their craft tied to a child's identity and to his or her intellectual and emotional development.

As a school gains a sense of readiness in all these groups, the next step is the alignment of administrative systems (or drivers) with the school's diversity goals. When the faculty meetings, the school calendar, the professional development programs, the in-service programs, the teacher-evaluation system, and the core values of the school are synchronized with one another around diversity and its pedagogical worth, a school knows that it has an institutional green light to pursue diversity work in a substantial way — that is, developing something that reaches way past the feel-good exercises of "food, folks, and fun" in the classroom. Diversity feels like an "add on" when it's not supported by such systemic functions of the school.

IDENTIFYING THE WORK

When schools have assessed where they are regarding DMEJ work, they'll most likely find that "where they are" is different from their peer schools. And when schools come to this realization, they tend to ask, "What's the best focus for our work in the areas of diversity, multiculturalism, equity, and justice: creating individual programs that address immediate needs or auditing institutional structures?"

Once again, the answer varies from school to school, depending on how far a school has progressed towards its goal of being an inclusive institution. However, the pragmatic answer that applies to all schools is this: The work is most effective when it meets the school where it is and progresses from there. In other words, honestly identifying where the school is, using the assessment tools and practices outlined above, is the key initial step in deciding what work (individual programs or structural audits) needs to be done next.

An analysis of a school's culture might, for instance, reveal that establishing an outreach program, housed in the admissions office and designed to recruit more students of color, might generate the sort of momentum that would cause a school to reexamine its admissions practices in general. On the other hand, if such a program were thriving in terms of attracting a diverse applicant pool, but the school was struggling in terms of admissions rates for that same group of students, a logical next step would be for that school to reexamine practices rather than create more new programs. Either way, knowing the starting point is crucial.

A tool we've used in our work that has proven to be especially effective asks schools to assess their culture and place themselves in one of six phases along a continuum: exclusive, passive, symbolic change, analytic change, structural change, or inclusive. Should you choose to use this tool to evaluate your own institution, keep in mind that your school might be at different phases for different areas of the school (curriculum vs. student support, for instance) and that your school might be at different phases for different aspects of diversity (socioeconomic status vs. sexual orientation). What this means, of course, is that you will have multiple starting points for your work, and that you'll need to coordinate that work in a meaningful, strategic, and appropriately prioritized fashion.

INSTITUTIONALIZING THE WORK

Ultimately, as you can see in the continuum, our goal is to help schools move to a place where diversity is part of the fabric of the institution. Naturally, then, schools interested in doing DMEJ work successfully should be thinking about working towards a coordinated initiative that touches all aspects of school life. The question, therefore, becomes, "How do we, as a school, transcend a model of special events or add-on programming and move towards a model that integrates diversity work into the fabric of our institution?"

The most critical step here is to understand that there are three key stages of the work:

Raising awareness

In this stage, there is a schoolwide effort to inform the entire faculty that DMEJ work is essential for a quality education today. Common elements include speakers, films, art exhibits, and other tangible, visible reminders of difference. Every school begins in this place, and it is absolutely necessary that they do so. It is crucial for the success of any initiative, however, that schools recognize that the work done in this stage is only an initial step that builds towards future work. Allowing the work to stay in this stage too long sends the message to the community that diversity work is an adjunct of school life — and will cause the larger initiative to fall flat.

Building capacity and accountability

Seldom do independent schools speak about diversity as a skill-based endeavor; it's our opinion that this oversight is one of the most common pitfalls of diversity initiatives. To be taken seriously, any initiative must have expected outcomes and growth points — things everyone in the school can be accountable for. This step, then, is where actual skill development comes forth from diversity training.

For example, a staple of diversity training is conflict management. While not evidenced often in our mostly cordial schools, conflict is nevertheless inevitable. Especially as we pursue a more diverse teaching faculty, cultural, personal, and professional viewpoints will undoubtedly intersect and clash. We should teach our faculty how to manage this aspect of a healthy, collaborative, community-building process in a way that is proactive and built on establishing solid relationships with colleagues.

Reaching integration and institutionalization

This rarely achieved state is where you see a change in the school community's population so that it now represents a broad spectrum of difference, where there is routine monitoring of "how are we doing" to sustain the gains and continue improvement, and where the school's practices change as a result of being organizationally aware of the impact of its decisions on underrepresented groups. At this stage, faculty meetings are used, among other things, to openly discuss the ways in which difference is interconnected in children's lives. The school calendar makes room for teachers and staff to practice dialogue skills about difference across the differences in the community. And the curriculum is not about simply including the experiences of darker-skinned peoples, but instead about encouraging critical analysis of race — focusing particularly on the voices heard and unheard, the perpetrators of injustice as much as the victims, and the way historic societal events parallel today's world.

We hope that you can see in our answers to these questions a few of the basic tenets we hold essential in addressing DMEJ issues in independent schools: (1) that schools must address these issues at multiple levels — the individual human level, the isolated

The Six Stages of Diversity

STAGE 1
Exclusive
School's mission, structure, and decision-making model is influenced entirely by the dominant perspective (white, male, Judeo-Christian, heterosexual, upper-class, able-bodied, etc.) and unabashedly so.

STAGE 2
Passive
School no longer markets itself as an exclusive institution, but it has done little, if anything, to change its mission or structure. Nothing about the school has changed in practice.

STAGE 3
Symbolic Change
School begins to address diversity with a limited definition of that term — that definition usually being limited to race, the most visible element of diversity. School begins efforts to diversify by recruiting a smattering of students and faculty of color, and goes to considerable lengths to publicize these efforts. Students/faculty of color must be the "right" students/faculty of color to thrive at the school. They must buy into the school's structures as they exist; those structures will not change to serve them.

STAGE 4
Analytic Change
School begins to ask questions about whether its structures are serving all its constituents as they need to. Often, the constituents have changed significantly in a way that prompts such questions. A danger here is that the school will get caught up in endless discussion, asking questions without being willing to provide concrete answers.

STAGE 5
Structural Change
School begins to answer the questions posed in analytic change stage. School does so by dedicating scarce resources — time, money, personnel — to diversity initiatives.

STAGE 6
Inclusive
Diversity, multiculturalism, equity, and justice (DMEJ) work is part of the fabric of the institution, fully integrated into school mission, structures, and decision-making process. It is important to recognize that this stage is a moving target, as diversity is not a static issue.

program level, and the institutional structure level, (2) that independent schools require independent solutions, so that no single answer to these sorts of questions applies to all schools, and (3) that schools are at different places from each other in their journeys towards becoming inclusive institutions, and that effective work in this area continually addresses where they are, not where they should be.

There are always lots of additional questions circling a diversity initiative: How do I justify the use of affinity groups? Do we really need a director of diversity? What's the next step after the MLK Day celebration? You've no doubt heard some version of these questions in your own school. And while we can't answer them for you without an intimate knowledge of your school, we hope that you see that asking the broader institutional questions and employing some version of our accompanying frameworks will lead you to a place where you can answer questions large and small. We also hope you see the value in making this effort.

From our perspective, the opportunity to address DMEJ issues in a meaningful way is an essential part of what makes an independent school great.

Abe Wehmiller is assistant director of the upper school at Lakeside School (Washington). At the time the article was written, **André Withers** was the assistant head of school at Lowell School (Washington, DC). He is now director of co-curriculum at the Madeira School (Virginia). They have presented a more detailed version of "Things That Make You Say 'Hmmm...'" at the 2006 NAIS People of Color Conference — including advice for individuals working within schools. This article first appeared in the Fall 2007 issue of *Independent School*.

…underneath the calm surface are torrents of equity, access, and opportunity that surge as a school's commitment to diversity takes hold…

Go Ahead, Open the Box
Assessing Diversity to Initiate Change

::

BY ERIC POLITE II

Inviting open discussion about a school's diversity initiatives and goals is often considered akin to opening Pandora's box. Do it and you run the risk of bringing all sorts of trouble upon the community.

But keeping the lid on these complex issues can have far worse consequences. Among other things, it can suppress frustrations and alienate members of the community, give the impression that school leaders are insensitive to the opinions and needs of others, and, ultimately, threaten the progress the school desires in its efforts to create and sustain a diverse learning community.

Better to invite discussion — or so we decided at the Gordon School, a nursery-through-eighth-grade independent school in Rhode Island. A year ago, we developed an assessment process designed to break through the barriers of political correctness (and independent school politeness) to reveal the honest subtext of the culture's feelings and thoughts on our diversity efforts.

This assessment focused on evaluating the progress on the goals outlined in the school's Strategic Plan for Racial Diversity and Multicultural Education, approved by its board in 2000. That plan proclaimed specific goals for the racial composition of its students, faculty, staff, and trustees and concurrently pressed the faculty to grow its practice. As a result, Gordon has increased its faculty of color from none in 1998 to eight in 2004, and its students of color from 11 percent in 1998 to 22 percent in 2004.[1]

As the school took on a yearlong review of a decade's worth of diversity work, it was clear that, in order to hold on to these gains and accurately project the future, all voices would need to be heard, even if the questions or viewpoints rattled the windows or unsettled longstanding assumptions about the school's purpose and mission.

THE COMMUNITY DIVERSITY ASSESSMENT

Titled the Community Diversity Assessment (CDA), the board-approved process provided parents, teachers, students, and trustees with the opportunity to speak their minds and write down their impressions, criticisms, and suggestions with regard to all aspects of the school's diversity work.

Advocates for the school's diversity focus spoke clearly, praising the tangible gains and pushing for more progress. Other people spoke more cautiously and offered advice. Still others shared strong criticism and, in some cases, resistance to further work. Altogether, the complete set of data — over 300 pages of Likert scales, written anecdotes, and transcribed interviews — is evidence of a decade's worth of focused, sustained work.

Wise to the culture's diverse opinions on work so central to the experience of children, Gordon leadership has crafted its next strategic agenda on diversity in ways that connect directly to the lessons learned from the Community Diversity Assessment. What follows is a review of those lessons. We offer it now to affirm the value of opening Pandora's box.

THE PARENTS: LESSONS OF AFFIRMATION, COMMUNICATION, AND ACADEMICS

In previous years, surveys and questionnaires failed to engage more than 10 percent of the Gordon parent community. Therefore, we were initially concerned with parent participation in the Community Diversity Assessment and, subsequently, the range of responses that complete anonymity would produce.

In the end, the success of the parent survey exceeded our expectations with a parent-participation rate of 44 percent and results that were overwhelmingly positive in

---

[1] As of September 2009, people of color at Gordon made up 27 percent of the student body; 20 percent of faculty, staff, and administrators; and 30 percent of the board of trustees. In addition to tracking these numbers, Gordon performs assessments at regular intervals that document how Gordon's diversity efforts have influenced individuals' experience of the school. Assessment tools have included focus groups, one-on-one interviews, and questionnaires.

praise of the school's work. Nearly half of the respondents acknowledged diversity as one of the reasons they chose Gordon, and more than half said diversity is a significant reason why they stay. Eighty-two percent of parents said that they were "proud of Gordon's commitment to diversity," and 91 percent said that they were "satisfied with their child's academic experience."

While the parent feedback was mostly positive, it was obvious that valuing diversity in principle does not always imply support for the practice of creating a racially diverse learning environment. On the surface, diversity is aligned with each individual's allegiance and institutional commitment to the democratic ideals of freedom, justice, and equality. However, underneath the calm surface are torrents of equity, access, and opportunity that surge as a school's commitment to diversity takes hold, simultaneously arousing the voices of resistance in the dominant culture.

One parent, for instance, wrote, "I believe that Gordon needs to balance its intent to create a 'diverse educational experience' with the need to maintain a certain standard of students." Another parent put it more bluntly: "My children are there for an education, not exposure to other ethnicities (that is my job as a parent)." Still another wrote, "Most of [my] misgivings are about the curriculum and the risk that political correctness will lead us into bad scholarship. I worry, too, that the debate on multiculturalism will divert the faculty's time and energy as they try to design creative and challenging academic assignments."

Another parent's comment echoed what a small percentage of parents felt: "Gordon wastes inordinate time and money on diversity and is pushing it to the point of creating ethnic and racial prejudice and tension where none previously existed."

These voices, which might otherwise be silent in the discussion, were very important for us to hear. We learned from them that myths and misperceptions arise in the absence of a clearly articulated (and regularly repeated) purpose and process for pursuing diversity as an institutional imperative. The lack of clarity leaves institutional diversity subject to individual interpretation. Subsequently, diversity initiatives can become the scapegoat for all of the school's issues and limitations, especially in times of crises.

In a community where everyone works together to advance the school's efforts, a well-informed parent and professional community is essential. The Community Diversity Assessment revealed places where communication and information would be helpful. For instance, the parent assessment identified a clear need for regular communication about the content of the school's multicultural curriculum.

We also found that multicultural curriculum and multicultural education carry little or no meaning for our parent body unless articulated as an educational imperative with tangible academic outcomes compatible with a shared interest in academic "excellence." Otherwise, many of these parents will continue to narrowly define anything multicultural as soft and second-rate, and they will perceive it as an imperative solely for students of color.

THE TEACHERS: LESSONS OF EVALUATION AND SUPPORT

Sometimes, the most conservative elements in school change can be found in the faculty. We were pleased to find that the faculty assessment data affirmed overall satisfaction with the work environment and a clear commitment to the school's diversity work. Eighty-six percent of the faculty expressed clear satisfaction working at Gordon. Eighty-nine percent said they believed that there was an institutional commitment to diversity at Gordon. Ninety-one percent agreed that a racially diverse and multicultural curriculum better prepare students for the "world beyond Gordon."

Two noticeable themes in the faculty assessment were a clear call for support in advancing multicultural practice and a demand for sustained progress in multicultural curriculum growth. We were pleasantly surprised to learn that teachers want evaluative feedback and consistent communication so that they could confidently pursue the curricular and pedagogic expectations of the school. As one teacher wrote, "Gordon needs to provide tangible resources that support the integration of multicultural practice in the classroom." Another said, "Hold us all accountable for pushing the envelope in multicultural practice which, in turn, would embolden each individual to seek more opportunities for personal and professional growth."

Another lesson learned from the faculty assessment is that teachers, as the old axiom puts it, can't teach what they don't know. In a section of the faculty survey on educational experience, the results revealed that the majority of the faculty's pre-service teacher education rarely included issues of multicultural education or preparation for teaching in diverse classrooms. In addition, many faculty members said they had no experience teaching in racially diverse classrooms (with more than 25 percent students of color).

Cleary, there is a need for hands-on support and practical resources to fill the gaps in education and professional experience that often fails to prepare teachers to confidently navigate diverse learning environments. Teachers requested specific support via reading lists, study groups, peer coaching, in-house workshops, and classroom observations. However, the consensus request from the faculty was collaboration with the director of diversity that would facilitate multicultural curriculum development and the professional growth associated with teaching from multiple perspectives.

THE STUDENTS: LESSONS ON IDENTITY AND RACE

On the whole, students expressed comfort and satisfaction with their academic and social experience at Gordon. Of the 143 middle school students who took the survey, 92 percent agreed that they are "happy at Gordon." They also showed an understanding of the multicultural education they were receiving, with 90 percent of the students affirming the value of a diversity of people and perspectives in the school.

While the student survey confirmed general satisfaction, we used a focus group to draw out the voices of students of color, believing that they are the best barometers of our progress in creating a student culture that supports diversity. This focus group produced a narrative of the experience of students of color at Gordon, revealing that they desire a stronger sense of inclusion and connection to their school. When asked what they would

How to Assess Diversity

All assessment starts with a problem. Organize a team of committed community members to identify the problem or problems to be addressed by the diversity assessment.

Once you've identified the problems, defined the purpose and the population(s) to be studied, calculate the human, physical, and financial resources the assessment will require. Things to consider include: the time and scope of the study, institutional resources, equipment, internal and external resources, marketing, materials, and compensation.

The integrity of the assessment process depends on creating a space for honest reflection. Open discussions depend on both the appearance and preservation of anonymity and confidentiality, particularly with issues of diversity. You should create a statement of confidentiality and anonymity for all surveys and vigilantly adhere to it when reviewing the data.

If you are considering interviews and/or focus groups, remember that outsiders can often ask questions that might be off-limits to insiders. External interviewers reduce concerns about confidentiality and anonymity, and increase the veracity of responses. Basic requirements for facilitators should be a background in education or counseling, experience facilitating dialogue, and impartiality. In addition, you should

assemble a team that best reflects your community with attention to racial diversity and gender balance.

How will the assessment data be used? The credibility of the assessment and its potential to initiate change depend on followup. A comprehensive diversity assessment must be followed by strategic action that builds on the collected data. It is imperative that your school community understands the assessment purpose and process, and that it views any plans of action that emerge from the analyses.

The assessment process will probably produce a considerable amount of data. Data is much easier to collect than to analyze, so think well in advance about who will review, code, and examine that data. You should consider the people in your school community who have knowledge of statistical analysis or educational research.

Ultimately, the assessment process will yield more questions than answers. Use the quantitative data — the surveys and questionnaires — as background information that is imperfect but pertinent. If the assessment combines quantitative and qualitative information (i.e., interviews and focus groups), then you are in a better position to make generalizations about the population under study.

— Eric Polite II

change about Gordon, the students in the focus group responded with "more students of color" and "a better understanding of how students of color feel."

The students of color also talked openly about their struggles to navigate the racially and culturally differing spheres of home and school, providing irrefutable evidence of the need to pay increased attention to the development of a healthy racial identity among students of color.

The student survey data also found that, for white students, Gordon is not only the primary site of their racially diverse friendships, but also the most racially diverse setting in their lives. Moreover, we learned that many white students feel some level of discomfort when addressing issues of race in the classroom. The student assessment confirmed the need to create more opportunities for interracial dialogue and to provide all students with the skills and experiences to confidently enter racially diverse settings at Gordon and beyond.

THE TRUSTEES: LESSONS ON LEADERSHIP

Given that the board of trustees is the body that decides which initiatives warrant allocation of time, energy, and resources, the board's advocacy for diversity is crucial to its success and survival.

Similar to the faculty, the lesson learned was that the board members can't lead what they haven't lived. The reality is that we have called on our largely white board members to lead in diversity work that, by and large, they have neither the training nor background to do with confidence. Leadership in diversity work does not require the same skills and experiences that trustees lend to work on other board initiatives like finance and marketing. While their engagement in board work is an extension of their professional lives, the skills and knowledge required for diversity work usually grow out of personal experience.

In the trustee assessment data, board members communicated a strong willingness and desire to assume a lead role in articulating the academic benefits of a racially diverse school and a multicultural education. But Gordon's commitment to diversity would quickly slide from important to illogical if it was only supported by platitudes and promises and not grounded in the commitment of a visionary and well-informed board. The Community Diversity Assessment highlighted the board's ability to clearly and consistently articulate and explain the school's strategic initiatives in racial diversity and multicultural education. As one board member put it, "I feel that I could be better equipped to play a leadership role and advance the diversity work. I am not sure how to respond to the question, 'How is diversity providing my child with a better education?' To this end, I would need more information in order to address the question, because I do feel diversity has a place in education."

The commitment came through loud and clear in June of 2004: The board of trustees voted unanimously in favor of two distinct plans designed to further the work initiated in June of 2000 when they approved the Strategic Plan for Racial Diversity. These two new plans, the Strategic Plan for Building a Racially Diverse Community and the Strategic Plan for Evaluating and Enhancing Multicultural Practice, represent strategic action that builds on the data collected from an involved and informed community of parents, students, and educators.

FROM AWARENESS TO ACTION

The board embraced the notion of a complete and thorough assessment and, in doing so, set in motion a process that uncovered both the challenges and opportunities for the next stage of the school's growth. However, sustained growth and momentum required that the assessment be followed by strategic action that builds on the collected data. Thus, the goals outlined in Gordon's revised strategic commitments directly correlate to the issues presented in the Community Diversity Assessment.

If knowledge is power, then providing the community — especially the parents — with clear and accurate information about the academic nature of multicultural education can produce articulate advocates for academic excellence through multicultural education. Accordingly, the plan details a schedule of written and verbal communication with parents about the content of the multicultural curriculum and the teaching practices that support it.

Given the aforementioned limitations of a largely white board in leading the school's diversity initiatives, the plan also states that they will "actively cultivate leadership and membership that understands and articulates the benefits of a racially diverse learning environment." To aid in this effort, trustees will receive a handbook to assist in orienting new and continuing trustees to the school's diversity work. In addition, the board will receive a yearly update on the tangible evidence of the educational benefits of this work so that each member can lead with confidence.

The new plan also seeks to engender an inclusive climate inside each classroom and throughout the school so that all students can reach their highest level of academic success. In response to the issues and themes presented in the student assessment, the new plan includes implementing the Open Circle social curriculum,[2] expanding the middle school advisory curriculum, and establishing racial affinity groups for students.

In response to the faculty request for support, evaluation, and accountability, the Strategic Plan for Evaluating and Enhancing Multicultural Practice calls for a "comprehensive professional development plan to improve and refine teachers' knowledge, skills, and approach to multicultural education." Professional development is linked to specific goals for each teacher and facilitated by a revised evaluation system that explicitly articulates expectations around each teacher's growth as a multicultural educator. In addition, the director of diversity job description has been revised to provide direct support and guidance to teachers in growing their multicultural perspective, pedagogy, and practice.

Institutions, almost invariably, do not change without the open discussion of real issues. The Community Diversity Assessment provided opportunities for this level of discourse. In opening Pandora's box, we at Gordon unearthed the hidden realities that move institutional change and strengthened our commitment to diversity.

As we build on this solid foundation of planning and persistence, only time will tell whether or not the Community Diversity Assessment moved the Gordon School to the next stage in this process. However, the direction has been established and the willingness to lead and teach to our goals has been reinvigorated. We believe that the Community Diversity Assessment can serve as a model, even as it is critiqued and improved, that other educational communities may use to initiate and sustain commitments to diversity that reflect the very best that independent education has to offer.

At the time this article was written, **Eric Polite II** was the director of diversity at The Gordon School (Rhode Island). He is currently the director of diversity at The Packer Collegiate Institute (New York). This article first appeared in the Fall 2004 issue of *Independent School*.

---

[2] The Open Circle Curriculum (grades kindergarten through five), developed at Wellesley College, integrates research findings in child development with the best teaching practices. The curriculum's holistic approach involves training the adult role models in a child's life to teach and embody principles of communication, responsibility, cooperation, respect, and assertiveness in order to facilitate healthy social, emotional, and intellectual growth in children. For more information, visit *www.open-circle.org.*

The Inclusive School
A Selection of Writing on Diversity Issues in Independent Schools

Once we are aware of what unconscious bias is….we can **build an inclusive organization** that gives everyone the opportunity to participate fully….

Bias Among the Well-Intentioned

How It Can Affect the Hiring Process

::

BY CHRISTINE SAVINI

In my work as a diversity professional, both as one school's long-term diversity director and now as a consultant and workshop leader for many schools, I have found that building a diverse faculty has been, and continues to be, a profound challenge for most schools, even after decades of effort.

It is my hope that the case study presented here, and the diagnosis and prescription stemming from that analysis, may shed light on one aspect of the challenges and suggest some means to overcome it.

A CASE STUDY

The following is a true story, which took place during one school year, with all identifying characteristics changed.

Sunny Valley School (SVS) is a 100-year-old, K–12 day school located in the suburbs of an eastern U.S. city. Nearly 24 percent of its 750 students are people of color. The head and board of trustees, having recently included support of diversity in the school's mission statement, also wrote in their strategic plan that they are committed to further diversi-fying the 100 faculty and administrators at the school. Currently, seven professionals of color work at SVS: an African-American admissions recruiter, two Spanish teachers from Latin America, a Chinese teacher from Taiwan, an African-American athletics coach, an African-American health center director, and a Latina diversity director.

Members of the faculty diversity committee have pointed out that, while they value what the school has achieved so far in creating faculty diversity, at 7 percent of the adult population, it doesn't come close to mirroring the school's student numbers or the pro-portion in the school's local area. They also note that no person of color teaches in the academic departments beyond the three faculty members who teach their native lan-guage, and that the only administrator of color works in the diversity office.

Sunny Valley School has tapped a variety of sources to obtain résumés of diverse candidates. The school has asked placement agencies to send résumés of their multicul-tural candidates. Also, SVS representatives annually attend the regional independent school diversity job fair and post the school's job openings on the local People of Color in Independent Schools (POCIS) listserve. In addition, SVS recently joined an area consortium dedicated to the recruitment of faculty of color. The head of school, Rachel Simon, is deeply engaged in a major capital campaign and building program, a priority of the board. Devising creative ways of managing an independent school during a time of national recession is also occupying much of the head's efforts during her second year in the position. At SVS, the head's role in the hiring process traditionally has come into play only after a department chair or the long-term dean of faculty, Clark Chase, rec-ommends a finalist to her as a department's choice.

Amid this setting, a retirement has created an opening in the upper school English department. The department chair, Heather Stone, an SVS graduate, says the depart-ment is "looking for someone who could teach the range in grades 9–12. We would like someone with a master's degree in English, some previous teaching experience, and particular strength in teaching writing. Another requirement is willingness to coach or advise a club or activity. And the department is also very interested in having a diverse candidate pool."

The English department has experienced little turnover during the four years that Stone has served as chair. Having risen through the ranks in the department, her expe-rience in hiring has been limited to filling a sabbatical replacement and a maternity leave. The head of school views this as an opportunity to diversify the English depart-ment. She is encouraged to hear the dean of faculty enthusiastically declare that the diversity director, Madeleine Rivera, "has been actively recruiting candidates of color from several sources for the position."

Rivera presents the résumé of a candidate of color she received from one of the teacher recruitment agencies. Keith Wood is an African-American English teacher with 20 years' experience on the secondary and college levels, who has spent the last five years at an international school in Paris. Wood wants to return to the United States and spend more time near his retired parents, who live within driving distance of SVS. Because Wood has independent school experience as both a student and teacher, along with a B.A. from Wesleyan University and Ph.D. from the University of Virginia, Rivera considers him a wonderful candidate for the highly academic Sunny Valley faculty. The agency's description also notes that Wood distinguished himself as a strong mentor of student writers at the three independent schools where he taught, securing publication of his students' work in many journals and their successes in several national student writing competitions.

Although Wood's academic credentials and teaching recommendations are outstanding, both Chase and Stone express reservations about inviting Wood for a visit. The dean says, "Given his age, 45, he'll be an expensive hire. I don't know if we can afford him." Stone adds, "Members of the department say they don't think that, after five years in Paris, he's looking at SVS seriously, given our location." She also notes the male majority in the department and that most of the faculty is over 40. She goes on to say that, "What we really need is a dynamic woman in her late 20s."

Rivera is disappointed at the decision, but moves on, encouraging Stone to consider a second candidate of color, this time a young woman she interviewed at the regional diversity job fair, Yvette Whittaker. Rivera learned that, as a high school student, Whittaker emigrated with her parents to Louisiana from their native Jamaica. She graduated with a 3.8 average from Louisiana State University in Shreveport, majoring in English and receiving teacher certification. She was hired to teach English in a public high school near Shreveport, where her principal and department chair praised her as their best teacher of writing. After three years of teaching, she attended graduate school at the University of Iowa, where she worked for two years as a teaching fellow in freshman composition, before completing her M.F.A. in Creative Writing. While at Iowa, one of her short stories was published in *The Southern Review*.

Stone tells Rivera that the department has strong concerns about what some members call "weak undergraduate preparation." Asked to elaborate, Stone speaks of Whittaker's attendance at "an unknown college." She says some department members also raised questions about "how American students would be able to decipher her Jamaican accent." Rivera, who had met Whittaker at the job fair, assures them that this is not an issue. Clark Chase responds by saying he doesn't "really know how to evaluate public school experience," and he isn't sure what sport Whittaker could coach.

Rivera has begun to grow frustrated with the responses to the two candidates of color and sets up a meeting with Chase, to whom she reports. Chase finds Rivera in the hall later that day and inquires about the meeting. Reminding him of the school's commitment to diversity, Rivera asks him to reconsider Yvette Whittaker's candidacy. She reiterates that she had met this candidate at the regional job fair and found her impressive. She also stresses that she is not asking the department to hire the candidate, but only to meet her. Chase tells Rivera that he will call Whittaker. A week passes, and Chase finally does call her, only to learn that she has just accepted a position at a nationally known boarding school in the same region.

Stone has moved on to set up interviews for some other applicants for the position. None are people of color. When the head of school asks Chase about candidate diversity in the English department search, he replies, "We had two candidates, but one was too expensive, and the other accepted a position at another school."

At this point, we can speculate about what the head and diversity director can do in response to the situation. But why did the dean of faculty and department chair proceed as they did? At the beginning of the search, both the dean and chair verbally supported Sunny Valley's commitment to diversity and inclusion. But something hindered them from acting as truly effective diversity allies.

UNCONSCIOUS BIAS

Most likely, both the dean and department chair were impeded by unconscious bias. Bias is a tendency to look at a situation from a specific and sometimes limiting perspective, based on past personal or hearsay experience. We all possess some forms of bias, which is part of normal thought processes. Beverly Daniel Tatum, president of Spelman College and an expert on the psychology of race, says that all of us are affected by "the cultural smog" we absorb through media stereotypes, family influences, life experience, and geographic isolation. To become effective diversity allies, we need to develop an awareness of the cultural smog we have "inhaled."

Those of us who possess some form of privilege are often unaware of our biases. And those of us who have sometimes been the victims of bias (women, people of color, gay people, disabled people, etc.) may be unaware that we may have internalized societal bias as well. Since we are unaware of possessing unconscious bias, its manifestation is unintentional and often expressed in subtle ways.

When discussing the concept of unconscious bias in my consulting work with schools, I often hear some variation on the phrase "but this is the country that elected President Obama," as if that proves unconscious bias is a thing of the past. Indeed, there has been a notable shift on the national racial landscape, but many schools have yet to experience the change. There are still few people of color who head independent schools. And while 40 percent of the Obama cabinet is composed of people of color, how many independent school administrative teams or boards of trustees look like the Obama cabinet? We still need to talk about how our unconscious bias plays out in our schools.

AVERSIVE RACISM

One form of unconscious bias is aversive racism, a concept developed through extensive research by John Dovidio, professor of psychology at Yale University, and Samuel Gaertner, professor of psychology at the University of Delaware. According to Dovidio and Gaertner, "Aversive racism is the inherent contradiction that exists when the denial of personal prejudice coexists with underlying unconscious negative feelings and belief" about people of color, particularly about blacks by whites. Those who experience feelings of aversive racism may regularly discriminate while maintaining a non-prejudiced self-image. The term "aversive" refers to maintaining a conscious commitment to principles of equity and finding the idea that they might be prejudiced to be aversive.

PROJECT IMPLICIT

Project Implicit — a study by Harvard University, the University of Washington, and the University of Virginia that has surveyed 4.5 million visitors in online tests of hidden racial bias — supports the research of Dovidio and Gaertner. The study found that 75 percent of whites tested from 2000 to 2006 had an implicit pro-white/anti-black bias. (In 2006, the researchers also found bias in white children as young as six years old.) The test involves measuring how reflexively a person associates positive and negative words with photographs of black and white people, and it is well described in Chapter 3 of Malcolm Gladwell's *Blink*. (You can test yourself at: *https://implicit.harvard.edu/implicit/*.)

In another study by faculty at the University of Chicago Graduate School of Business and the Massachusetts Institute of Technology, human resource directors were sent job applicant résumés to which names had been attached that were either "typical" of contemporary African-American names (e.g., Lakisha), or not overtly African-American names (e.g., Emily). The result? Human resource directors were 53 percent more likely to invite the neutrally named individuals to an interview — even though, when interviewed, those directors said they felt that they would be eager to invite diverse candidates to interview with their firms.

Why do we have this bias? Project Implicit found that "our brains make associations based on experiences and information we receive, whether we consciously agree with those associations or not." What does this bias look like? In contrast to the feelings of open hostility toward black people that characterize blatant racism, the negative feelings associated with unconscious bias are more diffuse, such as feelings of anxiety or uneasiness. Sometimes the feeling is one of ambivalence. This is usually due to a tension between wanting to be supportive of equity and having internalized our "cultural smog."

HOW IS UNCONSCIOUS BIAS MANIFESTED?

Unconscious bias results in a conflict between stated belief and actual behavior. A person may endorse equality and nondiscrimination and believe he or she is well intentioned, but act in a discriminatory way and justify those actions, quite sincerely, with reference to matters having nothing to do with race. Thus, at Sunny Valley, although the administrators' words, backed by the mission statement and strategic plan, affirm their commitment to diversity, they avoid hiring, or even interviewing, the available candidates, citing reasons not connected to race.

In our case study, there were several examples of discrimination based on factors other than race. The dean of faculty speculates, "At 45, I don't know if we can afford him." No one asks Keith Wood what salary range he may be looking for. Although

How a School Can Respond to Unconscious Bias in the Hiring Process

Provide bias awareness training for all who oversee the hiring process in the school.

Compile a list of faculty and professional staff of color, noting each person's position, tenure, and culture.

Analyze this data annually. Consider:

- which cultures are represented and which are not;
- in which departments and divisions;
- how long people of color have remained at the school and in which departments; and
- the adult percentages of color compared to the percentages in the student body.

Document your procedures for hiring teachers and administrators to ensure that all departments and divisions are following the same process. Review these procedures annually with new department chairs and administrators.

Document and track all candidates of color in all searches in all divisions and departments.

Review this accumulated data at the end of each school year. The head of school, division heads, diversity director, and human resources director should form the core of the review group.

Use this compiled information to develop a strategic plan focused on the hiring and retention of faculty of color.

The Inclusive School
A Selection of Writing on Diversity Issues in Independent Schools

the recruitment agency specifically noted Wood's geographic preference for SVS's area, Stone reports that her colleagues doubts that Wood will be interested in their area after working in Paris. Once again, no one talks to the candidate.

The department head reminds everyone of the majority of males in the department and of their ages, moving the focus away from race. "What the department really needs is a dynamic woman in her late 20s." But when presented with just such a candidate, bias continues, based on factors other than race. Despite the candidate's graduate degree at one of the most distinguished writing programs, the department focuses on "weak undergraduate preparation at an unknown college." The dean says he doesn't "really know how to evaluate public school experience." The chair claims that members of the department question "how American students would be able to decipher her Jamaican accent," without ever meeting the candidate to see if her accent is understandable.

In questioning what Yvette Whittaker could coach, the dean ignores the fact that SVS faculty may also advise a student activity, and he doesn't learn what extracurricular contribution she could make, again avoiding candidate contact. The person exhibiting aversive racism may avoid interracial interactions. In our case study, neither the department chair nor dean of faculty interviews either of the two black candidates, on the phone or in person, despite the fact that both candidates completely fill the department's requirements for the position. Chase delays calling Whittaker for a week, by which time she has already accepted another position.

HOW CAN SCHOOLS RESPOND TO UNCONSCIOUS BIAS?

First, schools need to have conversations with their adult communities about unconscious bias. Training on this subject cannot be optional if a school truly wants to ensure that all adults are effective allies for its diversity mission and that its community is authentically inclusive.

Schools also need to talk about unconscious bias outside of formal training — in board, administrative, and department meetings. Although doing so will make people uncomfortable initially, they must find the courage within themselves to take this step and trust in such conversations. As Beverly Daniel Tatum writes, "As a society, we pay a price for our silence [on these issues]."

Finally, administrators and faculty need to build in systems of accountability, creating written procedures and checking to see if those procedures are being followed. For example, at one school, a dean told me she was concerned about low academic achievement of black boys in the middle school. When I asked her about her conversations with the boys' parents, she told me she didn't contact the parents because she wasn't sure how they would respond. Parents in this case were not given vital information about their child until term grades were completed, depriving them of information and the opportunity to partner with the school to support their child. In this case, if there were written procedures for administrators to respond to students having academic difficulties, one of which was to have a conversation with the parents, the dean would know that contact was required. Even when procedures are in place, everyone, especially key administrators, needs to be aware of the tendency to avoid implementation when unconscious bias is present.

Written procedures for hiring and documentation of the decision process are much less common in independent schools than those for student records, whether in the dean's or the admissions office, but they are no less necessary. Returning to our case study, if Sunny Valley had written procedures requiring that, in every search, all candidates representing diversity should be contacted directly to ascertain their interest and availability, and that, given the competition for such candidates, contact must be initiated within a specified time of receiving the résumé, Keith Wood could have made clear his interest and salary needs, Yvette Whitaker's oral clarity would have been confirmed, and the school could have made an informed decision about whether to proceed in either case.

Once we are aware of what unconscious bias is, how it is manifested, and how we can respond to it, we can build an inclusive organization that gives everyone the opportunity to participate fully and contribute their talents, background, and viewpoints to our schools.

Christine Savini is principal consultant at Diversity Directions and director of the summer workshop, The Independent School Diversity Seminar. Diversity Directions has consulted to independent schools in 10 states, assessing school climate, mentoring diversity directors, and assisting with diversity strategic planning, recruitment and retention of diverse faculty, multicultural programming, and professional development. Prior to full-time consulting, she was director of diversity planning at Milton Academy (Massachusetts) for 17 years. She can be reached at *csavini@diversitydirections.com*. This article first appeared in the Winter 2010 issue of *Independent School*.

…a diverse community cannot come into being if a school is not **willing to work** specifically to face and address issues of class, race, and gender.…

Core Truths, Cultural Norms
Aligning Daily Practice with Diversity Goals

::

BY SHERRY COLEMAN

Most independent schools espouse the value of diversity in their vision or mission statements. While it is important that diversity be at the core of the school's mission, it is just as important that it be ingrained in the day-to-day life of the school.

Too often, diversity statements feel like idle words on a page that have little to no effect on the school community. In such schools, hiring practices and policies are not linked to mission, retention of faculty of color is not systemically addressed, and overall diversity goals are not established. Predictably, such lack of attention to defining what a diverse faculty means to a school community results in disappointment all around.

Why is it that some schools can espouse the value of diversity and yet not embed this belief in their daily life — their operations, policies, and practices? The lens of organizational theory offers significant insight into such an institutional disconnect.

ORGANIZATIONAL THEORY AND HEALTHY SCHOOL CHANGE

Economist Gareth Morgan, writing in his book, *Images of Organization* (2006), describes institutions as "organisms," unique living systems that also operate within a larger "complex ecosystem." In order to remain vibrant, an institution needs to nurture itself as an individual organism does, while also adapting to changes in its ecosystem. The danger comes when an institution thinks of itself as a "discrete entity" only, living in isolation from the ecosystem around it.

In my experience, this "organism" and "ecosystem" metaphor holds true for schools. Some have been able to evolve into diverse communities in response to changes in the world around them, while others clearly struggle. The latter happens, Arie de Geus argues in his 1988 *Harvard Business Review* article, "Planning as Learning," because "institutional learning is much more difficult than individual learning." When things are difficult, it's easy to put them off, choosing instead to manage and maintain the status quo. In some schools, it is exactly this sort of entrenchment that prevents them from revisiting the essential policies and practices that would actually lead them toward new visions of themselves.

The literature makes it clear that organizational culture is critical to the success or failure of any transitional efforts within an institution. In schools, the culture determines what is "normal," what matters most, and who "fits" into the environment. In an entrenched culture, a school community is unlikely to do something as basic as examining its hiring practices, which, of course, makes it difficult for a school to increase the number of people of color among its teachers and administrators.

More generally, a diverse community cannot come into being if a school is not willing to work specifically to face and address issues of class, race, and gender, as well as the tensions that can arise when the level of support necessary to sustain diversity is not there. In an entrenched culture in which such issues are not addressed openly, life can be difficult for newly hired teachers or administrators of color. They arrive because the schools says it wants to be a multicultural institution, and yet, they quickly discover that there are cultural codes or nuances of the community that elude them — and in many ways exclude them. They may be able to function in the school, yet they feel like perpetual outsiders. As others have described it, they feel like guests and not members of the club. It shouldn't surprise anyone that these talented educators will eventually move on.

On the other hand, a school that has effectively recruited and retained faculty of color has several characteristics:

- It is committed to a diverse school community;
- It affirms and values cultural pluralism;
- It understands how a diverse faculty adds to the discourse and the academic climate for students;

- It values new or differing teaching perspectives and points of view; and
- It considers cultural diversity as important as academic competence.

Such a school communicates the importance of diversity to the community through programming, curriculum, professional development, and a nurturing climate. It also reviews hiring practices across all divisions and departments to assure that these practices connect with its core beliefs. A head of school generally does not see candidates prior to reaching the finalist stage, but if key knowledgeable constituents are not part of a clear hiring process that includes a focus on diversity, many good candidates may be overlooked. School leaders who intellectually embrace the notion of diversity and of hiring a diverse faculty must also make that vision an active priority.

HIRING NORMS AND PSYCHIC PRISONS

When I began working in faculty recruitment 18 years ago, a division director described the ideal candidate using the analogy of the five Olympic rings. The candidate should have teaching experience, have taught at an independent school, have attended an independent school, have graduated from a highly selective college, and have had some coaching experience. For decades, that was the model of a "good" independent school candidate.

Today, a good hiring team must look beyond the Olympic rings for prospective candidates. Such a team acknowledges that great teachers come from a variety of backgrounds. It does not make assumptions about candidates based on its own limited knowledge. As a way of gathering broader viewpoints, it is not afraid to ask questions about things that are unfamiliar to its members, and it usually consists of a range of people who reflect the diversity the school hopes to attract. Such a hiring team broadens the focus rather than narrowing the lens to evaluate candidate viability. It takes time to assess the effectiveness of its hiring procedures. It can also acknowledge its successes and failures in order to make necessary changes to strengthen the process.

Morgan's metaphor of organizational "psychic prisons" is appropriate for schools that are unable to get beyond a set of norms that prevent them from adequately diversifying their faculty. He says that community members develop a "collective unconscious" by which the organization ends up with an unsatisfactory result and then rationalizes it. The Olympic rings analogy for a "good fit" is an example of this faulty rationalization. The rings represent mechanical hiring, focusing on what is familiar and comfortable. It does not bring relief from the "psychic prison" because it cannot lead to the sort of change a school says it needs.

I recently witnessed the release of a school from such a "psychic prison." The division director was looking for a middle school teacher. All candidates, the director initially said, should have at least five years of middle school teaching experience. One of my pet peeves is when a specific number of years of experience is a rigid determinant of effective teaching. I firmly believe that some people are instinctively good teachers while others need time to develop their skill. All candidates of color whose résumés we forwarded to the division director had teaching experience and all had advanced degrees, most from very selective colleges or universities. Yet none measured up to the "experience" yardstick, which demanded at least five years of experience in middle school. When I expressed my disappointment, I was told that, of the more than 80 candidate résumés received for the position, more than 30 had solid middle school experience, so it was easy to eliminate candidates from the pool. However, none of the 30 were candidates of color.

I expressed my concern to the department chair, who decided to attend our annual career fair to meet and interview candidates for the position. The head of school also thought it would be important to attend the career fair to meet some of the candidates. To make a long story short, one of the initially rejected candidates was invited to the school for an interview and ultimately hired. Both the principal and the department chair acknowledged that he was the strongest candidate in the pool. His skills and demonstration lesson were far superior to other candidates with solid middle school experience. The principal acknowledged that it was a terrible mistake to have initially overlooked this exceptional teacher. Making a paradigm shift by rethinking and challenging an existing norm is important to the success of hiring and retaining a diverse faculty.

Organizations must develop self-knowledge to move themselves out of the trappings of a "psychic prison." The trap of weeding out great prospective candidates before they even get to the starting line is a problem and is often grounded in superficial reasoning.

WHAT WE MEAN BY "BEST"

Schools can create barriers and not be innovative enough to find appropriate ways to dismantle them. In such cases, the barometer for success is based on the hegemony of the dominant group, and that becomes the gatekeeper that excludes many strong candidates. While the school's goal may be to select the "best candidate" for the job, it may be unable to step outside of the box that it created by setting up a rigid set of criteria for who meets its measure of success — for what "best" means. For these schools, hiring is a straightforward task that does not require them to move away from the assembly-line process. But by failing to find ways to hire a diverse faculty, they limit the opportunities

The Inclusive School
A Selection of Writing on Diversity Issues in Independent Schools

for their students to have the experience of having role models unlike themselves, and they weaken the strength of the academic discourse in the community.

I am reminded of an excellent young teacher, a gifted writer, who was enthusiastic about her work and the opportunity to share her passion with her students. Her instructional approach differed from other faculty members in some instances. She infused her lessons with literature that some of her students were not familiar with. She made connections between the classics and writers of color. The students relished the new discourse, especially the students who were often forced to code switch between their lives at an elite prep school and their lives as members of their cultural communities. Some parents initially concerned with her style soon came to respect her work. Nevertheless, her approach was not totally supported by a few of her department colleagues, which made her time at the school difficult and stressful — especially when she began to challenge her colleagues about their stereotype-laden views on some of the literature she used. The division director and the head of school supported her work and her ability as a teacher, but that did not change the opinions of the teachers who did not agree with her teaching style and pedagogy. She found the situation too much of a burden to bear and resigned after two years.

All organizations have a culture that influences their vision, philosophy, and patterns of operation. Their ideology and values are embedded in their routines and actions. As Gareth Morgan argues, creating new forms of organizational culture is challenging and difficult. Change is continuous, while culture develops through social interactions and connections. Having diverse voices represented broadens the discourse in a way that can bring institutionalized change and move the rhetoric of a diverse school community to one of permanence.

At the time of this writing, **Sherry Coleman** was the director of the Independent School Consortium (ISC), a diversity recruiting and retention organization based in Philadelphia, Pennsylvania. She is currently a diversity consultant. This article first appeared in the Fall 2010 issue of *Independent School*.

REFERENCES

Arie de Geus, "Planning as Learning," *The Harvard Business Review*, March-April 1988.

Gareth Morgan, *Images of Organization* (Thousand Oaks, CA: Sage, 2006).

For many people of color in the United States, life can be simultaneously euphoric and enraging.

Directing Diversity
Advice for Schools and Diversity Directors

::

BY ILANA KAUFMAN

The role of diversity director in independent schools has always seemed a bit peculiar to me. I officially held a version of the role for three years, and since then have remained in independent schools as an assistant head at Lick-Wilmerding High School in San Francisco.

Even when structured thoughtfully, the role of diversity director is rich with organizational contradictions. Diversity directors are simultaneously powerful and powerless, both leaders and followers, clear about their roles yet often lost in the larger organizational context.

It is the diversity director in whom we imbue our hopes for assuaging the angst that many students of color feel throughout their tenure in independent schools. We ask diversity directors to mitigate the circumstances that impede students of color from thriving in schools. And, indeed, it is the relationship of the diversity director with all school constituencies that creates the possibility for students of color who feel marginalized or under-represented to have a more vibrant, healthy experience in independent schools.

And yet while independent schools across the country are creating such positions and noting in their mission statements the importance of diversity for the students and the community, many educators in the position of diversity director express immense frustration with the work. For them, the position is too politically and emotionally charged, and is often structured in a way that makes it difficult to measure success. They feel discouraged and isolated in the community. They feel the weight of carrying the load alone.

What can schools do to assure a higher rate of success for diversity directors, and what can diversity directors do to help make their work more manageable?

WHAT SCHOOLS CAN DO TO ENSURE SUCCESS

Let's start with the schools. They can begin by remembering the essential purpose of the position: that the long-term goal of supporting students of color to be their best selves is central and calls for the intentional crafting of adult communities that mirror the diversity of the world so that all students, regardless of background or experience, see reflections of themselves in the faces of their teachers and administrators. School leaders should also skillfully craft a diversity director position in a way that honors the experiences of students and families of color and reflects the voice of the school community as a whole. To do this, a school needs to develop a thoughtful job description that unambiguously connects the diversity director's work to the school's mission, hire a diversity director who is a seamless match for the school community, and establish a strong and collegial team to support this individual. Schools that take these steps are schools that have a high likelihood of best serving the needs of students of color in their communities — and ultimately achieving the school's broader educational goals.

Schools also need to hone their systems thinking. They, too, often fall in the trap of forgetting their skilled systems thinking when it comes to working on issues of diversity. While the "encounter group" models of the past have some value, we are talking about schools here, not support groups. Maybe leadership teams should wear lanyards around their necks that say "WWSD." When things appear to be falling apart, the question we should be asking is, "What Would Senge Do?" (If you're not familiar with the work of Peter Senge, please read *The Fifth Discipline* and its companion piece, *The Fifth Discipline Fieldbook: Strategies and Tools for Building a Learning Organization.*) To my administrative brothers and sisters, I offer lessons we at Lick-Wilmerding learned over the years. Our insights come from careful research, thoughtful and intentional design, and, at times, controlled chaos. And while I do not intend to sound doctrinaire, the suggestions below are tried and true. They have been refined over the years with the help of colleague diversity directors and heads of school.

- **Publicly mandate, through the school head and board members, a focus on diversity.** If there is no mandate made public by those in positions of leadership and governance, the community will be sent the message that the place of diversity work is, in fact, on the margins, rather than central to the school's mission and vision. Sending this message of marginalization simply perpetuates the systemic problems that inhibit students of color from fully blossoming and is counterproductive to a school's good intentions.

- **Design a comprehensive diversity strategic plan with a scope of at least five years.** When thinking through a systems lens, successful strategic plans demand a minimum of at least that much time. Design your diversity strategic plan using the same skilled thinking that goes into other school plans. Identify your goals and objectives, outline the phases, build in appropriate assessment, and understand the resources necessary to bring your vision to fruition. And don't forget to ask members of the community for contributions — they will be your conscience.

- **When possible, hire a diversity director who is a person of color.** The goals of bringing a diversity director into our communities center on (1) meeting the needs of students and families of color, and (2) supporting the entire community to find deep meaning in working on issues of diversity. To that end, it is imperative that the diversity director be able to share similar experiences and perspectives with many of your families of color and connect with and galvanize the community as a whole. While this might seem to be a tall order, diversity work demands that we challenge and stretch ourselves.

- **Spend significant time developing precise thinking about the diversity director's "roles, authority, and boundaries."**[1] Write a thoughtful and manageable job description that appropriately situates the diversity director within the larger organizational context. Also, have clarity about who supervises this individual, how he or she will be evaluated, and the extent of his or her responsibilities. Managing staffing expectations and assumptions is a key ingredient in the recipe for organizational success.

- **Locate and commit substantial resources.** I'm talking money, staffing, institutional visioning, decision-making, and time. Unlike launching a tutoring or debate program, diversity work is comprehensive and involves all aspects of the community. And the work of diversity director is full-time. If your vision is far-reaching, and your

---

[1] The phrase "roles, authority, and boundaries" is borrowed from educational consultant Debbie Freed. She uses the term in "Shaking Up the System: Have We Lost Our Way?" (*Independent School*, Winter 2000, p. 76) in a section on how school leaders manage expectations and assumptions.

goals appropriately lofty, the diversity director needs resources to successfully fulfill the objectives outlined in his or her job description.

DIVERSITY DIRECTORS: ALIGNING INSTITUTIONAL AND PERSONAL VISION

If building a sustainable, inclusive community requires an independent school to have a thoughtful vision, by extension, the person charged with helping to usher that vision to fruition must have an equally unambiguous and transparent agenda. Among other attributes, he or she also must have a great deal of confidence in his or her knowledge base, abilities, and sense of moral purpose. In addition, "hustle," thick skin, and endurance will serve him or her well.

For me, in deciding to become my school's dean of multicultural affairs, my agenda was and continues to be simple: I want to help give the marginalized — folks of color, women, religious minorities, gays and lesbians, and the disabled — a roadmap to aid the navigation of independent schools as organizational systems. As I see it, the systems that keep individuals and groups from experiencing schools in ways that are equitable are simply that, systems. When enough key people who can decode the systems and translate them for others are in place, it is more likely that those who have been traditionally marginalized will be able to skillfully negotiate their way to the metaphoric table — to move gracefully and deliberately from margin to center. It is my personal hope, and the community's hope at Lick-Wilmerding (and, I assume, at other independent schools), that once playing fields are leveled, experiences shared, and knowledge, vocabulary, and systems co-created, all members of the community can happily, equally, and vibrantly co-exist.

It is important, too, for those who accept the challenges of being a diversity director, that they accept the fact that this work is not easy. For many people of color in the United States, life can be simultaneously euphoric and enraging. And existing within such a bifurcated reality often calls us to work in settings where we can contribute in ways that change the lives of young people, so, ultimately, they can help change the world. Many people of color who accept the position of diversity director feel the pulse of this call-to-action in their veins and accept the challenge of reshaping the culture of many independent schools into successful, sustainable, inclusive communities.

HOW TO SURVIVE AND THRIVE

Attempting to build an inclusive independent school community is the kind of work that is very much all or nothing. I am convinced that it does more harm than good to launch a diversity program if a school community is not prepared to commit to it for the long haul, come rain or shine. And it is predictable that opening the Pandora's box of inclusion (with its revelation of many forms of exclusion) will trigger some hard times, noble intentions notwithstanding.

I have also learned that, as the work gets underway, it becomes increasingly vital to bring into the community only people who are committed to the effort. At Lick-Wilmerding, we thus try to be crystal clear with prospective teachers, students, families, and trustees about our values and the work in which we are involved. As a consequence, we tend to attract people who also are genuinely committed to our mission and vision. This does not mean that everyone at Lick must be a "diversity coordinator" or show his or her multicultural credentials upon arrival. But it does mean that we need and expect every member of our community to bring a determination to do his or her part.

In the end, it is the diversity director, or in my case, the dean of multicultural affairs, who must be clear, centered, and capable enough to facilitate this process. Those of us in (or aspiring to be in) such a role cannot be egocentric, hardheaded, or omniscient. In most instances, in fact, those assuming such a role actually know very little about how schools as systemic institutions work. You might have an innate sense of the theory behind the practice — maybe even a B.A. in sociology or anthropology — but the daily systemic dynamics of schools are characterized by complexities and subtleties requiring knowledge and wisdom that most new diversity directors are only beginning to fathom. In addition to viewing the beginning phase of this position as a mandate to move up the organizational and cross-cultural-theory learning curves, you must also be able to make a firm commitment to being a team player and to trusting your colleagues to do their jobs, to work for your success, and to "cover your back."

Before accepting a diversity director position, then, it is critically important to assess the likelihood that you will be joining a good — no, a great — team. By the grace of God (and the invitation of my head of school), I landed in the company of people who know what they are doing and who always work by design rather than by chance. The team is skilled, compassionate, and highly competent; moreover, they are learners as well as teachers, and they demand that all who are part of the team believe deeply in the same philosophy. That demand translates into endeavors and programs that are strategic, transparent, highly energized, morally grounded, full of integrity, and effective. What's not to like?

"Doing diversity" in independent schools is not for those who hyperventilate or get woozy at the emergence of confrontation or discomfort. The truth is that this work is, for me, a calling. And I think it should be a calling for anyone who accepts the work. That belief allows us to get up daily no matter how gray the skies may seem. Happily, Lick-Wilmerding and I found each other because the stars aligned. (Yes, this is California, and we spoke in these terms when I signed my contract.) As the dean of multicultural affairs, with my charge and community clearly in mind, my learning curve has been steep, and I've begun to develop what I believe are some general rules to live and work by:

- **Scour your head's bookshelves for reading recommendations.** Make note of the journals on his or her coffee table. Ask for citations that speak to his or her knowledge base and then read even more. All that you are able to glean and contextualize for your work will serve you well.

- **For diversity directors who are people of color, enter situations that are not comfortable.** Go to those places where you are the only person of color. There, you will learn the inner workings of a school, you will rub elbows with folks whom you need to know and who need to know you, and you will develop the skills and thick skin necessary to meet the obligations of your charge. You will take some lumps, so be ready to take the high road, always presenting your best, most learned, circumspect, and professional self.

- **Invite and be open to feedback and constructive criticism.** Pay special attention to how you are playing to your audience and how others perceive you. No one knows better the impact of your intentions than those who experience your efforts.

- **Don't pout when you fail to get your way.** Either make the system work for you or collaborate with your team to change the system so that it can work better for a larger spectrum of constituents.

- **Never throw tantrums when upset or unsuccessful.** Once you abandon professionalism, you can expect to be marginalized as a lone ranger, a maverick, or even worse, someone who 'is working through his or her own stuff on the school's time." Always stay strong, think hard, call upon your allies, and breathe. There are a thousand more battles to be fought, and you can't afford to exhaust yourself or undermine your credibility by sweating the small stuff. Having said this, it is also vital that you maintain a support group outside the school to whom you can vent and from whom you can gain perspective.

- **Exercise extreme caution when times get hard, because they will get hard.** Consider calling upon your mentors, allies, colleagues, and friends for counsel, support, and perspective. And be very circumspect about quitting out of anger or in protest — this can hurt you, your community, and your mission. But, most important, quitting can damage the faith invested in you by those who brought you to their school. If you come into a school to do this work and end up making a mess and leaving, chances are the school and your people will find themselves many steps behind where they were when you arrived.

WE MAY NEVER REACH THE MOUNTAIN TOP...

Defining success when doing diversity work is, at best, a tricky business. Schools tend to focus on quick-fix solutions in order to quiet those who trumpet a school's perceived shortcomings or to try to make folks feel better when they experience inequities. All too often, schools default to the "faces and foods" game, where brown faces are tallied and cultural cuisine is featured. The purpose of the former is to provide a quantitative measure of success, while the latter seeks to connect people through their stomachs. While not intrinsically bad, neither moves a community very far down the road to true cross-cultural understanding, appreciation, and empathy.

The numbers are important, of course; school communities that value diversity seek to have a critical mass of students and faculty of color. But quantity without depth and quality is a recipe for disaster. While posters, cultural days, and exotic assemblies can paint a veneer of inclusion, limiting a school's efforts to such window dressing has two unintended consequences. First, it can insult the people it is supposed to celebrate. In fact, some of our students at Lick-Wilmerding have said "food, faces, fiestas" is on a par with naming a boulevard after Martin Luther King, Jr. when that street is in a broken-down neighborhood in a city that has no intention of addressing the neighborhood's real issues and problems. Second, "food, faces, fiestas" often has the consequence of reinforcing the misconception that building an inclusive community is easy work.

In fact, the work is much deeper and requires exploration of extremely difficult themes. Usually it necessitates rethinking and re-engineering the school culture. We have found that, while difficult, going deep and grappling with complex issues can yield profound results, as it reinforces a sense of personal and collective responsibility and mutual reliance. This common bond is essential if a school community is to move beyond Band-Aid solutions — ethnic dinners, "drive-by" diversity training, and cultural speaker series — to incisive, comprehensive, and holistic initiatives that capture and address the authentic needs of all constituencies.

At the time this article first appeared, **Ilana Kaufman** was the assistant head of school for academic affairs at Lick-Wilmerding High School (California). She is currently head of Windrush School (California). This article first appeared in the Summer 2003 issue of *Independent School*.

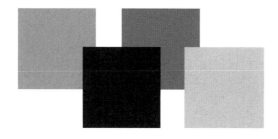

Significant evidence suggests that **students learn best** in racially heterogeneous learning environments.

Diversity Directors As Leaders

Making the Case for Excellence

BY ELIZABETH DENEVI AND MARIAMA RICHARDS

Now is not a good time for those of us who see ourselves as diversity advocates in schools. In a recent NAIS survey, diversity was not included in the list of 22 challenging aspects of the job that heads of school were asked to rate.[1]

Although some surveyed heads did list "diversity" as another area of concern, the fact that it didn't make the list of top challenges assumes that, for most schools, diversity has been adequately addressed or is not an issue requiring great focus.

Yet, in reality, nagging issues remain in independent schools: persistent low numbers of teachers of color, flat admission numbers for students of color, lack of people of color in department head or other senior administrative positions, few heads of color, lower expectations and performance of students of color, white allies growing frustrated with the lack of institutional commitment to antiracism, persistent issues of sexism, and growing socioeconomic stress for families trying to afford independent school tuitions.

---

[1] 2007 NAIS Head of School Leadership Challenges Survey, Summary of Findings, December 2007.

As colleges and universities look for students with greater leadership skills in the area of cross-cultural communication, most independent schools, it seems, still question the real value of a multicultural education. It may be the moral thing to do, but will it really make kids smarter? In fact, it will, but continued misunderstandings about multicultural and equity pedagogy, along with ongoing systems of resistance and oppression, have kept substantive diversity efforts at bay in our schools.

Our contention is that schools can't achieve excellence without clear strategic diversity goals and informed personnel to lead the process. Diversity directors who are well versed in multicultural education and who have a clear mandate and job description can coordinate and facilitate such initiatives and programs. They can serve as resources for all constituents and provide a crucial piece of knowledge that other administrators may not bring to the table. Perhaps the inability of schools to achieve greater equity is directly related to practices that have often marginalized diversity advocates as opposed to using their expertise to create a strategic vision. To move our schools forward, we need a more dynamic conception of leadership that recognizes the value of and necessity for multicultural educators and administrators.

We serve as co-directors of diversity at Georgetown Day School — founded in 1945 as the first racially integrated school in Washington, DC — and we also consult with other schools around the country. We continue to meet smart, talented teachers of color who have suddenly become diversity coordinators or directors with no job description, no experience or relevant training, and no budget. Many of them teach a full load in addition to working on diversity programs. It shouldn't be hard to see how this is a formula for failure. And, indeed, school communities too often end up blaming the diversity coordinator (who just "couldn't make it work") for the school's inability to move forward on issues of diversity.

In other schools, one routine argument we hear often is that, since diversity is everyone's job, we shouldn't relegate the responsibility to one person or office. Yet, when applied to other areas, this rationale rings hollow. Schools expect all staff members to be technologically proficient, but we are unaware of any school that doesn't have qualified, designated, and highly trained staff members to direct technology efforts. And even though we are all responsible for the welfare of children in our schools, most schools have a dean of students or a similarly appointed position. Yet diversity remains an area guided by a particularly fuzzy logic, as if an extensive body of research and scholarship dating back over 60 years has not firmly established multicultural and anti-bias education as a discipline and field of expertise.

The Inclusive School
A Selection of Writing on Diversity Issues in Independent Schools

There are positive signs on the horizon: the research proving that academic excellence is dependent on racially diverse learning environments, the Association of Independent Maryland Schools (AIMS) statement on diversity and its accreditation tool, more white teachers committed to challenging racism, and the growing number of young professionals of color who are interested in teaching in independent schools. Independent schools are, in fact, strategically poised to help lead education throughout this century, but only if they are willing to take a hard look at the progress they've made with respect to diversity and the distance they still have to cover.

What follows is a comprehensive list designed to show how diversity impacts every area of school life and why it needs to be at the top of the list of both future challenges and opportunities. With this all-encompassing view, it is essential to have designated, empowered staff members who can design and implement a strategic plan for diversity and who can work with the board, other administrators, and the head of school to bring about lasting and effective change.

DIVERSITY = ACADEMIC EXCELLENCE

Significant evidence suggests that students learn best in racially heterogeneous learning environments. Studies led by Patricia Gurin, professor emerita of psychology and women's studies at the University of Michigan, have shown that students who experience "the most [racial] diversity in classroom settings and in informal interactions with peers show the greatest engagement in active thinking processes, growth in intellectual engagement and motivation, and growth in intellectual and academic skills."[2] Additionally, the field of multicultural education has provided years of research on the relationship between multicultural teaching practice and increased student engagement and performance.[3] Although there have been ongoing critiques of multicultural education, both the research and testimony from teachers demonstrate overwhelmingly that teaching from multiple perspectives and having a multiplicity of voices in the classroom is more challenging, more rewarding, and very simply, produces better educated students who can engage with each other and their world in a more authentic and productive way.[4]

THE DEMOGRAPHICS OF FULL ENROLLMENT

As the U.S. population becomes more diverse and as tuitions continue to rise, schools will need to diversify their outreach efforts and recruitment of families. In addition to

---

[2] Expert Report of Patricia Gurin, *www.vpcomm.umich.edu/admissions/legal/expert/gurintoc.html*.

[3] James A. Banks and Cherry A. McGee Banks, *Handbook of Research on Multicultural Education* (San Francisco: Jossey-Bass, 2nd Edition, 2003).

[4] James A. Banks, *Introduction to Multicultural Education* (Boston: Pearson, Allyn & Bacon, 3rd Edition, 2001).

outlining the value of diversity in independent schools, the AIMS statement recognizes that "the ability of AIMS schools to thrive in the future will depend in part upon their ability to make good on the promise of diversity ideals by implementing concrete and far-reaching changes."[5] What is true in Maryland is true throughout the country. Schools have to think critically about how they market and make new populations aware of the value of an independent school education. This may mean more targeted outreach efforts to particular constituencies. Our school, for example, holds an admissions open house for gay and lesbian families so prospective parents understand our institutional commitment to supporting all families in our school community. Of course, it also means that schools need to back up their marketing language and outreach with a thoughtful commitment to diversity and multicultural education in order to support all children who enter the schoolhouse.

EFFECTIVE LEADERSHIP AND FEWER HEADACHES

An insufficient approach to diversity almost always ends up wreaking havoc in a school. Effective leadership not only helps schools make the transition to inclusive communities, but it also does so with fewer headaches. What does effective diversity leadership look like? In our experience, it requires diversity directors who are members of the senior administrative team and who work with all constituencies to ensure strategic planning and implementation of equity initiatives throughout the school.

By way of illustration, the Georgetown Day School Senior Administrative Team currently has 11 members representing all three divisions and includes the head of school, diversity and business offices, principals, development and admissions offices, and directors of curriculum studies and technology. Each week, we hold an administrative dialogue to look at emerging issues with the hope that multiple perspectives will be considered before any decision is made. Additionally, we function under the premise that the principles of equity and justice should be applied to all areas of the institution. In many schools, all too often, diversity practitioners are left out of this process. As a result, every racial incident or complaint is a "surprise" that then needs to be handled. In contrast, our collective vision allows the school to stay ahead of the curve. Not only are we prepared to have the difficult conversations when they arise, but we are also knowledgeable enough to know what challenges are on the horizon. This is not to say that we aren't still floored by some of the things that happen, but our process is one of growth, rather than recovery.

[5] Association of Independent Maryland Schools, Diversity and Independent Schools, *www.aimsmd.org/upload/DiversityStatement.pdf.*

MISSION-DRIVEN CHANGE:
CULTURALLY RESPONSIVE TEACHING AND LEARNING

Integration of diversity efforts with a school's mission is one key to successful change. And a clear understanding of multicultural education directly aligns with mission-driven work. Just as mission statements articulate common beliefs and commitments, multicultural education is based on a guiding set of principles, the core premise being the successful education of all children. In our work, we often highlight the triumvirate of hiring, professional development, and evaluation as one place to begin a strategic commitment to increasing equity. By ensuring a diverse candidate pool and having all candidates meet with the diversity director or directors and the head of school, as well as with other relevant administrators and faculty, a school sends a clear message about its mission during the application process.

Finding racial diversity is often referenced as the biggest challenge that schools face. While racial diversity is an extremely important goal, it is just as important to hire teachers, regardless of race, who are aware of their own racial identity and who understand how their race impacts their teaching process. At our school, once staff members are hired, they all complete a training session with the diversity office at the beginning of their first year, so we have an opportunity to engage more fully in issues of diversity. Additionally, we offer in-house training opportunities and encourage all staff to seek out other diversity training beyond the school.

Finally, any evaluation process has to include an assessment of staff members on their commitment to the school's diversity mission and their ability to teach and learn in ways that support a diverse learning community. Without this kind of accountability, a school's efforts can fall short because, just like our students, we ultimately know that what we are graded on matters most.

ENGAGED AND EMPOWERED STUDENTS

Empowered students are much more likely to find success inside and outside of the classroom, and can be our best advertisement to our larger communities. As directors of diversity, we believe that our foremost responsibility is to the students. If students do not see themselves reflected in all aspects of school life such as governance, the curriculum, or cultural celebrations, they are less likely to feel ownership of the school community. We monitor all three of these areas while also developing relationships with the student body to promote self-advocacy. By supporting affinity groups and open forums, we help students have a voice in the welfare of the school.

ENGAGED AND EMPOWERED STAFF AND FACULTY

One of the key reasons teachers like working in independent schools is the relative freedom to develop their own curricula. Georgetown Day School teachers also often cite our commitment to issues of diversity and social justice as one of the main attractions to working at the school, and we actively involve staff in the creation of diversity programming and classes. Like the students, we have staff affinity groups and opportunities for professional development and growth, such as our annual Staff of Color retreat, our SEED group (Seeking Educational Equity and Diversity), and our staff Gay/Straight Alliance.

INVESTED FAMILIES (WHO WILL GIVE TO THE ANNUAL FUND)

It is key that development offices know the power that diversity programming can have on parent philanthropy. When families feel welcomed and included, they are more likely to financially support the school. Often in schools, parent associations seem to be run by the same group of folks: those who are affluent, not racially diverse, and mostly female. As a result, many families are reluctant to get involved if they don't feel as if they fit the profile. With this challenge in mind, our Parent Service Association (PSA) chairs created regular meetings with the diversity office to better understand the work that we do, including our support of the Parents of Students of Color and the Parent Gay/Straight Alliance. Through these dialogues, the PSA reached out to the other parent leadership groups, and, once that happened, it radically changed parent participation. For the first time, fathers were doing more volunteering at cookouts; they were conducting school tours and leading community-service trips. Parents of color chaired the annual auction, dramatically changing the look and feel of the event.

In the end, this inclusiveness meant more financial and emotional support of the school. To show their support for the work of our office, the Parents of Students of Color gave a collective financial gift to the school. Also, five years ago, we increased our efforts to make Georgetown Day School a safer space for same-gender families and LGBT students. It was through these efforts that LGBT alumni and their parents renewed their financial commitment to the school.

One line of thinking in many independent schools is that diversity programming will anger those alumni who want a school culture to remain the same. There are plenty of examples where this clearly isn't the case. And, more to the point, what this thinking overlooks is the number of folks who have disconnected because a school has failed to meet their needs.

MORE PRODUCTIVE WORK ENVIRONMENT

The research of Claude Steele, a social psychology professor and dean of the school of education at Stanford University, on stereotype threat — the threat of being viewed through the lens of a negative stereotype or the fear of doing something that would inadvertently confirm that stereotype — is one example of how the failure to address inequity can lead to an unproductive workplace.[6] This kind of fear and threat of judgment does not allow staff members or students to do their best. By being explicit about expectations, challenging prejudice and bias, and actively educating students about stereotypes and how they function, we can dramatically improve the quality of a school's culture.

STRONG COLLEGE ADMISSIONS

This year, the University of Michigan included the following essay assignment on its undergraduate admission application:

> We know that diversity makes us a better university — better for learning, for teaching, and for conducting research." (UM President Mary Sue Coleman) Share an experience through which you have gained respect for intellectual, social, or cultural differences. Comment on how your personal experiences and achievements would contribute to the diversity of the University of Michigan.

Schools that help students think critically about diversity and explore issues of social justice will better prepare students for colleges that are actively seeking leadership in the area of diversity. Our college counselors regularly cite the ability of students to write and discuss experiences related to diversity and equity and how that ability sets them apart from other candidates. Similarly, college representatives who come to GDS comment on how our students seem to know who they are and how their identities impact the larger community. Many have commented on the fact that we have an affinity group for white students committed to anti-racism. Since colleges actively recruit for all kinds of diversity, they are looking for students who have strong cross-cultural communication skills and who know how to be successful in a diverse learning environment.

ASSESSMENT AND ACCOUNTABILITY

In a recent article from DiversityInc.com, Weldon Latham, a senior partner and chair of the corporate diversity counseling group at the law firm Jackson Lewis, discussed the value of assessing the climate and culture of diversity in the workplace as a smart

---

[6] Claude Steele, "Thin Ice: Stereotype Threat and Black College Students," *www.theatlantic.com/doc/199908/student-stereotype*.

business strategy.[7] Many schools are resting on their proverbial laurels with regard to diversity work and are vulnerable to a diversity crisis. In our experience, the best schools, like the best businesses, consistently monitor, assess, and improve their schools' climate for diversity and equity. This means that schools need qualified professionals who understand organizational development and the role of diversity and multiculturalism in the culture.

These points delineate a vision of school leadership that places equity at the center, as opposed to the margins, of both our daily and long-term work. Each year, we hear from the participant schools of the GDS Equity Collaborative,[8] a diversity strategic planning program, that they want their schools to be more equitable; they just don't know how to get there. What they are essentially asking is for school leaders to become better allies and advocates for change in order to reclaim with pride the term "diversity" and resist efforts to "find another term." Creating a truly diverse learning environment should be the work of all of us who want to best serve children and their families. In order to ensure excellence and to systematically increase diversity and equity, schools must start with trained and informed personnel and a strategic commitment to being the best they can be.

Elizabeth Denevi and Mariama Richards are the co-directors of diversity at Georgetown Day School (Washington, DC). This article first appeared in the Spring 2009 issue of *Independent School*. Elizabeth Denevi is also the author of "White On White: Exploring White Racial Identity, Privilege, and Racism," which appeared in the Summer 2004 issue of *Independent School*.

---

[7] Weldon Latham, "To Avoid Costly Litigation, Assess Your Diversity," *DiversityInc.com*, September 2008.

[8] For more information on the GDS Equity Collaborative, go to *www.gds.org/collaborative*.

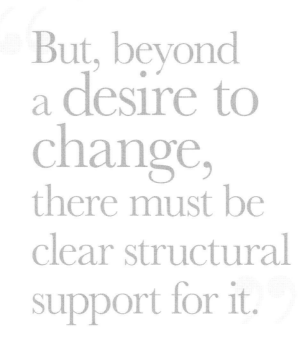

"But, beyond a desire to change, there must be clear structural support for it."

Leading the Way
Why a Diversity Committee of the Board Is a Must for All Schools

::

BY CHRISTOPHER MARBLO

The benefits of being a more diverse school — as opposed to a relatively monocultural school — have never been more apparent. As our world continues to "flatten" and intercultural contact becomes the norm, as our own country becomes more diverse in a variety of ways with each passing year, and as cognitive and intellectual diversity are seen as precursors to excellent schools and institutions,[1] it becomes untenable for school leaders to believe that there is educational excellence in schools with a narrow representation of adults and students.

If schools truly want to meet the needs of their students, prepare them for the realities of the world, and teach them to be moral leaders of the future, then schools must become more diverse, more inclusive.

---

[1] Scott E. Page, *The Difference: How the Power of Diversity Creates Better Groups, Firms, Schools and Societies* (Princeton, NJ: Princeton University Press, 2007).

But, beyond a desire to change, there must be clear structural support for it. In particular, two essential conditions must be in place for progress to be made. First, the school leadership — the head and trustees — must make diversity a primary goal. The head and board must be clear with all constituents that increased diversity is good for the school and that everyone must take actions that demonstrate this commitment. Second, a school must have structural vehicles in place to bring about progress and forward motion. Such structures allow for the thorny issues of diversity to be debated and resolved, they lead to the development of clear policies and support systems, and they assure that the necessary resources — of time, power, money, and people — are allocated to the cause.

At The Town School (New York), we created and revised three important structures to help us move our diversity agenda forward. The first was to establish a senior-level director of diversity position that is part of the school's leadership team. The second was to redefine the purpose of our Parents' Association Diversity Committee by broadening its scope to examine all aspects of diversity, not just race. Interestingly, attendance at these meetings quadrupled — and understanding of, and buy-in to, our diversity initiatives grew. The third, and in some ways most important, change was to create a board-level diversity committee. We knew that the board of trustees had to demonstrate diversity leadership, and we felt that there was no better way to do this than to create such a committee.

IF YOU BUILD IT, THEY WILL LEAD

Of all the constituents of our school, however, the board was the least comfortable with its role in moving the school's diversity efforts forward. While there was support for increased diversity, some trustees had reservations. So we had conversations about what diversity was and talked about why the school should be more diverse — essentially, why this was valuable to our overall educational mission. Finally, we strategized about how the board could — and should — move our diversity agenda forward.

Eventually, the board members made it clear that they were willing to support and trust the school's diversity initiatives, which, by this time, had found articulation in a strategic diversity plan. However, they were not quite ready to lead the process, and we knew why. They needed a vehicle to focus their leadership in this area. They needed a structure to continue their deliberations, to debate policy, and to stake a leadership claim. In short, they needed a diversity committee of the board. Adapting the "Field of Dreams" principle — "If you build it, they will lead" — we constructed our diversity committee from the ground up, and provided the board with a structure that allowed it to contribute to and lead our diversity initiatives.

Our first job, however, was to define exactly what the diversity committee of the board would do. We were explicit that it would not duplicate the work of the staff or the parents' association committee. Ultimately, we focused on four areas: (1) anticipating and setting policy, (2) working with the finance committee to frame and understand the resource needs (fiscal and human) necessary to greater diversity, (3) being leaders — both symbolically and through action — of our diversity initiatives, and (4) ensuring that the school's climate and culture are healthy.

Issues of policy surrounding diversity are notoriously difficult and sensitive. Financial aid, admissions, and hiring practices can all be greatly influenced, for good or bad, by policy decisions aimed at greater diversity. We knew that we needed the diversity committee to tackle these issues when they came up, to study their ramifications, and to make recommendations to the full board. Recently, the committee examined financial-aid policies for our pre-kindergarten students. While many schools do not offer financial aid for these students, we decided to do so because it was directly related to our goal of attracting and keeping families of differing economic backgrounds. We know more policy issues will arise in the coming years, and I am grateful that we have a board diversity committee to help us analyze them and eventually recommend policy actions to the full board.

The diversity committee also audited the cost associated with diversity. Frankly, we thought it was important for the diversity committee to examine the nuances of this topic before it went to the finance committee for further discussion; simply put, the members of the diversity committee look at these financial issues through a different lens than those on the finance committee do. This alternate view is essential to making sure that our financial policies are not only justifiable from a monetary viewpoint, but also from a broader mission-based and human perspective.

In addition, the simple fact that we have a diversity committee of the board has proven to be enormously beneficial. The symbolic and actual power that the committee has and displays speaks loudly to all constituents: faculty, families (current and prospective), and potential employees. I have seen this most noticeably with prospective families and employees. The existence of the committee says something clear and vital about what our school stands for, about what matters most. In short, people notice — especially those who are underrepresented in the independent school community.

BEING PROACTIVE AND READY FOR THE FUTURE

One thing is certain about diversity and schools: While the promise of genuine transformation is present, the potential for conflict and strife is, too. We have come to expect that it is natural for tensions, disagreements, and discomfort to occur as we step deeper into diversity. Issues of race, identity, culture, class, and sexual orientation, among others, are all both personal and political, and, hence, potentially contentious. You can approach this reality in two ways: be ready for it and proactive or be unprepared and reactive. Having structures in place has helped us to respond in a healthy and mission-based manner. Our director of diversity, parents' association diversity committee, and board diversity committee have all helped to keep conflict to a minimum.

The diversity committee of the board is arguably the most important structure in this regard, for it provides a neutral, but powerful, setting to help the leadership of the school make informed decisions about diversity. Having institutional commitment behind diversity in the form of the committee takes some of the pressure off individuals, especially the director of diversity. The issues that arise tend to become institutional, not simply personal, and while this proposition poses some risks, it also offers great opportunities. The diversity committee also keeps us honest and aware; we remain mindful of the policies and concerns that are important to diversity; and this stance helps us to avoid the type of conflicts that often spring from unintended thoughtlessness.

We devote considerable resources on the board level to all aspects of school life, and we are, of course, working to ensure that the school thrives now and in the future. Indeed, given that diversity is important — and will only grow in importance in the coming years — it's hard to imagine why a board would not establish a diversity committee to lead in this area. The buildings and grounds of the school warrant a board committee; surely, the diversity initiatives of the school deserve one as well. It would seem that a school is setting itself up for poor performance if it denies the importance of diversity on the board level, and, while a diversity committee is but one way for the board to acknowledge this importance, it is arguably the most significant one.

INSTITUTIONAL IDENTITY, MISSION, AND THE QUEST FOR EXCELLENCE

Independent schools and their identities — and reputations — are often tied to a few important beliefs. Academic excellence, clearly, is the most important one. But how many independent schools link their identity and mission to diversity — to the ideal of a well-functioning, inclusive community? How many link diversity with educational excellence? As Joe Healey, then head of Ethical Culture Fieldston School (New York), and now with University Liggett School (Michigan) wrote, "In a school, diversity is first and foremost a learning tool. We would no more imagine a school without math or science, foreign languages, or physical education than we would imagine a school without diversity of opinion and belief. If the quality of a school can be measured by the quality of its conversations, then a school with limited or narrow stories to tell cannot be truly great."

A board of trustees, as the guardian of the mission and the future of a school, absolutely needs to be in the middle of these issues and debates.

Our experience with creating a diversity committee of the board has been nothing but positive. The very process of thinking about the committee — what it would do, how it would be structured, and how it would advance the mission of the school — was very useful and instructive. We had many substantive discussions about the core issues of diversity, about the realities of our world now and what we imagine it will be in the near future, about our school's institutional commitment to excellence and justice, and about what role the trustees should play in all of this. Ultimately, the board decided to be active participants and stakeholders in our diversity initiatives. In retrospect, this was a wise decision, and one that will positively impact our school for years to come.

Boards of trustees must, in one way or another, confront diversity in concrete and proactive ways, yet I still get the sense that many schools think it is not all that important. The world and future say otherwise. If we are to prepare our students for an increasingly globalized society, if we want our students to know how to interact well with and learn from people from different backgrounds and with different beliefs, if we want our students to have a deep understanding of the human value of equity and justice, we need to lead in these areas. Fortunately, we are in an ideal position from which to lead, given our cultural and academic freedom. Novelist Anais Nin wrote, "Life shrinks or expands in proportion to our courage." It is my hope that more independent school boards will have the courage to be champions of diversity.

Christopher Marblo is head of school at The Town School (New York). This article first appeared in the Fall 2007 issue of *Independent School*.

Whites in independent schools typically have the **privilege** of feeling as though **they belong.**

Addressing White Privilege In Independent Schools

Frequently Asked Questions (and Their Answers)

::

BY GREG BLACKBURN AND TIM WISE

In recent years, independent schools have begun to move beyond discussions of racial diversity and multiculturalism into weightier considerations of the race and class inequities that continue to plague our nation. As part of this process, many independent schools have initiated conversations about white privilege and the way it operates within the independent school environment.

It is hoped that, by raising awareness about white privilege and institutional racism, our schools will redouble their commitments to creating equitable educational experiences for all students, faculty, staff, and parents.

Yet, because discussions of privilege and inequity can prove contentious, objections are often raised. Some people believe there is no such thing as white privilege and that conversations about such topics are "liberal" propaganda. Others acknowledge the existence of white privilege but contend that discussing it only leads to greater division. They suggest we avoid the matter of privilege in favor of a continued focus on diversity and "appreciation for difference." Others are new to the conversation and are often confused as to what is meant by white privilege in the first place.

It is with these objections and concerns in mind that we offer the following set of frequently asked questions about white privilege and answers to those questions. It is our hope that, by providing this resource, the conversation about white privilege can continue, even when the participants in that dialogue don't always agree. By coming to better appreciate the seriousness of the issue, even persons with different ideological positions should be able to engage in respectful discussion, and then agree to work together toward the creation of more equitable and inclusive independent school environments.

What is white privilege?

White privilege is any advantage, head start, opportunity, or protection from systemic mistreatment, which whites generally have, but people of color do not have.

Our family worked hard for what we have. Why should whites be blamed or criticized for being successful?

Discussing white privilege is not about blame or criticism. It's about making sure we understand the factors that contribute to racial inequality. Hard work has been part of the reason why individuals have succeeded, but unearned privilege has also been part of the explanation. Just as many whites have worked hard, so have millions of people of color, and yet, because of discriminatory barriers and fewer connections, they have been less able than whites to access, among other things, elite educational opportunities.

Even when parents work hard to provide for their children, once those children take advantage of the opportunities provided, they benefit from someone else's effort. So, unless one believes we "deserve" our families, the transmission of intergenerational advantage, even if initially secured by hard work, has not been earned by many young whites attending independent schools today. This is especially true because white families often accumulated their professional credentials and wealth in a system that restricted the ability of people of color to do the same. Whites have worked hard, but they have also been favored in employment, housing, and schools.

Finally, many privileges enjoyed by whites aren't things that can be earned, but instead are benefits that come to whites merely by virtue of being white in a mostly white space. Whites in independent schools typically have the privilege of feeling as though they belong. They can feel confident that their presence won't be questioned or presumed to be the result of someone rigging the game on their behalf. This is true even for children whose parents or grandparents attended the same school. Rarely do legacies (who are

The Inclusive School
A Selection of Writing on Diversity Issues in Independent Schools

overwhelmingly white) have to worry about people thinking they don't belong in a prestigious school, or that standards were lowered for them. Even when a legacy's academic credentials are unimpressive, it is rarely suggested that he or she doesn't belong. On the other hand, students of color often confront the assumption that they were only admitted to a selective school because standards were lowered to foster diversity.

White students also have the privilege of not having to overcome racial stereotypes in the classroom, while students of color often feel as though they have to work especially hard to disprove negative assumptions made about members of their group. Among the stereotypes that students of color often feel the need to disprove are beliefs that they are less intelligent and less hardworking than white students or are only good at certain things — like sports for black kids, or math and science for Asian students.

Aren't you confusing race and class? Yes, independent schools are places of economic privilege, but why bring race into it?

Independent schools are often rooted in a history of racism and white privilege. Some were only formed after public school integration began, specifically by those who didn't want their children going to school with African Americans. Other schools have been around much longer and were clearly established — often as reflected in their early mission statements and certainly in the way they functioned — for the education of wealthy, Christian, and explicitly white children. For persons of color who are considering such schools for their children, worries about whether their kids will be fully accepted are real and understandable. For whites, not having to worry about how a school's history, traditions, and origins might feel alienating to them and affect their ability to truly fit in is another example of privilege.

Even independent schools with progressive educational philosophies tend to have mostly white boards. What's more, their policies, practices, and procedures have been implemented by mostly white leadership on behalf of mostly white students and families. Although these people may have the best of intentions, rarely will they have been required to consider the distinct needs of (and pressures experienced by) families of color in their schools.

Research has found that students of color in mostly white schools, regardless of their family's economic status, experience a "burden of representation" not generally experienced by whites. This burden refers to the way in which black and brown students feel the need to succeed, not only for their own sake, but also for others of color coming after them. Such students often feel as though failure or underperformance on their part may reinforce stigmatizing group stereotypes and negatively impact others from their group.

Even affluent students of color in independent schools contend with these stereotypes in ways that white students typically will not. Often, students of color are presumed to be poor and on financial aid (and therefore somehow less deserving), even when they are neither poor nor receiving much, if any, financial assistance. Likewise, they may be presumed less capable, and thereby they experience anxieties about proving their abilities to others. These anxieties can have profoundly negative consequences for academic success, as well as physical and emotional well-being. Not having to worry about overcoming stereotypes in class is a substantial privilege for white students.

Finally, students of color have the pressure of trying to fit in within two different worlds: forced into an emotional and psychological tug-of-war between the need to fit in and succeed in the dominant culture, on the one hand (which independent schools are often very good at preparing them to do), and maintaining a feeling of connection to their racial or cultural group, on the other (something to which our schools have often given little thought). That white students typically do not experience this conflict is yet another way in which white privilege exists in independent schools, separate and apart from economics.

Nowadays, our mission statements include sections on diversity, and teachers and administrators are committed to inclusion. So how can white privilege still be a problem?

Yes, schools may now have diversity clauses as part of their mission statements, but is the school's commitment to diversity fully "operationalized" throughout the institution? Does it play a role in the establishment of policies, practices, and procedures? Are hiring and admission decisions made with an eye toward maximizing diversity and equity? Are candidates for admission, faculty positions, or administrative jobs screened not only on the basis of traditionally understood qualifications, but also on their commitment to the mission of the school, including its focus on diversity and equity? If so, how is this done? If not, why is it not done? And how can a school be truly committed to such principles while doing little to prioritize them in their daily operations? If diversity becomes just a buzzword or a nice aspirational goal — but one that doesn't require us to rethink existing conceptions of qualifications, standards of excellence, or what constitutes a "good school" — white privilege will be maintained.

As for teachers and administrators, how deep is their commitment to diversity and equity? When candidates are evaluated for jobs, or students are evaluated for admission, do these teachers and administrators evaluate them with traditional tools alone — which often view accomplishment in a vacuum and ignore the person's access to opportunity or lack thereof — or do they use a more holistic conception of merit that considers what candidates have accomplished or how they have performed relative to prior access? If schools make hiring or admissions decisions on the basis of test scores, years of experience, or experience teaching in a school like the one to which the applicant is applying, they may inadvertently reinforce white privilege. Such schools would favor whites simply because whites would have had more opportunities to teach in such places, and for longer than persons of color, or because white students would have had more exposure to the kinds of materials found on standardized tests, relative to students of color. The evaluations might then have little to do with merit, would perpetuate white privilege, and would actually undermine the diversity component of the school's mission.

Traditional evaluation tools reward the advantaged for having had more opportunity to begin with. Though a candidate of color may have slightly less experience or a somewhat lower test score than a white candidate, it may be that, relative to that person's starting point, the person of color's achievements are actually more impressive and indicate perseverance and potential that would translate to success in an independent school. A true commitment to diversity and equity takes this into account throughout the institutional process.

But we're already bending over backwards to recruit students of color and provide them financial aid, we've made our curricula multicultural, and we have all kinds of diversity programs. Hasn't the pendulum swung too far to the other side?

If it seems as if schools are "bending over backwards" for students of color, this is only because for so long schools did almost nothing to recruit such students or to make the curricula more inclusive. Given where we come from, any attention to these issues may seem like a lot. But rest assured, it is whites who continue to receive privilege in independent schools. Schools typically have far more white children who are legacies, come from other well-connected families, or are siblings of previously admitted children than they have students of color. Yet, rarely is it suggested that schools are bending over backwards for such white students, as if to imply that something is untoward about their presence.

It is actually rare for independent schools to deliberately recruit or seek students of color. But when such actions are taken, there are several good reasons for the practice. First, because of the history of racism, families of color are less likely than white families to have prior connections to independent schools. As such, they may not be aware of the steps involved in applying, or know which forms to fill out or how to set up a school visit or evaluation for their child. Having less familiarity with the process can be intimidating and dissuade families of color from pursuing independent school options for their children. This would then deprive our schools of many incredible children who would contribute much to our institutions. By engaging in deliberate recruitment, independent schools can provide families of color with the same information, knowledge, and confidence that our white families so often already have.

Secondly, unless independent schools send a clear signal about our desire for and commitment to diversity, families of color might be hesitant to enroll their children. Knowing that their child would be significantly underrepresented is a source of anxiety for many families of color. Deliberately seeking out students of color only seems like "bending over backwards" because such efforts are not needed to recruit a healthy number of whites. But this is due to privilege — specifically, the privilege of being able to take for granted that you belong in a particular place and will be seen as belonging there by others.

As for financial aid, it is often assumed that such aid is mostly for students of color, and that most students of color receive substantial assistance. But this idea is often false and rooted in outdated stereotypes. It is true that, when independent schools began to racially diversify, the children of color entering the institutions were often from economically marginalized families. But compared to prior generations, today a much larger cohort of financially comfortable families of color send their children to independent schools, as do many more cash-strapped whites who receive financial aid. Yet the stereotype about who receives financial aid persists.

Having said that, why is the provision of generous financial aid to deserving students of color a problem? The premise of the complaint — or characterizing such aid as "bending over backwards" — seems to be that students of color from low-income backgrounds don't really deserve to be in independent schools. But shouldn't schools seek to educate highly capable students from all kinds of backgrounds, irrespective of financial need? Indeed, one could even argue that students of color from lower-income backgrounds who strive and achieve, despite not having had the advantages so common to many white students, might actually be more deserving of admission than those who have had a wealth of opportunity since birth.

As for curricula, despite some changes, the overwhelming majority of the material studied in school — from literature to history to art and music — continues to be that of European or "white" origin. The reason multicultural education efforts may seem preferential to people of color is due to white privilege: in this case, the privilege of not having to see your group's narrative, or the pre-existing curricula, as a racially-specific one. Whites have never had to think about the literature, art, or history we studied as white, even though for the most part they were. When your group's experiences are considered the norm, they don't have to be racially labeled. So, we don't have an official "White History Month," even though most every month functions as though it were.

As for programming, though such events are often valuable, they can sometimes be little more than celebrations of the food and holidays of racial and cultural "others" — hardly the kind of efforts that erase the privileging of the dominant group. Learning about Diwali, Chinese New Year, or Kwanzaa doesn't challenge the dominance of whites within our schools. In fact, because such celebrations sometimes allow students and families to view the traditions of non-whites as "exotic," they may (absent a discussion of power and privilege) serve to reinforce the privileging of whites, whose traditions are deemed normal and mainstream, as opposed to the strange and fascinating rituals of "others."

Doesn't talking about white privilege reinforce division by making whites feel guilty and people of color feel like victims? Shouldn't we be color-blind, instead of focusing on divisive subjects like this?

Racial division existed long before conversations about those divisions began. Blaming the conversations for the problem they seek to address is like blaming the speedometer in your car for the speeding ticket you just received.

Ultimately, this question presumes that, if we don't bring up the subject of racism and white privilege, people of color won't think about it and tension will be avoided. But people of color know that racism and white privilege are real and damaging factors in their lives. Sadly, it is white people who often deny the problem and refuse to speak of it. This refusal to engage is a source of much of the tension between whites and people of color. By avoiding the discussion, those of us who are white give the impression that we either don't care about the life experiences of people of color, or worse, that we simply don't believe people of color when they claim to have been harmed by racism.

And far from seeking to instill guilt, these conversations can point whites in the direction of greater alliance with people of color by engaging all stakeholders in the creation of more equitable structures. A school that embraces color-blindness merely blinds itself to the consequences of color, making it harder to ultimately address those consequences and create equity. If schools strive not to notice color — the very category that triggered unequal treatment and unearned privilege to begin with — how are they to then engage members of the community in a discussion about color-based injustice?

One way to foster healthy discussions about these subjects is to create affinity group structures, whereby people of color provide support to one another and whites striving to be antiracist allies do the same. Although affinity groups are structured as intraracial groupings, over time they can spark productive interracial dialogue as well because some of the conversation-stopping and tension-creating comments that might otherwise be made in mixed company can be tackled first in a less tense and more secure environment.

Won't too much emphasis on diversity or changing the curriculum water down our academic standards? Colleges want students who can do high-level work. Isn't this additional stuff extraneous?

Colleges want prepared students, to be sure. But, increasingly, they consider the ability of students to succeed and thrive in diverse and equitable environments part of what it means to be prepared. Institutions of higher education are preparing their students for the real world, in which most people are poor, non-white, non-Christian, and don't speak English. To think that equity and diversity are extraneous is the ultimate white privilege and conceit: Only those in the dominant group could think themselves sufficiently educated even as they remain largely ignorant of the cultures, histories, or literature of others.

It is also white privilege to think that the existing standards — simply because they have long worked for some — are truly demanding, and that diversity and equity efforts would amount to lowering them. In fact, standards are regularly altered to reflect the times in which we live. Until a half-century ago, few elite schools taught any American authors; by and large, only British literature was considered worthy of being taught. Now we would consider many American writers, poets, and playwrights as central to the canon. Why should we view the inclusion of persons of color within that canon any differently? There is no objective scale, after all, by which their work can be deemed inferior. Only privilege and racism would lead one to assume that diversity sacrifices excellence.

Similarly, if admission or hiring standards have previously rewarded those who had more opportunity from the start, then by no means can they be considered objective or valid. Altering the criteria used to select students or faculty does not amount to lowering standards so much as recalibrating our interpretation of what it means to be qualified in a global and interconnected environment and within institutions whose mission statements increasingly prioritize diversity, inclusion, and equity.

Ultimately, undoing systems of inequality and privilege is everyone's business. To live up to the more lofty parts of our schools' missions and to fulfill the obligation to equal opportunity in which our nation professes to believe, white privilege must be addressed and ultimately rooted out of our institutions. Addressing this privilege will not be easy. Much of it is longstanding, and the people who benefit from it have grown accustomed to the way things are. But the way things are must change. We do none of our children any favors by educating them in spaces of profound racial inequity.

At the time of this writing, **Greg Blackburn** was head of The Caedmon School (New York). He is now head of St. Philip's Episcopal School (Florida). **Tim Wise** is an independent school parent and author of *White Like Me: Reflections on Race from a Privileged Son*. He can be reached at *timjwise@mac.com*, or through his website, *www.timwise.org*. This article first appeared in the Spring 2009 issue of *Independent School*.

'Change is a
process,
not an event.'

The Road from Here

Where Independent Schools Are on LGBT Issues, and How to Get to Where They Need to Be

::

BY KEVIN JENNINGS

In the winter 1989 issue of *Independent School*, I wrote an article entitled "Opening Closets and Minds" that marked, in some ways, the beginning of a revolutionary change in how independent schools addressed lesbian, gay, bisexual, and transgender (LGBT) issues. Over the past 15 years, innumerable schools have expanded their non-discrimination policies to include categories like sexual orientation and gender identity; hundreds have established Gay-Straight Student Alliances; and, in some boarding schools, LGBT couples are now house parents.

These changes have hardly happened in a vacuum. They reflect shifts in societal attitudes towards, and in the legal status of, LGBT people in the United States and abroad. These shifts have resulted in an increase in the number of states that prohibit employment discrimination based on sexual orientation from two in 1989 to 14 today, as well as the granting of marriage benefits equally to opposite-sex and same-sex couples in Massachusetts and Canada.[1]

So, are we done? If not, what's next?

Over the past four years, the Gay, Lesbian, and Straight Education Network (GLSEN) has done extensive research among students in independent schools, creating the largest-ever data set on LGBT issues in independent schools — with a broad-based sample of 6,532 students from 20 schools in 14 states, from both coed and single-sex schools as well as boarding and day schools. This data, coupled with the lessons we have learned from other research and a decade and a half of working directly with schools, gives us a clear picture of what problems still exist, what interventions work, and how schools evolve with regard to these issues.

WHERE ARE WE NOW?

For those who believe we're done with anti-LGBT prejudice in independent schools and can now move on to other issues, the results of the GLSEN Independent School Study are startling. Anti-LGBT language remains rampant on our campuses: 75 percent of students report they hear it frequently or sometimes, and only 25 percent say they hear it rarely or never. Anti-LGBT language is seemingly still socially acceptable on the typical independent school campus. Given that this data is from schools that were willing to work with GLSEN, and therefore might be assumed to be more proactive and inclusive on LGBT issues, we may be able to assume that the real numbers would be higher if we had a completely random sample of independent school students, as "hostile" schools — more on them later — self-select out of working with our organization.

The key determinant of the prevalence of such language seems to be the composition of the student body — in short, the more boys, the higher the frequency of anti-LGBT language. Ninety-five percent of students in all-boys schools report hearing such language frequently or sometimes, as opposed to 72 percent in coed schools and 35 percent in all-girls schools. For those working in all-girls schools, however, two cautionary notes are worth keeping in mind. First, the all-girls data set is the smallest of the three in our survey and, thus, may not be as representative as the others; second, recent research has found that girls act out their bullying behaviors though actions such

---

[1] Since the time this article was written, a number of other states have legalized same-sex marriages, including Connecticut, Iowa, New Hampshire, Rhode Island, and Vermont, as well as the District of Columbia. California recognizes same-sex marriages that existed prior to the passage of Proposition 8 in November of 2008. Still other states grant spousal rights for same-sex couples, including California, Oregon, and Washington. Domestic partnerships are recognized in Hawaii and Maine. New York and Maryland also recognize same-sex marriages from other states.

Stages of Development

When it comes to LGBT issues, schools progress in stages. Once a school is clear where it stands in terms of development, it can then begin to work for change. The four stages are:

- **Hostile,** where LGBT issues are not addressed and there is overwhelming opposition to so doing.
- **Resistant,** where some individuals have begun to address the issues, but the community as a whole and the school as an institution have not committed themselves to a process of change.
- **Open,** where basic policies have been put in place to insure equitable treatment of LGBT people, but there is not a commitment to a process of continuous improvement. (Interestingly, one independent school teacher recently convinced me that these schools were better described as "passive" than "open," and we plan to incorporate this suggestion into future editions of *The GLSEN Workbook*.)
- **Inclusive,** where both the community and the school as an institution are engaged in a continuous process of self-examination and improvement with regards to LGBT (and other) diversity issues.

as social shunning rather than overtly hostile language, which would not be measured in our survey. In other words, girls may not be complete angels just because their numbers are lower than these for boys in the survey. But it seems indisputable that boys are more prone to use and tolerate anti-LGBT language, and it is incumbent upon educators working with them to study the culture of boys to understand why.

GLSEN has also begun to gather data on the prevalence of racist language on independent school campuses and, while the incidence of such language is lower than anti-LGBT language, it is hardly uncommon. Twenty-seven percent of independent school students surveyed reported hearing racist language frequently or sometimes on their campus, as opposed to 75 percent who hear anti-LGBT language. That is not to say we're "better" on racist language (I think we'd all agree that an incidence rate of 27 percent is too high), but it is instructive to note that we seem to have made more progress on reducing racist language than anti-LGBT language.

Why? One obvious reason is that both our society as a whole and many independent schools in particular have been working on issues of racial justice far longer than LGBT issues, so a greater degree of progress would be predictable. Our data seems to suggest that independent school students have internalized the idea that racist language is socially unacceptable to a greater degree than they have with anti-LGBT language.

I draw this conclusion from the following data. First, intervention rates are not startlingly different on racist versus anti-LGBT language. For example, 73 percent of students say they "rarely/never" witness intervention when racist language is used, as opposed to 92 percent when it comes to anti-LGBT language. Thus, fear of "getting in trouble" with teachers cannot solely account for the difference. The second point involves where they hear the language. Frequency of both anti-LGBT and racist language is low in classroom settings (8 percent for anti-LGBT and 9 percent for racist), perhaps in part because of the greater degree of structure found there and perhaps because of the presence of adults as well. But there is a marked jump in the frequency of anti-LGBT language in student-controlled spaces that does not occur when we look at racist language. For example, 68 percent of students say they hear anti-LGBT language sometimes or frequently in hallways (750 percent higher than the rate in classrooms) compared to 26 percent who say they hear racist language (slightly less than 200 percent higher than the rate in classrooms). There seems to be a degree of self-policing or social unacceptability to racist language that keeps its incidence relatively low across settings; the same is not the case when it comes to anti-LGBT language.

And such language matters. While many students may say "That's so gay!" to describe things they don't like in general rather than in an explicitly homophobic way, the impact on LGBT students is still profound. In GLSEN's 2003 National School Climate Survey (a biennial study of LGBT student experiences in public, independent, and parochial schools), we found that 71 percent of LGBT students said that they were moderately or extremely bothered by such language. It contributes to a hostile school climate that explains why, in our 2001 study, 51 percent of LGBT students in independent schools reported that they did not feel safe on their campuses. Sadly, despite the progress that has been made, anti-LGBT language and attitudes still pervade independent schools, with real consequences for students.

WHAT WORKS?

GLSEN's model of school change is found in a publication called The GLSEN Workbook, which speaks of how three major components of school life must be addressed to create safer school climates. They are:

- **Policy,** such as nondiscrimination and benefits policies, set usually by boards of trustees.
- **Programs,** such as training, library resources, and both curricular and extracurricular offerings, shaped by administrators and teachers.
- **Practices,** such as the prevalence of anti-LGBT language on the campus and the actions of teachers, primarily shaped by students and teachers.

Fortunately, GLSEN found that schools can have a measurable impact on student achievement in each category by taking certain steps. Among them are:

- **Inclusive policies.** LGBT students in schools with policies that did not include categories such as "sexual orientation and gender identity" had absenteeism rates that were 40 percent higher than those who did (36.5 percent versus 26 percent, respectively).

- **Inclusive programs.** For example, LGBT students who had a diverse curriculum that included positive portrayals of LGBT topics were 27 percent more likely to say they felt like they belonged at their school.

- **Practices that show teachers are supportive.** LGBT students with supportive teachers had GPA's that were nearly a full letter grade above those who did not (3.1 vs. 2.8, respectively). Anecdotally, students report that "distinguishing behaviors" such as intervention when anti-LGBT language is used and inclusion of LGBT topics in the curriculum are common ways they measure teacher supportiveness.

These findings remove some of the guesswork out of creating an inclusive school climate where all feel they belong and can achieve academically, and they provide invaluable guidance for schools looking to "do the right thing."

HOW DO WE GET THERE?

Virtually all educators are familiar with the basic precepts of developmental psychology and how human beings evolve from infants to toddlers to adolescents to adults, with each stage bringing different challenges and joys. The same process is true of schools, especially when it comes to diversity issues. School climates can be measured and schools can objectively determine at what stage of development they are when it comes to LGBT issues (see sidebar on page 105).

A standard feature of GLSEN's staff development work with independent schools is to ask the faculty as a whole to complete the assessment tool found in *The GLSEN Workbook* to see where their school falls on this spectrum. From experience, I can tell you that many staff members are startled to discover that their school is not as far along as they had thought. As one school head put it to me, "I realize now I have been confusing our intentions with our actions. I think, in our hearts, we're all committed to treating LGBT people equally, but we haven't really done the work to change our school so that this is actually true." That just about says it all.

I believe strongly in the adage "Change is a process, not an event." A red flag goes up for me every time an independent school calls and I hear something like this: "We 'did' racism last year and this year we want to 'do' homophobia. Can GLSEN help?" What exactly did they "do" to racism, I wonder, as they clearly could not have made it go away in a single year? We need to reframe the work of creating inclusive schools so that it is no longer based on a checklist mentality of "a thing to be done." Instead, we must understand it for what it is: a continuous process of learning in which, yes, there will be things to be done but, once they are, we will find new challenges and new things to do. If we view the process of creating inclusive schools as a journey rather than a one-time task, we'll all be much better off. Clearly, the journey for independent schools on LGBT issues has been fruitful since I first wrote in these pages in 1989, but we're hardly home yet.

Kevin Jennings is the founder of GLSEN and its executive director until 2009. From 2009 to 2011, he was the assistant deputy secretary for the Office of Safe and Drug-Free Schools at the U.S. Department of Education. He is currently the CEO of the nonprofit organization, Be The Change. This article first appeared in the Fall 2004 issue of *Independent School*.

"When people
don't have
knowledge,
they often react
with fear...."

When Chris Becomes Courtney

Preparing a Pre-K–8 School Community for a Transgendering Student

BY JOHN PETERMAN

On their first day of the 2008 school year, the eighth graders are unusually boisterous. This is it. They're at the top.

It is the beginning of their last year at Brookwood School (Massachusetts), and it feels magical, yet strangely ominous. Shrieks of excitement explode from two friends who haven't seen each other in three months. They hug and dance and both babble into each other's face at the same time, understanding everything and nothing at all.

As the students make their way into classrooms, our eighth grade English teacher appears at my side looking rather concerned. "Thought you'd want to know that Chris is wearing a dress." It is the first line of a dramatic play that unfolds on the Brookwood School stage for the next nine months.

In truth, it came as no surprise that Chris was wearing a dress, although the last time he wore one to school was three years before in fifth grade. Given Chris's history, we all knew it was not a prank or an act of defiance. It certainly wasn't a disciplinary issue. We were all aware that Chris had announced he was gay during his seventh grade year and, at the time, had wondered whether he was struggling with gender identity. We knew the dress was something to take seriously. Fortunately, the sexuality education and sexual diversity consultants who had come to work with Brookwood parents and faculty over many years had helped prepare us well for this eventuality.

Regardless, we had an immediate major disruption to the first day of school. We had to get Chris out of the dress while not totally embarrassing him or causing a scene. The last thing we wanted was an explosive reaction from parents that would hurt Chris and potentially turn the school year into a battleground.

I asked Chris's advisor to talk with him and, if need be, call his parents so that they could deliver dress code pants to their son. (What are they thinking, anyway, letting him out of the house like that?) A little while later, Chris's advisor came to my office to report back.

"Well, it turns out that Chris left his house in trousers and hid the dress in his backpack. He changed in the bathroom before first period, and I told him he needed to

Guidelines for Parents of Gender-Variant Children

Lynne Michelle Howard

Five years ago, my now-13-year-old daughter transitioned to being the girl she always said she was. After having worked with many families with transgender kids and co-founding a support group in Colorado, here is my advice.

- Don't be afraid to let kids explore gender differences. It's normal and healthy. Don't make a big deal out of it. Parents can't make their kids gender variant.
- If a child tells you s/he is a different gender or that s/he hates her/his body parts, don't scoff. Kids going through a "phase" rarely use these words.
- Not all children have words for explaining to adults that their brain and spirit do not match their body. Don't assume they aren't gender variant if they don't actually tell you they are.
- Support gender variant kids from an early age. Understand that gender variance is not the same thing as sexual orientation. It is about who people are, not about sexual attraction.
- Studies show that some humans "understand" if they are boys or girls as early as 18 months.

- Don't let your fears of being judged affect how you decide to support your child. More people than you think are aware of transgender issues, and they are more supportive than you might assume.
- Reach out for those who have been on this path. Groups like TYFA (*www.imatyfa.org*) and PFLAG (*www.pflag.org*) can help you find professionals who can help as well.
- Make sure your professional is qualified. Therapists without experience in gender issues can hurt more than they help.
- Your child has more rights than you think. Don't let one negative school administrator or teacher be the last word. The groups that I've mentioned previously can help.
- Educate, love, and support. These kids have the highest suicide rates of any youth group. They need support and understanding from everyone.

Lynne Michelle Howard lives in Boulder, Colorado, and is the co-founder of Trans Youth Education and Support Colorado (*www.tyes-colorado.org*).

change back into pants. He wasn't too happy. But that's not the whole story. Apparently, he emailed his friends last night and told them he was now a girl and they should call him Courtney from now on."

I sank in my chair knowing we were all in for a long and bumpy ride. We all loved this boy and wanted him to be safe.

From the day that Chris had worn a skirt in fifth grade, we had worked with him, his parents, and teachers in offering support for his gender identity search. Back then, no one much cared that he chose to wear a skirt, and his teacher did a wonderful job of leading class discussions around inclusivity and self-expression. She spent many hours with Chris as he struggled to come to terms with his feelings. In seventh grade, he announced to everyone that he was gay, which prompted a series of meetings with his parents and his therapist to ensure that we were doing all the right things to support him. At the time, students and parents who knew were either supportive or silent on the issue.

But eighth grade was a different story. Working with a transgender student would require us as a community to make many decisions for which we had no road map. We knew immediately that if, in fact, Chris would be publicly transitioning to Courtney during his/her eighth grade year, silence and support would no longer be the universal response from parents. We also knew that we would stand behind him through this journey no matter how difficult it would be for Brookwood. But we needed time to prepare. We needed time to educate the community while respecting Chris's need to express himself as Courtney — even though he was years away from sex reassignment surgery, should he choose to pursue it. (Not all transgendered individuals do.) To complicate the matter further, Chris, by nature, was anything but patient and, understandably, oftentimes assumed that those in authority should not be trusted. We knew that he would see our need to take the time necessary to prepare our community as being a rejection of his immediate need to express himself.

In the first hours of that first day, we were thrust into planning mode. We listed everything that we needed to consider and then suggested ways to move forward. The thoughts and questions quickly bounced off the walls of my office.

- "We need to talk with the eighth grade. They are confused."
- "Our teachers need training."
- "We have to get Chris's parents in right away."
- "What about bathrooms?"
- "What if he wants to play field hockey?"
- "Will he graduate in a dress?"

- "What about the eighth grade buddies in third grade?"
- "Will he sleep in the boys or girls room during the eighth grade overnight trip?"
- "We need help with this."

My assistant knocked on the door, interrupting the strategy session. "I just had a phone call from an angry eighth grade parent, and he said he is on his way to school to speak with you." It was starting.

After a very brief conversation with the fearful and anxious father, I finally had the chance to meet with Chris. He told me that he had been in therapy all summer with a transgender specialist and that he had been diagnosed as a transgender candidate. He wanted everyone to call him Courtney. I explained to Chris that we supported him completely, but everyone was not yet ready to accept him as Courtney. "We can tell everyone to call you Courtney, but we would rather have them accept you as Courtney, and that means they need to understand what you now know about yourself. As much as this is so very real and true for you, it will be confusing and scary for others. When people don't have knowledge, they often react with fear, and that reaction may end up hurting you. I am not going to let that happen even if you don't like the way we decide to do this. So, we need you to be patient. We are going to ask your therapist to come to school and speak to students and teachers. They need to know what you know. We also need to communicate this situation to the Brookwood parents. That is going to take a while, and until then, you will still be called Chris and will follow the dress code for boys."

Chris sat there, staring at the floor. He was angry. He wanted it all, immediately. He was 13. Most of all, he was ready and anxious to live as his true gender — and more than ready to stop living with the profound psychic disequilibrium that came with having to be and pretend to be what he was not.

Over the course of the next few days, we formulated a plan to move ahead. I informed the president of the board of trustees and promised that a course of action plan would be sent to all trustees. We made a list of what needed to be done, and we assigned responsibilities to various administrators and the school's consulting psychologist. Our list included:

- Establish ground rules for Chris so that he is clear about our expectations of him as we educate our community.
- Immediately set up a meeting with Chris's parents and therapist.
- Contact experts in the field for advice.
- Inform all faculty and staff of the situation.
- Hire an expert to train our faculty on all issues related to transgender teenagers.

- Select the best professional to speak with students in our upper school, grades six through eight.
- Write a letter to all Brookwood parents explaining the situation and the school's position on the issue.
- Set up a date for an evening information session for parents.
- Make decisions about the accommodations needed once Chris officially "becomes known" as Courtney.

When we met with Chris's parents and his therapist, we reassured them that the school was fully supportive of making accommodations for Chris throughout the school year. They understood and appreciated that we needed time to train faculty, educate parents, and communicate with the at-large community. We agreed that Chris would continue to use the name Chris, dress according to boys' rules, and participate in boys' activities until we had fulfilled our obligation to all constituencies. We estimated that it would take three to four weeks to accomplish everything, and we urged Chris's parents and therapist to help Chris understand the necessity of remaining patient.

A week later, Chris's impetuosity got the best of him. He came to school wearing a short skirt, high heels, and an abundance of jewelry and makeup. He quickly informed other eighth graders that he would not speak to them unless they addressed him as Courtney. Following the understood agreement, a teacher escorted Chris to my office, and I called Chris's father to come to school to take Chris home. I then sat next to Chris on my couch. "Chris, your teachers' hearts are in this so deeply that I refuse to let you sabotage our efforts," I said. "We are going to make sure that you have a safe and supportive eighth grade year. I know you don't understand why we just can't make it happen. But right now, you are making it more difficult for yourself and for us." After Chris left with his father, I received the first of several ultimatums from one of our parents. It was a short phone conversation.

"I didn't send my daughter to this school expecting I would have to talk with her about sex when she was still in kindergarten. This situation will be a constant disruption to her, and unless it is resolved, I will take my daughter out of school. By the way, I have talked to a lot of other parents, and they feel the same way." At the moment, he was in no mood for discussion, so I simply invited him to the planned parent information session and told him the school and Massachusetts law stood firmly behind Chris as a Brookwood student. The father did not attend the session. His daughter stayed in school.

After holding successful faculty and student meetings conducted by transgender specialists, we hired Deborah Roffman, nationally known author of *Sex and Sensibility*, to conduct our parent information night. The turnout was more modest than I had expected, with more supporters than opponents attending. There was some tension, lots of questions, and many outspoken advocates for Chris and his family. Overall, the parents came away from the meeting with a deeper appreciation for and understanding of transgender youth. Momentum and support was clearly in our favor. The time had come for Chris to officially become Courtney.

Guidelines for Schools Working with Gender Variant and Transgender Students

Engage in professional development programs for faculty and staff in the area of Gender and Sexuality Diversity (GSD). Ideally, this work is begun before there is a particular student or family that necessitates it.

Create and enforce nondiscrimination and anti-bullying/anti-harassment policies that explicitly protect gender identity and sexual identity.

Emphasize school rules and policies that address the emotional and physical safety of all students. Data indicates that those students who are able to be open about their gender identity and sexual identity in a safe environment feel more part of the school community and do better academically.

Provide educational programs about GSD for parents and students. Creating an informed, inclusive environment is a community-wide effort.

Be mindful that standard bullying prevention programs often do not explicitly address GSD as an area of concern.

Use school forms and applications that are inclusive of all gender and sexual identities and family structures. Make sure language that refers to identities and families is inclusive in all written materials.

Ensure that your academic and social curriculum regularly integrates history, information, and events that recognize GSD.

Consider a gender-neutral or flexible dress code. Permit students to comply with the dress code in their affirmed gender.

Honor preferred names and pronouns. There are ways to comply with record-keeping regulations and also allow a student to identify in her or his affirmed gender.

Avoid gender-segregated activities for P.E., lining up, etc., or create groupings that allow for flexibility.

Provide gender-neutral options for bathrooms, changing areas, locker rooms.

Develop clear guidelines for gender variant and transgender students regarding athletic teams participation, overnight trips, same-sex activities and clubs, etc. These students need clear rules and expectations just like all students do.

Respect students' right to be "out" about particular aspects of their gender and sexuality identity, as well as their rights to privacy. Not all students or families want to be spokespeople or activists for these issues.

Recognize that the needs of gender variant children and transgender teens are similar to and different from students who identify as gay, lesbian, or bisexual.

Provide GSD resources to all community members. Make sure your library has accessible information and that your Internet filters do not prevent students, faculty, or parents from finding relevant information.

If you have a gender variant child in your school, put together a team, including a professional therapist and/or consultant, to create plans and approaches on a case-by-case basis. Each child and school community has particular needs that can best be addressed with a collaborative consultation model.

Understand that for gender variant children, transgender teens, and their families, a private school may be seen as their best option. These schools have the ability to create community, policy, programs, and curricula that reflect an independent vision of inclusion and equity.

Remember that helping your school community examine unhealthy gender-role stereotyping is a benefit to all, not just those students who are gender variant.

On the day before Courtney began her Brookwood experience as a girl, we met with the eighth grade one more time. We told them it was OK if they made mistakes during the transition. We reassured them that we all might use the wrong pronoun or call her Chris instead of Courtney. It would take some adjustment for all of us. We told them that we had put an athletic locker in the unisex bathroom near the locker room, and Courtney would use that space to change and as a bathroom. Since Chris had only intended to participate in coeducational afterschool athletic programs, Courtney would do the same. I then thanked the eighth graders for their incredible support for their classmate. We all knew that their unwavering support for Courtney was the single most important factor in the eventual acceptance shown by the entire community.

I think all of us were amazed at how smoothly the rest of the school year unfolded. Our teachers, trustees, and parents shared a sense of pride in the way our community came together around Courtney and her family. We all knew this was only a small step in her journey, but it was a big step for us.

Graduation day, June 14, 2009. Courtney's name was called, and she stood to make the walk onto the stage to receive her diploma. She wore a simple white dress. Her auburn hair now reached her shoulders. Those in attendance stood to applaud as Courtney's broad and steady smile revealed her teenage braces. Like all the other girls, Courtney's steps showed a slight wobble in the unfamiliar high heels.

John Peterman is the head of Brookwood School (Massachusetts). This article first appeared in the Summer 2010 issue of *Independent School*.

REFERENCES

Emily A. Greytak, Joseph G. Kosciw, and Elizabeth M. Diaz, *Harsh Realities: The Experiences of Transgender Youth in Our Nation's Schools* (New York: GLSEN, 2009).

Stephanie A. Brill, S. and Rachel Pepper, *The Transgender Child: A Handbook for Families and Professionals* (San Francisco: Cleis Press, Inc, 2008).

Susan Lee, *When It Counts: Talking About Transgender Identity* and *Gender Fluidity in Elementary School*, *www.genderspectrum.org*.

"Schools not only socialize students **academically,** they also socialize students **racially.**"

The Success of African-American Students in Independent Schools

::

BY EDITH G. ARRINGTON, DIANE M. HALL, AND HOWARD C. STEVENSON

Over the past five years — at the request of concerned independent school educators and with funding from independent schools and a grant from the National Institute of Mental Health — we've conducted extensive research[1] on the experiences of African-American students in independent schools.

(See sidebar on pages 128–129 for the genesis of this project.) Based on this research — which we've named the Success of African-American Students (SAAS) in Independent Schools project — we would like to share three main points about the experience of black students in independent schools:

1. Promoting black students' connection to the school community and their emotional health is key to their academic success.

---

[1] A note about the sample: Qualitative data is culled from individual interviews with 65 male and female students in grades 6-12 and focus groups with upper school students (6-8 students per group). Quantitative data is from two waves of data collection. In the first wave, 109 students in grades 5-12 completed survey questionnaires. There were 59 female and 50 male students. In the second wave of data collection, 122 students completed survey questionnaires. Of these students, there were 54 male and 68 female students.

2. Schools not only socialize students academically, they also socialize students racially.

3. The experience of racism is a reality for black youth that can compromise the quality of their school experience and tax their emotional resources.

EMOTIONAL HEALTH AND SUCCESS IN SCHOOL

We begin with our assertion that promoting black students' connection to the school community and their emotional health is key to their academic success.

Our research (here and elsewhere) indicates that, for black students, success is best defined by a strong sense of connection to the school community; a positive sense of self across contexts, but especially in the school; social and emotional health; and a racial identity that would serve as a resource as they develop, but particularly when students encounter racism. In our interviews with students for the SAAS project, it was also clear that their experiences in these areas varied.

When we measured the students' self-esteem across the home, school, and peer contexts — all three areas being important contexts of socialization for youth — students reported above-average levels of self-esteem in all areas with the highest levels of self-esteem reported in the home environment. There was a statistically significant difference[2] between the students' self-esteem at home and at school, with school self-esteem being lower.

Students assessed the climate of their schools by responding to a number of questions about learning satisfaction, teacher support, school fit, and perceived quality of education. On average, student responses to the school climate questions were positive. For example, a clear majority reported that they had social and cultural opportunities at their school (64 percent) and that they were satisfied with the quality of education they received at their school (85 percent). Fifty-six percent said that the teachers cared for students, and an overwhelming majority said that the education they received at their school would prepare them for college and life (91 percent).

Yet while student responses to most of the questions about school climate were positive, there were statistically significant differences between the students' reports of school fit and their reports of learning satisfaction, teacher support, and quality of education. In fact, students' reports of school fit were lower than their reports in any other area. Three-quarters of the students said they had to make special efforts to fit into their school communities; 82 percent reported that they had had negative experiences at their school; and 40 percent did not believe that their school treated all students the same.

---

[2] All of the mean differences and correlations reported throughout this discussion are statistically significant at the .05 probability level.

When we explored the students' "psychological sense of school membership" (PSSM), the results were similar to what was found with school climate. PSSM is the extent to which students feel that they belong in their school and are deemed to be respected and contributing members of the community. The average response of students in regard to PSSM was moderately high. For example, 70 percent of the students reported that there was a teacher or adult they could talk to in the school, 72 percent reported that other students liked them the way they were, and 82 percent believed that people in the school knew that they were capable of doing good work.

Similar to the school climate results, while black students' overall PSSM was moderately high, there were other areas in which their connection to the school community was not strong at all. Sixty-seven percent reported that they had, at one time or another, wished they were in a different school, 70 percent believed that it was hard for people like them to be accepted at their school, and 62 percent thought they did not belong in their school.

Although levels of emotional distress were low for the black students in our study, relationships did exist between distress and self-esteem, school climate, and PSSM. More specifically, as emotional distress increased, esteem at home, with peers, and especially in school decreased — as did perception of the school climate and PSSM. In terms of anger expression, when distress increased, anger control decreased, and anger suppression and anger acting out increased. Only anger control is related to self-esteem for students, with higher anger control related to higher levels of peer, home, and school esteem. More positive evaluations of the school climate and stronger PSSM are related to higher levels of esteem across all areas, but particularly so in relation to school esteem.

The question of how black students are doing in independent schools has no simple answer. It is true that black students value their relationships with teachers and peers, the resources that exist within their school, the preparation for college admission and success, and the training they receive for future endeavors. However, some aspects of independent schools leave a number of students feeling at times as if they do not fit into their school environments and that they have a tenuous connection to the school community in some areas. We believe that black students in independent schools can feel both connected and disconnected to their schools. This is because they encounter people and resources that affirm them within the school at the same time that they confront challenges to their sense of self and community.

Promoting black students' connection to the school community will require continued work to affirm them while addressing the existing challenges they face. Our research indicates that schools need to better explore how race is addressed in schools and how students experience racism. In discussing these challenges we move onto our second point: *Schools not only socialize students academically, they also socialize students racially.*

RACIAL SOCIALIZATION

In the introduction to *Visible Now: Blacks in Private School*, Diana T. Slaughter-Defoe, a professor at the Graduate School of Education at the University of Pennsylvania, and Deborah J. Johnson, a professor of family and child ecology at Michigan State University, assert that "all children carry the culture of their communities and families into their schools." In a truly multicultural school, students carrying the culture of their community and family to school would not be an issue, as the cultures of all racial and ethnic groups would already be represented and respected in the school.

However, the multiracial composition of the United States has not often translated into schools with racial or cultural diversity among students. In the case of independent schools, the most recent statistics on the racial composition of the schools in the National Association of Independent Schools (NAIS) indicates that approximately 82 percent of students are white, 5 percent are black, and 12 percent are other students of color (NAIS, 2000). The faculty and administration of these schools is predominantly white as well. Given the racial composition of independent schools, the school context for black youth is *racially dissonant.*[3]

Racial dissonance becomes even more meaningful when we focus on the broader context of *whiteness* that exists in predominantly white schools and how it relates to socialization. In school, youth learn what is expected of them in their roles as students and as citizens in the larger world. In independent schools, the majority of students are white, and significant economic resources are available to prepare students to enter into places and positions of power and prestige. Consequently, whiteness and privilege will shape the rules concerning what is appropriate behavior, which attributes are valued more than others, and how people are supposed to interact with one another in and out of the school community.

As members of groups that are not socially and economically advantaged in the same way whites are, black students and other students of color in independent schools benefit from acquiring the academic and social knowledge that will position them for success in college and their careers. Connecting with possible future leaders in society and, more important, potentially becoming one of these leaders are other advantages

---

[3] Gray-Little & Carels (1997) define "racially dissonant" school contexts as school environments where a student's racial group makes up 20 percent or less of the student body. By this definition, independent schools are clearly racially dissonant contexts for black students and other students of color.

of attending independent schools. But by attending independent schools, black students must also grapple with implicit and explicit messages that the community they represent is less valued in school than the majority community.

Addressing the latter concern becomes complicated in schools where teachers and administrators are ambivalent about how they should deal with racial and cultural diversity. From our interviews with white teachers, it seemed clear that, in the interest of treating all students equally, many of them don't want to focus on racial and cultural diversity. But, ultimately, this view tends to trivialize diversity as being something that is just "skin deep," thereby sending the message to students that since "we are more alike than different" there is no need to discuss race and diversity. Such messages perpetuate the "myth of sameness" identified by psychotherapist Kenneth V. Hardy, which discourages a critique of how race may impact who is deemed to be successful in school, how school may be experienced differently by students based on their community membership, and what members of the entire school community learn about people different from themselves. If no one challenges the myth of sameness when there is evidence that real differences based on race exist within the school, it is harmful for all members of the community.

We cannot overstate how important it is to be cognizant of the messages that students and adults in the school community convey about race. These messages have an enormous influence on shaping the learning and social environment for black students. This leads us to the last major point we want to emphasize: the reality of race and racism for black youth.

RACE AND RACISM IN INDEPENDENT SCHOOLS

Whether it was through our interviews with students or information gathered from surveys, it was clear that race and racism matter for black youth in and out of school. Racial identity and racism[4] surfaced as topics of discussion in nearly all of our interviews and were significantly related to a number of different indicators of success in our analysis of the survey data.

In terms of racial identity, almost all the students who participated in our research project viewed the black community and their membership in it in a positive way. There was more variability in terms of how important being black was to students and how

---

[4] We define racial identity as how students see themselves as members of the black community, their understanding of what other people think of black people, and the meaning that race holds in their lives (Sellers, Smith, Shelton, Rowley, & Chavous, (1998). Our definition of racism is the expression of prejudice and discrimination on an interpersonal level so that it is subjectively experienced by individuals (McNeilly, Anderson, Armstead, Clark, Corbett, Robinson, Pieper, & Lepisto, 1996).

they believed other people evaluated the black community. In fact, our research clearly indicates that black students will engage with race in different ways because of their unique characteristics, developmental history, and experiences across social contexts such as the family and neighborhood. As students get older, race and racism can play larger roles in their school experiences.

Along with their racial identity, students also discussed encounters they had with racism in their schools in many of our interviews. Very few students described dealing with crude expressions of racism, such as being called a racial epithet or hearing a racist joke, and none described any physical altercations motivated by racism. The questionnaire we used that focused on racism asked students about their experience with any of approximately 40 events or situations that could occur at school, in public, on the job, or when hearing racist statements. Students reported that, on average, they encountered approximately half of the events or situations over the last year at least once.

Some of the most relevant events and situations included: being followed while shopping (47 percent), believing that white people act surprised at their intelligence or hard work (43 percent), people thinking students will act out their stereotypes of how they think a black person is supposed to act (school sports, style of dress, speech, etc.) (41 percent), and feeling it was necessary to change their speech or appearance when around white people (40 percent). While some of these events occurred outside of the school (e.g., being followed while shopping), the other events can and did occur within the school setting.

In response to their experiences of racism, students reported feeling angry and strengthened most often (particularly in school and in the public realm). Feeling strengthened as a response to racism may seem counterintuitive. However, students who have been proactively racially socialized by parents and other adults so that they have coping responses ready when they encounter racism may report being strengthened because they are able to deal with racism in a healthy way. Indeed, across all of the domains we assessed, students reported "speaking out" or "proving them wrong" as the coping responses they used most often, particularly in school or when they heard racist statements. Being able to take a stand of some sort when confronting racism may serve to empower students and ultimately strengthen them. In that regard, proactive racial socialization would be invaluable for students.

The black students' experience of racism in and out of school is important to address because, for a number of students, racism adversely affects their emotional and psychological coping within school. As students report more school-related racism, their sense of connection to the school community, or PSSM, and evaluation of the school climate decreases. Conversely, their emotional distress and anger expression (specifically, anger acting out) increases. Similar relationships hold for racism experienced in and out of school, such that the more students reported racism in school or in public, or the more they heard racist statements over the last year, the lower their school self-esteem.

From our interviews with teachers, we have gleaned that many do not view discrimination as a problem that their students currently face in school. And while students described situations that we felt were racism related, some students did not name the experiences as racism. We think the hesitance on the part of some teachers and students to see racism in the schools is likely due to their holding definitions in which racism is thought only to be the more overt and crude types of discrimination.

Racism in today's society often takes a subtle and more covert format, involving stereotyped thinking and diminished or lowered expectations for black students. Given the anxiety around the topics of race and racism, the tendency for some in the school community to deny or downplay racism is understandable. However, it is detrimental for students, and especially so for black students — for whom race is central to their identity — to not have an opportunity nor a vocabulary to name, discuss, or change their reality. Discomfort on the part of adults or students in the school community in discussing racism will not prevent students from having these experiences. Indeed, discomfort and silence in regard to racism will unfortunately make the students' ability to cope effectively with racism more difficult, since students will not have the resources to draw upon when they need them.

Moreover, given our assertion that schools are racially socializing environments, not talking about race and racism does send messages to the members of the school community. Not discussing race and racism, particularly when it is in the format of denying their relevancy, also leaves notions of privilege and whiteness unexamined. As a result, black students and all members of the school community are left without the tools to work through the role race and racism play in their school experiences. Race and racism do matter in how students experience their schools, and it is only by directly addressing how they matter that their negative impact can be reduced.

PROMOTING THE SUCCESS OF BLACK STUDENTS

Given our assertions and findings, what do we suggest that the independent school community do to promote success for black students? We have a number of recommendations.

First, it is necessary that schools recognize the diversity among black students in their community. Acknowledging that black students are diverse in and of themselves should alleviate some of the reliance on stereotypical thinking — and the bias that results from it that students report encountering in and out of school. This is important to address because black students who have more personal experiences with racism in and out of school have a lower sense of school membership and school esteem.

Second, without understanding and examining how the contexts of whiteness and "niceness"[5] surround and silence race dialogue, school programming for students of color is likely to fall short of reducing the emotional distress they experience in their schools. To reduce stigmatization, honest and open discussions must occur on whiteness, the power and privilege that are related to it, and the expression and experience of racism within independent schools. Since the wider sense of community for all students and adults is compromised when racism is left unexamined, conversations on race and racism should be held across and among the various constituencies in the school community. Talking about race and racism is not something only black people and other people of color should do. While interracial dialogue that directly addresses race, racism, and privilege may be difficult to engage in, it is necessary that these conversations take place. Such discussions would represent proactive socialization around race and help promote the emotional health and school connection of black students.

Third, for black students and other students of color to feel as though their communities are as valued as the majority community within their schools, the numbers of students of color must increase. It is necessary for schools to bolster or remain committed to recruitment and retention efforts so that the number of black students and other students of color within independent schools becomes a viable force. In this way, students from all communities will have a voice in their schools.

Finally, the identification of programming to cultivate stronger connections to the school community for black students and to enhance the emotional health of students should be a school goal. This is particularly necessary for students who are more aware of the dynamics of race, racism, and privilege in their schools since these students have lower levels of PSSM and evaluations of their school climates than other students do. Schools can accomplish this in a number of ways, but we believe that organizations where youth from the same or similar racial communities can come together and be emotionally reinforced within the school setting, or affinity groups, are especially effective.

We see multiple implications for the overall development and in-school experiences of black students who attend predominantly white schools. Problems arise for black

---

[5] In independent schools, we discovered a systematic "niceness" that masked the hesitance of the schools to fully engage with the research. It took a long time for us to read through this niceness and understand that, while many of the people we encountered in the schools were pleasant to us and spoke encouragingly about our work, we were still not making the progress we had hoped. This same niceness manifests itself in a desire not to discuss the hard issues of race and racism in many schools.

students in these schools when the significance of race is denied or downplayed, or when there is no acknowledgment of the messages sent about race and how it impacts success in the school community. Students must still learn, grow, and thrive within this atmosphere, and, as such, independent schools have a responsibility not only to pay attention to the academic achievement of black students, but also to tend to the emotional and structural challenges these students face daily.

It is our belief that every independent school should view the positive development and mental health of black students as an equally meaningful barometer of success as their PSAT/SAT scores, grades, athletic accomplishments, or admission to the "right" colleges. Anything less would be a failure to provide black students with the education they deserve.

At the time of this article's publication, **Edith G. Arrington** was a postdoctoral research fellow at the University of Pennsylvania's Graduate School of Education. She is now deputy director of the Robert Wood Johnson Foundation's New Connections program. At the time of this article's publication, **Diane M. Hall** was program coordinator of the Psychological Services Masters Program at the University of Pennsylvania's Graduate School of Education. She is currently a behavioral scientist with the Prevention Development and Evaluation Branch in the Division of Violence Prevention at the National Center for Injury Prevention and Control (NCIPC). **Howard C. Stevenson** is associate professor in the Psychology in Education Division and co-director of Clinical Training for the School, Community, and Child Clinical Psychology program at the University of Pennsylvania's Graduate School of Education. This article first appeared in the Summer 2003 issue of *Independent School*.

REFERENCES

Amanda Datnow and Robert Cooper. "Peer Networks of African-American Students in Independent Schools: Affirming Academic Success and Racial Identity," *Journal of Negro Education*, 65 (4) (1997): 56-72.

Bernadette Gray-Little and Robert A. Carels. "The Effects of Racial Dissonance on Academic Self-esteem and Achievement in Elementary, Junior High, and High School Students," *Journal of Research on Adolescence*, 7 (2) (1997), 109-132.

Kenneth Hardy. "The Theoretical Myth of Sameness: A Critical Issue in Family Therapy, Training, and Treatment," *Journal of Psychotherapy and the Family*, 6 (1989), 17-33

George Wilson Saba, Betty M. Karrer, Kenneth Hardy (Eds.). *Minorities and Family Therapy* (New York: The Haworth Press), 17-33.

Maya D. McNeilly, Norman B. Anderson, Cheryl A. Armstead, Rodney Clark, Marcella Corbett, Elwood L. Robinson, Carl F. Pieper, and Eva M. Lepisto. "The Perceived Racism Scale: A Multidimensional Assessment of the Experience of White Racism among African Americans," *Ethnicity & Disease*, 6 (1996), 154-166.

NAIS Statistics 2000: Volume I (Washington, DC: National Association of Independent Schools, 2000).

Robert Sellers, Mia A. Smith, J. Nicole Shelton, Stephanie J. Rowley, and Tabbye M. Chavous. "Multidimensional Model of Racial Identity: A Reconceptualization of African-American Racial Identity," *Personality & Social Psychology Review*, 2 (1) (1998)18-39.

Diana T. Slaughter-Defoe and Deborah J. Johnson (Eds.). *Visible Now: Blacks in Private Schools* (Westport, CT: Greenwood Press, 1989).

The Story Behind the Research

Around the time that Howard Stevenson, an African-American psychologist and professor at the University of Pennsylvania Graduate School of Education was consulting with the family of an extremely bright African-American male perceived as "difficult" at the independent school he attended, a group of independent school educators, administrators, and others concerned with the experience of African-American males in their schools was beginning to form. The group became the African-American Boys Coalition (AABC), and its focus of concern was the disproportionate numbers of black boys who were viewed as having either academic or behavior problems, or who were leaving the schools they attended — either on their own accord or at the schools' request.

For the most part, AABC members were faculty, administrators, and staff of color who had keen insight into the experiences of black males in their schools. As the AABC became more active and vocal in its advocacy for black male students, it came to the conclusion that research should be undertaken to address the demands from the various constituencies that wanted more than the testimony of the AABC that black males were experiencing difficulty in their schools.

Having worked with Howard Stevenson on other clinical and research projects involving the well-being of African-American males, some members of the AABC believed that its advocacy efforts would be informed and supported by working together on a research project. The Success of African-American Males (SAAM) in Independent Schools was created from this collaboration. The schools that collaborated with the Penn team on SAAM were generous enough to provide some financial support to help get the project up and running. Once the research team received additional funding from a federal source, SAAM quickly became SAAS, the Success of African American Students (SAAS) project. More resources allowed the work to include both boys and girls, as well as support the collection of longitudinal data over several years.

From speaking with members of the AABC and drawing on the experience of various members of the research team, we compiled a collection of questionnaires and created a set of interview and focus-group questions that we thought addressed the different facets of the experience of black students in independent schools. Student perspectives were at the heart of our research endeavors, but we also believed hearing what parents, teachers, diversity coordinators, and alumni had to say was important to deepen our understanding of the many factors that contributed to students' success. In that vein, we planned to ask parents to complete survey questionnaires, to interview teachers and administrators, and to conduct focus groups with parents, teachers, and alumni.

Moving from the planning stages into actually conducting interviews and focus groups or collecting surveys was easier said than done. Despite the similarities among the schools, each was unique in terms of the culture of its community and how diversity was (or was not) addressed. While the schools that were part of the SAAS always appeared to be willing to address diversity in its broadest sense, we continued to encounter resistance to the work. As opposed to our previous work in public schools where resistance was more overt, and therefore easier to identify, a systematic "niceness" in independent schools seemed to mask a hesitancy to fully engage with the research. It took longer for the Penn team to read through this niceness and understand that while many of the people we encountered in the schools were pleasant to us and spoke encouragingly about our work, we were still not making the progress we had hoped.

We mention all this because an analysis of the process of working with independent schools and their various constituents says a great deal about the sensitivity schools have toward diversity and racial issues in school. There were members of the different school communities who did not view work on SAAS as a priority or see why the work was necessary. Additionally, a significant number of parents of black students chose not to participate or have their children participate in the SAAS project. From information we gathered from families, we learned that some parents were concerned that SAAS would focus on their children and their supposed problems and not explore the role the school played in their children's adjustment. Other parents expressed a concern that, by participating in SAAS, their children would be stigmatized or suddenly made aware of racial differences.

With the help and support of AABC members and parents, we were able to learn from the challenges we encountered along the way and successfully complete many of the goals of the SAAS project. We conducted individual interviews with students at three of the four schools and with teachers at two schools. We held focus groups with alumni at three schools, parents at three schools, and teachers at one school. Due to some of the previously mentioned challenges, we were not able to collect surveys from students at all four schools simultaneously in the first few years of the project. After we addressed the challenges, we were able to collect surveys from students and parents across all four schools for two consecutive years.

—**Edith G. Arrington, Diane M. Hall,
   and Howard C. Stevenson**

The confusing and sometimes painful struggle of students who are coming to terms with their racial and ethnic identity is an added dimension that independent schools do not always take into account.

Understanding the Latino Experience

::

BY MARIAN CAVANAGH AND MARÍA A. LÓPEZ

Maggie Alonzo was a sixth grader in a Los Angeles magnet school when she was given a full scholarship to attend a K–12 independent day school in an affluent section of the city. She liked her new school and participated in a wide range of activities.

She is smart, highly motivated, and had the support of her Mexican-American parents. Her mother, in particular, saw an independent school as the road to her daughter's college education. She was right. Maggie excelled and went on to graduate from Stanford University in the spring of 2003.

And yet, Maggie says, during those seven independent school years, "I never walked home from school or had people sleep over. No one knew my family — no one met my mom. When I would talk about my [school] friends at home, I'd have to show her a picture." Her father considered not attending her high school graduation ceremony. "He was worried that he would feel out of place or have to act differently."

"At home," says Maggie, "I wanted and needed a sense of my culture, but I never felt I could bring that to school. I used to check my culture at the door."

In June 2003, one month after Maggie graduated from Stanford, the U.S. Census Bureau reported that Latinos are now the nation's largest minority group at 38.8 million people, surpassing the African-American population by half a million.[1] Approximately 13 million Latinos are children under the age of 18. And yet statistics from the National Association of Independent Schools (NAIS) released in March 2003 show that fewer than 13,000 Latinos are enrolled in independent schools. In comparison, almost 35,000 were identified as Asian Americans and more than 26,000 as African Americans. Among other groups of color, 13,587 students were identified as a multiracial," 6,128 as Middle Easterners, and 866 as Native Americans.[2]

Over the last 10 years, national representation of ethnic groups of color has certainly increased in independent schools (as of spring 2003, the number stood at 20 percent), yet the Latino population has grown from 2.3 percent to just 2.7 percent. Considering the Census 2003 figures, this is a dismal growth, especially in areas of the country where large populations of Latinos reside. While it is impossible to address within this article the many complex reasons why Latinos are underrepresented in independent schools, some larger issues can be identified.

Certainly there are socioeconomic factors, since the Census survey shows that only 26 percent of full-time, year-round Latino workers have incomes of $35,000 or more, compared with 54 percent of whites. "Most independent schools were founded by well-to-do families for the education of their children," notes Sam Salas, of Breck School (Minnesota). Salas, from Chile, is one of the few Latino heads of independent schools in the country. "These schools are usually not in neighborhoods with lots of Latinos," he adds, "so families would have to travel to another socioeconomic level for their children to attend." Religion, family traditions and expectations, and lack of awareness that options outside the public school system even exist may also contribute to the low numbers.

In many schools, outreach efforts have historically focused on the African-American population. "They are wrapped up in the thought that diversity equals African Americans," says Rosalia G.H. Miller, of Nicaragua, who is a faculty member at National Cathedral School (Washington, DC) and president of the Latino Student Fund, an organization that helps broaden educational opportunities for Latino students in the area. Encouraging all schools to look at diversity more broadly is essential, Miller emphasizes. "But we are talking about 'culture,' not just 'color.'"

---

[1] The estimated Hispanic population of the United States as of July 1, 2009, was 48.4 million. According to the 2010 U.S. Census, Hispanics constituted 16 percent of the nation's total population. In addition, about 4 million reside in Puerto Rico, a Caribbean U.S. territory.

[2] According to the NAIS statistics for 2010–2011, the numbers of students of color in NAIS member schools have increased to over 19,000 Latinos, 31,000 African Americans, 39,000 Asian Americans, 29,000 Multi-Racial students, 1,000 Native Americans, 7,000 Middle Easterners, and 6,000 Pacific Islanders. Relative to the overall U.S. population, Latino enrollment in independent schools is still low.

"The cultural piece does continue to make us feel disengaged," adds Carmen Nieto, whose family is from Puerto Rico. Nieto has taught Spanish for many years at the university and high school levels; she now works with middle schoolers at The Park School (Maryland). "There's no real understanding among the general population of 'What is Latino?' Color is not the thing that defines us, and we don't have the heritage and the history in this country that African Americans do." Even in independent schools, she says, it's hard for Latino students to relate to multicultural efforts. "And it's not because they're not interested. It's just that you can't put everyone in the same box."

The confusing and sometimes painful struggle of students who are coming to terms with their racial and ethnic identity is an added dimension that independent schools do not always take into account. "Part of high school culture is that you want to blend in," says Maggie Alonzo. "Kids are scared; you don't want to give other people a reason to make fun of or criticize you. I always felt outside of everyone else, separated from other people, but was never able to openly acknowledge this feeling. I wanted to be one person, but I was always divided." In her senior year, she found her voice; Maggie organized her school's first multicultural students' club where she and others felt free to talk openly.

Joaquín Vega, a 1997 graduate of an independent religious day school, was the only Latino male in a class that included just a handful of people of color. Though he wanted to go to a public high school, his parents — both from Puerto Rico — perceived that an independent school would offer a more responsible peer group. "I didn't feel like there were people who really understood where I was coming from. I wanted to connect to some degree with my background, but I really had no sense that this could be done." Like Maggie, he eventually chose to take an active role as a senior in his school's expanding multicultural efforts, becoming a group leader in a student-led outreach program.

When they were ninth graders, Alan Hernandez and Luis Genao, both from New York City's South Bronx neighborhood, were recruited from their public schools and, as sophomores, attended an East Coast boarding school. Alan, from a deeply religious Puerto Rican family, had been valedictorian of his ninth grade class. Luis, whose family is from the Dominican Republic, was a self-described "disillusioned student." They both knew that the opportunity they'd been given was enormous and were determined to make the most of it.

Wanting and needing to be a part of their new environment, they say, was an eye-opening and sometimes humbling experience that required distancing themselves from their old friends and, to some extent, even from their own families. "It was a good experience, but a hard one," says Luis. Their pronounced New York accents were a cause of embarrassment. The food was a surprise ("breakfast for lunch" and the omnipresent peanut butter and jelly sandwich); the clothing a mystery (boat shoes and alligator shirts); and the social interactions unfathomable (casual, bantering conversations between students and teachers). "Being bilingual and bicultural has its advantages, but it can also present many challenges," says Luis. "There was a duality of consciousness that had to be learned. It was hard to connect with friends from home after being away at school."

While it could be argued that some of these struggles are an inherent part of transitioning into independent schools and school life in general for all students, other people believe that independent schools need to make a more conscious effort to understand and accommodate Latino students and their families. Regardless, it is worthwhile to examine what practices and efforts have proven successful in attracting and retaining Latinos.

Malcolm Gladwell's *The Tipping Point: How Little Things Can Make a Big Difference* suggests that small things can produce enormous change. The theory, says Gladwell, "requires... that we reframe the way we think about the world." Schools might consider some of the following steps if they are truly committed to offering Latinos a more welcoming, safe, and inclusive environment.

BE MINDFUL AND RESPECTFUL OF THE LINGUISTIC VARIANCES OF THE SPANISH LANGUAGE.

"Language is inextricably bound to identity," says Beverly Daniel Tatum, president of Spelman College. It is "not only an instrumental tool for communication, but also the carrier of cultural values and attitudes." In Spanish, the broad range of colloquial variation in diction, speech patterns, vocabulary, and vernacular use creates a sense of identity and pride distinct to each region. This can create unexpected problems, even in areas that might seem safe bets for success for Latinos, such as a Spanish language classroom. One student described his surprise and embarrassment as his teacher repeatedly corrected his pronunciation, even though his language use was faithful to his cultural heritage.

"We can say we're bilingual, but there are still those subtle tones of your culture and of your values that can cause confusion," notes Carmen Nieto. "Even voice level is an issue. In my (Puerto Rican) culture, we frequently raise our voices, and that can be misunderstood. Some people think we're yelling, but we're not; it's just part of the culture."

RECOGNIZE THE IMPORTANT ASPECTS OF LATINO CULTURE: FAMILY, RELIGION, AND DISCIPLINE.

Strong family values, religious beliefs, and a sense of discipline can play important roles in often tight-knit and multigenerational Latino families. The *Los Angeles Times* recently stated that more than a quarter of Latinos live in families with five or more people, compared with 11 percent of whites. Since families are valued both as a cultural touchstone and as a source of social support, states Luis Genao, "whenever you have a school that does not bring the family along, it causes a strain on that family."

"Latino families want their children to know where the boundaries are," adds Nieto. "Authority has to be acknowledged all the time and be in place. There's a kind of psychology at work in many independent schools that wants to let the students make the important decisions. That's not necessarily part of the Latino culture; the thinking is different."

Both secular and religious schools might wish to be explicit with Latino students and their families about the schools' values, religious traditions, and expectations for student conduct. As head of school at Breck, Sam Salas has met with parents and their children together to discuss their school experience. "This has generated healthy expression of feelings, suggestions for improvement, and the organization of schoolwide events to celebrate their culture," he states. "I believe the main point here is listening to them. We seldom do it. We feel we know the formula; they think we know better and do not dare challenge us. These conversations changed from venting to taking responsibility to educate the community. It has been a very good experience."

PROMOTE OPPORTUNITIES FOR STUDENT-ADULT RELATIONSHIPS.

Given the hallmark of strong teacher-student relationships in independent schools, it is not surprising that a personal relationship with at least one adult member of the school community is always cited as a pivotal factor in student success. "Students greatly benefit from someone whose job responsibility entails being engaged and conscious of what's going on," Luis Genao says. But those connections can also be less structured. Maggie Alonzo found a mentor in her school's admission director. "I was at home in his office," she says. "He talked with my mom and never made me feel like I was overreacting. He helped me clear things up in my head."

Happily, advisory systems now in place in many independent schools ensure that such relationships are given an opportunity to develop and flourish so that students may be valued for who they are as individuals.

What's in a Name?

There is continuing conversation at the national level regarding the precise definitions of Latino and Hispanic.

Beverly Tatum notes in *Why Are All the Black Kids Sitting Together in the Cafeteria and Other Conversations About Race* that "although non-Latinos often use the word Latino to refer to a racial group, it is an error to do so." She goes on to say that "the term Hispanic was used by the Bureau of the Census as an ethnic label and not to denote a race, because Hispanics are a racially mixed group, including combinations of European White, African Black, and indigenous American Indian. It is possible for an individual to identify himself or herself as ethnically Hispanic and racially Black or White at the same time."

Juan Gonzalez, author of *Harvest of Empire, a History of Latinos in America*, believes that neither [term] is totally accurate but both are acceptable."

In this article, we use the word Latino. The choice was made for both linguistic reasons (the word follows Spanish gender rules) and political ones (word choice varies in different geographic regions of the country). The purpose was to talk in broad terms about races and cultures, not of one place but of many, that all share a connection to the Spanish language.

— **Marian Cavanagh and María A. López**

CREATE A STUDENT SUPPORT GROUP.

A club or student support group with an active presence and high visibility — one in which thoughts, ideas, and opinions are respected, welcomed, and taken seriously — is a must for providing a true multicultural experience. Although not all students will choose to be active participants, others need and want such a regular physical and emotional forum that is built into the fabric of the school.

ENSURE THAT NO STUDENTS ARE LEFT STRANDED.

New students can often feel a sense of isolation, especially during less structured activities such as recess and lunch. This sense is not always easy to prevent, since activities will vary depending on student age and school procedures. However, students of color can feel it more strongly if they are struggling with issues of racial and ethnic identity. Thus, ensuring that all students — not just Latinos — have a seat next to others, particularly at the beginning of a school year, is crucial to diffuse any social discomfort.

A poignant reminder of this sense of isolation: One student we interviewed was so anxious to avoid finding a place to sit in the dining hall that, for nearly a year, the student ate lunch in a bathroom stall.

HAVE INTERPRETERS AVAILABLE FOR CONFERENCES OR OTHER SCHOOL VISITS.

When possible, have a Spanish interpreter available to assist families so that the student is not burdened with this role. It is important that an interpreter is able to handle confidential subjects with great care.

- Be sensitive to critical issues: finances and transportation.

- Examine the hidden cost to students and their families of attending the school and share this information with families so they can plan accordingly. That includes everything from the cost of an athletic uniform and tickets to school dances to transportation.

- Show consideration during classroom conversations relating to how students spend their holidays and free time. "In this country," says Carmen Nieto, "material issues are very important. It affects the families that are working two or three jobs trying to survive and compete with groups that aren't in the same league financially. It happens with adults, so it's really hard for kids."

- Develop a discreet disbursement system for students who are on financial aid. Some schools have all students purchase "extra" items such as dance and concert tickets at the bookstore, with transactions linked to the school's database so that information remains confidential. "I never talked about my financial status with my friends," remembers Maggie. "If I couldn't go somewhere because of the money, I never let on. Homecoming was supposed to be a big family day and was made to sound like a low-budget event. But if you bring three kids, with face painting, booths, snow cones — it gets to be expensive. My mother didn't want to disappoint us, but we couldn't afford it."

- Provide a transportation system that complements the efforts of the admissions office, allowing qualified students and their families to consider the school as a viable option. This might entail rerouting bus service or facilitating the organization of carpool groups. "Transportation isn't always addressed with families," says Nieto. "If the student has to take the train to school, that's an expense that's not reimbursed. When students receive financial aid, they shouldn't just become numbers. Someone should be saying, 'What's going to make it possible for these students to stay?'"

ESTABLISH HIRING PRACTICES THAT PROMOTE LATINO VISIBILITY.

While every position within a school can serve as a positive role model for students, it is important to include Latino representation in positions of authority and as a visible presence in the community. Students should be able to witness success and see themselves at all levels of the school hierarchy. Hiring practices should reflect the fact that not all Latino teachers aspire to teach Spanish or even to be involved in diversity initiatives.

Latinos are frequently found in a school's foreign language department, but are less prevalent in other faculty, staff, administrative, and board positions. Jose Molina, of the Gilman School (Maryland), says the need for more Latinos in "substantive" roles in independent schools is an urgent one. "I'm talking about administrative positions, not just Spanish teachers," he says.

"It's up to school heads and governing boards to commit themselves to the task," agrees Sam Salas. "Attracting and retaining Latino teachers has to do with leadership." All across the country, job fairs specifically for graduating students of color are good resources for independent school administrators.

INVOLVE LATINO FAMILIES IN THE ADMISSION PROCESS.

Invite Latino parents to be members of the school's welcoming committee, supporting the admissions process throughout its various steps, including open houses, campus tours, and welcoming phone calls.

PROVIDE KEY INFORMATION IN SPANISH.

Guarantee that all families are well informed by having key information and deadlines made available in Spanish. Material such as the NAIS/SSS Parent Financial Statement in Spanish (which assists families in applying for financial aid) ensures that students with potential for success will not be penalized for the linguistic limitations of their parents.

UNDERSTAND FAMILIES WILL HAVE VARYING DEGREES OF FAMILIARITY WITH AMERICAN CULTURAL NORMS.

Like their children, some Latino parents are more familiar with some mainstream American customs than others. What for most Americans may be considered routine experiences — such as sleepovers, summer boarding camps, and leaving home for college — may be less commonplace in other cultures within the United States.

HELP FAMILIES DECIPHER A SCHOOL'S HIDDEN CULTURE.

Every new family has a lot to learn regarding "Who's who." Knowing to whom one can turn when a problem arises facilitates getting the problem solved. A school's culture can become so ingrained as to be nearly invisible to insiders, but it is a dividing wall for newcomers. Providing new families with the basic information to navigate the system of daily school life helps reduce confusion and misunderstanding.

VALUE THE SMALL GESTURE.

As with any newcomer, a word of welcome can go a long way in making a person feel valued. Diane Dunning, admission director at St. Stephen's and St. Agnes School

(Virginia), stresses the importance of the personal greeting. "I am usually stunned by how often kids or parents of color will say how much it meant to them that someone said hello. Small gestures can make a big difference."

ORGANIZE INCLUSIVE EVENTS.

Make school events multigenerational when possible, and vary the time of day at which events are held to take into account family members' work schedules. Because school is the only place where all community members share common ground, host as many meetings and events as possible on campus, as opposed to private homes, hotels, or other locations.

USE THE RESOURCES OF THE GREATER COMMUNITY.

Mine the area for agencies or organizations that provide support services, scholarship or intern opportunities, and cultural validation for Latinos. Building relationships with such entities can be mutually beneficial.

At the 2003 NAIS Annual Conference, Costa Rican President and Nobel Laureate Oscar Arias urged schools to keep expanding their multicultural efforts. "It is our values that determine our priorities," Arias stated, "and from these flow our actions." As school cultures evolve, keeping these ideas more central to a core mission should surely be a priority.

At the time this article was written, **Marian Cavanagh** was director of communications at Menlo School (California). She is now the communications director at Flint Hill School (Virginia). At the time this article was written, **María A. López** was director of community life at The Langley School (Virginia) and a board member of the Latino Student Fund. She is now the head of the middle school at Keys School (California), and an emeritus board member of the Latino Student Fund. This article first appeared in the Winter 2004 issue of *Independent School*.

"Upward mobility through academic achievement becomes the **most viable option,** as a wider variety of opportunities for success have not traditionally been available."

The Model Minority Myth
Implications for Independent Schools

::

BY GISELLE W. CHOW

From a distance, Asian American Pacific Islander (AAPI) students appear to be our great success story in education. As a population, they are over-represented among winners of National Merit Scholarships and U.S. Presidential Scholarships, and they are undergraduates at the country's most prestigious universities.

They make up three to five times their proportionate share of architects, engineers, physicians, and college professors. They score higher on the SAT and ACT than any other racial group, particularly in math. According to published school report cards mandated by the No Child Left Behind Act, they are often grouped with whites in terms of academic achievement. Sometimes they are found to be achieving at rates above that of white students. If we believe that achievement scores are valid measurements of student success, then the AAPI community has nothing to worry about. As a result, AAPI students are often held up in the public eye as the model minority, worthy of respect, praise, and emulation.

So what's the problem?

Upon closer scrutiny, the AAPI story changes, becoming cloudier. First, the academic, social, and emotional experiences of AAPI students are far more varied and nuanced than most of us think. More importantly, the model minority stereotype, rather than being helpful for the AAPI community, tends to silence and render invisible the complexity of the AAPI community. Because of its subtext — if one minority group is an exemplary model, what's wrong with the other groups? — the stereotype also isolates the AAPI community from other communities of color. And in schools, it tends to lead many educators to make broad assumptions about all AAPI students and thus to overlook the actual needs of individual students.

The truth matters here. People of AAPI descent in the United States comprise more than 50 different and distinct ethnic groups, But if aggregated as a single racial group, usually under the label "Asian American," they comprise merely 4.5 percent of the overall population — lagging behind both African Americans and Latinos, at about 13 percent and 15 percent, respectively. As a result, AAPIs are often viewed as a monolithic group with generalized experiences. This tendency is compounded by the fact that the majority of research and the stories we hear in the news media mostly focus on only those of the largest, and most established and successful AAPI ethnic groups — namely Chinese, Japanese, and Korean, whose larger numbers can relegate other AAPI ethnic groups to statistical insignificance.

Among other things, the tendency to generalize skews our perceptions of the needs of specific AAPI communities, and influences the decisions schools make about the kinds of programs they provide and for whom. It also affects how teachers and peers view individual AAPI students. Sometimes the pervasive quality of the model minority stereotype can even limit the way these students are able to see themselves.

THE MODEL MINORITY STEREOTYPE EXPOSED

One need only look back a few decades to see that what many people assume is true of most AAPI students today is the result of a relatively recent stereotype. In the 1960s, the news media broadly applied the label of the model minority to newly arrived Asian immigrants, who were upheld as models of racialized success in the United States. Before that time, from about 1850 to the post WWII decade, Asians in the U.S. were, as educator and researcher Jean Yonemura Wing puts it, "dehumanized as an unsavory foreign contaminant — portrayed as uncivilized, sinister, heathen, filthy yellow hordes that threatened to invade the U.S and 'mongrelize' the white race."

Today, it is easy to forget that 30 years of deeply ugly anti-Asian sentiment in

California led to the Chinese Exclusion Act in 1882, the first major law in our nation's history to bar immigration from a specific ethnic group. It is also easy to forget that this law was extended several times, and only repealed in 1943, when China had become a strong U.S. ally against Japan.

However, in the 1960s, the Japanese and Chinese in the U.S. became the somewhat unlikely subjects of "success literature," in which they were touted in the national press as singular examples of the American Dream achieved. For those in power, the development of this model minority myth was a useful counterpoint amid the growing social unrest in the 1960s in the wake of the Watts riots and from the emergent Black Power Movement. Here was a racial group that could seemingly do it all, without complaint and without government aid. This story struck a deep chord with much of the American public as it offered an alternative perspective to those who claimed that the struggles of minority groups were due to racist policies and behavior in the nation. In this regard, the model minority stereotype created the context for the AAPI community to be used as a racial wedge between whites, on the one hand, and blacks and Latinos, on the other. The very presence of a model minority narrative, in which one racial group is held above others for being successful, regardless of the conditions placed upon them, implies that racial groups that have not done the same are somehow at fault for their own position in society.

THE AAPI EXPERIENCE

The AAPI community is far from monolithic. It comprises people from a region that includes Far East Asia, Southeast Asia, the Indian Subcontinent, and the Pacific Islands, with over 100 languages and dialects represented. Given the vast geographic range, there are large differences in religion, cultural beliefs, and practices. In the U.S., the AAPI community differs in all these ways in addition to socioeconomic status; competence in speaking, reading, and writing English; the generational distance from the immigrant experience; and the contexts in which various groups have immigrated to America.

In actuality, AAPI students represent both ends of the achievement spectrum. They are at once our nation's highest achievers and those most in need. In the national conversations regarding the achievement gap, AAPI students are often given small mention or little regard. But particularly vulnerable are Southeast Asian and Pacific Islander students — such as the Vietnamese, Laotian, Hmong, Tongans, and Native Hawaiians — whose dropout rates are among the highest of any group. These groups are also less likely to receive the language support they need as students and come from families that are highly likely to live in poverty. Moreover, according to the last U.S. Census, about

10 percent of AAPI women in America have less than a ninth grade education, more than twice that of white women. Such facts help us know that the proliferation of the stereotype of the impossibly nerdy and bookish Asian is a woefully limited and partial view of the real experiences of this diverse racial group. There is no single or singular AAPI story.

Additionally, AAPI students do not perform equally well in all subjects. AAPI college students who attend four-year universities earn disproportionately fewer bachelor's degrees in the humanities than any other racial group. With 66 percent of the current AAPI population in the U.S. speaking a language other than English at home, many more students than acknowledged often need developmental work in reading and writing English in both high school and college.

Recently, some researchers have questioned the notion that excelling in school is an inherently "Asian" family value. They suggest instead that the AAPI students that have excelled have done so because of the lack of opportunities and limits placed upon them in other areas of life. Upward mobility through academic achievement becomes the most viable option, as a wider variety of opportunities for success have not traditionally been available. Historian Liang Du writes, "Facing the open or hidden racism and discrimination, there were not many choices left other than the 'hard way' of striving for academic achievements. It was one of the few options that were left open through which they could possibly make it."

While AAPI students are over-represented in some colleges and universities, they also suffer from the lowest acceptance rates of any group. In many cases, it has been found that non-AAPI candidates with similar academic credentials have gained admission to certain universities over AAPI candidates. The more stringent criteria for AAPI candidates clearly points to a double standard, or a two-tiered system to college admissions that is institutionally racist. It is also crucial to remember that not all AAPI students attend four-year colleges. In California and Nevada, for instance, over half of college age AAPI students attend community colleges.

AAPI students are also not "trouble-free," as compared to other students. In the context of schools in the U.S. that are predominantly white in terms of faculty makeup and governance, as well as the culture of the school itself, AAPI students who may seem meek or mild are often ignored and less scrutinized than other students. Teacher beliefs about their achievements and high capacities for learning are sometimes assumed and unfounded. One study found that teachers in some kindergarten classrooms spent up to five times the amount of time with students who were either deemed by the teachers to be "difficult" or with students who were high achievers than with other students.

When interviewed, the teachers in these classrooms grouped AAPI students with the high achieving group. But they only spent a fraction of their classroom time with these students, notably not aware when one was found to be completing the same puzzle over and over again, or another was discovered sitting silently by a window, staring outside for the duration of the morning work time.

Because AAPI families sometimes subscribe to the belief that the school is the ultimate authority regarding their children's education, and some parents and schools struggle with language barriers, AAPI parents are not always advocating for their children as other parents might and are less connected to their children's experiences in school.

OBSCURING THE NEEDS OF THE AAPI COMMUNITY

For those working in schools, the nature of the model minority myth creates a significant barrier to understanding and noticing the depth of discrimination against Asian Americans. It also makes it difficult to believe that AAPI adults do not earn as much as their white counterparts with the same education, are often the victims of hate crimes, or have relatively few culturally relevant social programs. In schools, the myth obscures the need for culturally relevant educational support.

The myth also serves to divide the AAPI community from the struggles of other people of color. In this way, the "gift" of the model minority label ultimately upholds systems of inequity by pitting people of color and various groups against each other. Frank Wu, an Asian American law professor and author of *Yellow: Race in America Beyond Black and White*, explains how a racial hierarchy is created, "that denies the reality of Asian American oppression, while accepting that of other racial minorities and poor whites. Model minority is a poisonous prize, because the stereotype will only be wielded in defense of the racial status quo." In this context, researchers Miranda Oshige McGowan and James Lindgren point out how "whites will remain on top, African Americans on the bottom, with Asian Americans sandwiched in between." We see this played out most prominently in California where both affirmative action opponents and proponents have used the AAPI community against the interests of blacks and Latinos.

In 2007, according to the U.S. Department of Health and Human Services, AAPI women aged 15 to 24, as well as AAPI women over 65, had the highest rates of suicide among all women across all ethnic and racial groups in the nation. Additionally, one of every two of these women would have encountered obstacles in obtaining care because of language differences. Since 1996, over half of Cornell University's student suicides were committed by students of AAPI descent. As a group, AAPIs are less likely to seek

Asian American and Pacific Islander (AAPI)

"Asian American" is a term used to describe American individuals who have origins in one or more of the 28 Asian nations that include the following:

INDIA	LAOS
BANGLADESH	MALAYASIA
CAMBODIA	PAKISTAN
CHINA	THE PHILIPPINES
INDONESIA	SRI LANKA
JAPAN	THAILAND
KOREA	VIETNAM

It is also important to note that there are a great many Asian ethnic groups within Asian nations to which people may identify, irrespective of national origin, such as the Hmong. The Hmong people are an Asian ethnic subgroup not represented by any particular nation, but whose diaspora is spread across large portions of China, Vietnam, Laos, and Thailand. "Pacific Islander" is a term used to describe native Hawaiians and others

living in the U.S. protectorates, as well as American individuals with origins from one or more of the 19 Pacific Islands, which include the following:

FIJI	NORTHERN MARIANA
GUAM	ISLANDS
HAWAII	PALAU
MARSHALL ISLANDS	SAMOA
(INCLUDING THE	TAHITI
CHAMORRO PEOPLE	TONGA
MICRONESIA	

AAPI is therefore an inclusive umbrella term that seeks to connect and unify both the Asian American and Pacific Islander populations in the United States and its protectorates. At the same time, it is important to note the vast differences that exist within the AAPI population and the variety of languages, dialects, ethnic groups, religions, and cultural beliefs represented.

mental health services or self refer because of deep cultural stigmas. While there are efforts to provide culturally relevant services in certain areas of the country, the lack of AAPIs that pursue health care, education, and social services as career paths themselves contributes to keeping certain subgroups within the AAPI community culturally and linguistically isolated.

IMPLICATIONS FOR INDEPENDENT SCHOOLS

It is significant that, while the AAPI community constitutes a scant percentage of the overall U.S. population, AAPI students make up the largest racial group of students of color in NAIS-member schools — and have for at least 30 years. Thus, it behooves all of us working in our schools to consider how we can ensure that AAPI students receive the support they need. Given what we know about the AAPI community at the national level, how do we apply this knowledge to better serve and engage students and families in our schools?

Who Are You Serving?

The best place to start is by taking a closer look at the AAPI students in our student population. Who are they? Are they predominantly affluent Korean boarding students whose families do not reside in the United States? Are they immigrant Chinese students with strong connections to language and family and whose parents do not speak English and therefore do not come to school events? Are they the children of Cambodian refugees? Are they transracially adopted Asian children? What if you serve multiple groups of AAPI students? How do you begin to treat each student as an individual with a singular story?

Knowing your students well is a key to educating them well. To this end, it's essential that we recognize the great variance in their life experiences.

Realize We Are Making Value Judgments

As teachers, we must recognize that we see and value certain behaviors in our classrooms from our particular vantage points as agents in schools with deeply held cultural beliefs that are largely invisible to us. When we understand that, we can start to ask important questions. To what extent, for instance, do we unconsciously reward AAPI students for being docile or quiet? As one AAPI student has noted, "They (white teachers) like us because we're not black." While this is the sort of comment that takes us aback, it's also worth asking to what extent we, in fact, reward AAPI students for not behaving like students from other racial groups.

Independent schools are still places that are affluent and predominantly white in numbers and culture — even schools that express an interest in diversity and actively seek out students of color. Because not all students fit this affluent/white profile, it's always important to examine the reasons for seeking out and admitting students of color. With AAPI students in particular, we need to examine our expectations of them, the behaviors we value in them. Do we expect that AAPI students will need minimal support? Do we assume that they will be academically successful and then not worry about them in class?

The reality is that students may be quiet and docile in class without understanding what we are trying to teach. A student may keep meticulous notes in class without truly understanding key concepts. Students may appear to have it all together, but that doesn't mean they don't feel intense pressure on a number of levels, including pressure to live up to the model minority stereotype. Too often, doing so is the only way some AAPI students feel they can be known and seen in school.

Ultimately, in the name of quality education, we need to surface and dismiss all the cultural assumptions we carry about AAPI students and start to take them at face value.

Debunk the Model Minority Myth

If we know that the model minority myth is ingrained and pervasive in the culture at large — and that it is not only damaging to AAPI students, but also to the broader school community — what are we doing to educate ourselves and the rest of the school community about stemming the power of this myth?

In particular, educators can take an honest look at how the myth plays out in their classrooms and schools. Does the high achievement of some AAPI students make us feel justified in our pedagogy for all students? To what extent do we believe that, if the Asians can do it, everyone else can as well? Do we steer AAPI students toward certain courses but not others? Do we make assumptions about the colleges they should attend and the majors they should pursue? What are the messages, intended and unintended, that are conveyed to AAPI students when we act this way? What are the messages we send to the rest of our students? How is this damaging everyone?

If the stereotype exists widely in the culture, then it will also exist within your school. If assumptions arising from the stereotype are not proactively addressed, they will persist.

Find Bridges and Connections

The challenges and struggles of AAPI students should be seen as part of a broader context that includes the struggles of all students of color. Examine the diversity efforts at your school. From an institutional perspective, are AAPI students included in those efforts? Does your school offer a picnic at the beginning of the school year to welcome African American families to the school, but not one for AAPI students and families? Have you provided translators for Spanish speakers at school events but not investigated which AAPI families might need the same service? What messages, intended or not, do such decisions send?

Listen to the Students

Listen to the voices in your AAPI student groups or clubs. If your school doesn't have such a group, consider calling together a focus group of students so that they can speak candidly about their experiences in your school. While this should not take the place of the important work of adults (we certainly don't want to place students in the position of doing the work around issues of equity that adults need to do for themselves), we need to spend time paying attention to the stories and experiences of AAPI students — both inside and outside of school. It is important to acknowledge, for instance, what a student feels when teachers get him mixed up with the other Asian student in his class for his entire four years of high school, or when a student feels as if she is the spokesperson for her race when the class is studying the Vietnam War. We need to listen when AAPI students speak of the higher standards they feel are placed upon them compared to other students, or the expectation placed on them to out-perform others, as well as the derision they feel from classmates as a result. We also need to listen when they tell us that they don't get equal playing time on the field, and they suspect it is because of race, or when they are not seen as "appropriate" for the lead in the school play.

Such stories are everywhere. We just need to ask and listen, then accept their reality and their truth — and not rationalize or explain it away.

Keep Asking Yourself, What Are We Not Seeing?

Finally, it is important to continually ask ourselves what we are not able to observe. If we pay attention, issues we thought didn't exist in our schools will start to surface. As all independent schools become more diverse — in all diversity's definitions and forms — faculty and staff need to get beyond mere cultural competence. We must learn to see everyone — students and adults — in terms of their unique perspectives, informed by racial heritage, gender, sexual identity, socioeconomic status, religion, age, life experience, and so on. It is only then that we can see both the benefits and the limitations of each of our perspectives.

Staying vigilant in this way will allow us to see our AAPI students and families more clearly. And if we see them more clearly, we can provide the sort of support and guidance they need to thrive in our schools.

Giselle W. Chow is dean of equity and instruction at Lick-Wilmerding High School (California). This article appeared in the Winter 2011 issue of *Independent School*.

All students need to feel affirmed and there are significant ways schools can make sure their Asian and Asian American students feel that they are an integral part of the community....

A Lasting Impact

Supporting Asian and Asian American Students

::

BY AYA MURATA

When people ask me what I do at Phillips Academy (Massachusetts), I wish I could just say something simple like, "I teach math," since it easily satisfies the curiosity of the questioner. Instead, I have to tell people that I serve in an administrative role as a dean and as the advisor to Asian and Asian American students.

The latter role often elicits a variety of follow-up questions. What does being the advisor to Asian and Asian Americans students mean? Why does this position exist? Is it really necessary?

Implied in such questions is a feeling either that Asian and Asian American students don't really need our focused support or that the questioner had not considered the possibility before.

My favorite questions, however, comes from educators who understand that the specific needs of Asian and Asian American students are too often overlooked in school. When I tell them what I do, they respond, not with puzzlement, but with excited curiosity, "What can our schools do to best support our Asian and Asian American students?[1]

---

[1] For the purposes of this article, I define "Asian" as non-US citizens who live outside of the United States (e.g., the student who is a Japanese national and whose place of residence is other than the United States) and "Asian American" as U.S. citizens and U.S. permanent residents (e.g., the American citizen of Asian ancestry whose place of residence is somewhere in the United States). I also include students of mixed heritage Asian background and transracial and transnational Asian adoptees under the umbrella of Asian and Asian American.

The short answer is that we can — and should — do a great deal.

ACKNOWLEDGING ALL STUDENTS

Phillips Academy established its Office of Community and Multicultural Development in the late 1980s with a single advisor for black and Latino students. Shortly thereafter, the academy recognized that other constituencies on campus could be further supported by similar advisors. Thus, the school established the positions of international student coordinator; advisor to gay, lesbian, and bisexual students ("transgender" has recently been added to this title); and advisor to Asian and Asian American students. In creating these positions, the school recognized that the transition and experience of particular groups of students might be different and, in certain ways, more challenging than the transition and experience of students in the white American, straight majority.

I stepped into the role of advisor to Asian and Asian American students in 1994, excited by the opportunity to mold and shape this relatively new position. In this role, I serve in two major areas: (1) support for Asian and Asian American students and (2) development of activities and programs to assist the community (students, staff, and faculty) to learn more about and better understand Asian and Asian American history, culture, and issues. I develop both informational and social programs relating to Asia and/or Asian and Asian American issues. Such programs have included a study of Phillips Academy's Asian and Asian American students' experiences, an Asian Arts Festival (an annual event raising awareness and showcasing Asian food, art, culture, and talent), faculty development opportunities, an alumni and student event, various guest speakers and performers, and social activities such as trips into nearby Boston.

Additionally, as faculty advisor to student organizations such as the Asian Society, I work with student leaders to develop social activities and educational programs and to lend support. Other organizations under the umbrella of the Asian Society include the Andover Japanese Connection, the Andover Korean Society, the Chinese Taiwanese Student Association, and the Indian and Pakistani Society. Along with student leaders and the other faculty advisors to these clubs, we work to recognize and support the school's Asian and Asian American students and to continue to educate the ever-changing community of students, faculty, and staff regarding the issues and challenges these students face.

Why does this position exist at Phillips Academy and why should it exist in other schools? Because Asian and Asian American students in independent schools confront a number of distinct and complex issues, including but not limited to:

- Experiencing a sense of invisibility particularly in the dialogue about race;
- Shouldering and managing (and in the case of Asian international students, learning about) the label of the "model minority" and other limiting and damaging stereotypes;
- Balancing and negotiating the line between being an American (referring specifically to white American values and images of beauty) and yet honoring and appreciating their Asian heritage;
- Coming into their own sense of authentic being as they explore their identity and what role being Asian plays in that identity development; and
- For international students, understanding what it means to be Asian in America, particularly in cases when they move from the racial majority to the racial minority.

While some students will never cross my doorstep, the importance of having a specific advisor dedicated to Asian and Asian American students cannot be overstated. It says to these students and students who identify as Asian and Asian American, "You are important; you are recognized; and we acknowledge that your experience may differ in some ways from your peers." These students often feel that that they are expected to perform well in the classroom, stay out of trouble, and contribute to the community in particular areas. They can feel that their concerns and challenges are invisible or, worse, dismissed because they are expected to be the "model minority."

The term "model minority" was coined by William Petersen in his 1966 *New York Times* article "Success Story: Japanese American Style." Petersen used the term to underscore his belief that Asian Americans are successfully integrated into American society, are achieving the American Dream, and are thriving — due to their hard work, perseverance, emphasis on education, and strong family values. Unfortunately for all, this stereotype has persisted ever since. It is inaccurate, of course, because it assumes that the experiences of all Asian Americans are identical. More importantly, it is detrimental because, among other things, it renders invisible the real struggles and challenges facing Asian Americans, serves to justify ignoring the critical needs of the Asian American community, and drives a damaging wedge between Asian Americans and other minority groups.

For Asian and Asian American students, the feeling of invisibility can be further compounded when schools discuss issues of race — since, often times, the conversation quickly falls into a black-white paradigm, with Asian and Asian American students left asking, "What about us?" Indeed, some schools or educators use the term "students of color" to refer only to their black and Latino constituencies, which further renders the Asian and Asian American student community invisible. When topics of race are raised, it is crucial that-schools recognize all students of color. Alongside black and Latino students, Asian and Asian American students want to be engaged in these conversations because they are, in fact, racially located in particular ways in America and also experience both blatant and institutional racism.

THE BURDEN OF STEREOTYPES AND ASSUMPTIONS

Compliant, good at mathematics, accomplished musicians, self-sufficient, and hard-working. This is a partial list of racial stereotypes and assumptions that some people mistakenly see as "positive" and, in so doing, do not acknowledge the limiting and damaging effects that such stereotypes have on Asian and Asian American students.

In classrooms, these students have to regularly negotiate comments and expectations from both teachers and peers that can annoy, belittle, or dismiss them and their individual abilities and accomplishments. When college admission decisions are released and cum laude lists announced, Asian and Asian American students are barraged by remarks that are drawn from crude racial stereotypes and serve to diminish one's achievement or sense of self. Furthermore, depending on the school, if an Asian or Asian American student is the only Asian or Asian American student in a class or dorm, or on a playing field, adults and fellow students often look to that student to speak on behalf of his or her race or ethnicity or expect him or her to comply with their idea of what it means to be "Asian."

These kinds of experiences build over time and become an additional burden — one which Asian and Asian American students need to negotiate on top of the everyday trials and tribulations of being students at independent schools. Some Asian and Asian American students grow increasingly fatigued by the comments, questions, and jabs about "not needing to work hard to succeed" and "being foreign" and "being un-American." Consequently, they feel they must retreat to a safer and more supportive group of peers and, in some instances, this inadvertently prevents them from engaging in the wider community.

Some students experience other emotions such as anger and sadness. Some subsequently have issues with self-esteem or self-hate. Adolescents most often pick up their own sense of self from what others see and reflect back to them — so it makes absolute sense that many Asian and Asian American students begin to hate the self that is "Asian" because it seems to cause them the most pain and alienation. The statistics from the U.S. Department of Health and Human Services are startling and cannot be ignored: "Asian American women ages 15-24 have the highest suicide rate of women in any race or ethnic group in that age group."

In an Asian Society meeting at my school last year, students discussed what it meant to be an "American." They shared stories of the tightrope some of them felt they had to walk between the white American values they were raised with in their schools and through the mass media (e.g., freedom of expression and independence) and the Asian values and traditions their parents have taught them (e.g., obedience and respect) — some of which are in deep conflict with one another. Other students talked about feeling more American — which they described as "mainstream, white" — in their outlook and values, while simultaneously knowing that, in most settings, people see their Asian face first and often assign stereotypes accordingly, particularly the view of Asians as the "perpetual foreigner."

Asian and Asian Americans have a markedly different experience and perspective. Asian American students, for example, recounted with frustration the number of times people told them they spoke English very well or asked, "Where are you from?" expecting an overseas locale. When given a U.S. locale, the questioners pushed to know the students' "actual" origins. Compare this to the Asian international student who swells with pride when complimented on his or her fluent English skills and thinks nothing of responding with his or her hometown abroad.

Still other students in our Asian Society meeting discussed feeling pulled in opposite directions by their Asian and non-Asian friendship groups and struggling with the pressure to choose between them. Each choice comes with its own set of stereotypes, such as being labeled with the derogatory terms "banana" or "twinkie" (yellow on the outside, white on the inside) simply for hanging out with white friends, or a "FOB" (fresh off the boat) for choosing to spend time with their Asian or Asian American friends.[2]

It is important for these constituencies to talk to one another about such issues and for non-Asians to understand these crucial differences as well. In the end, as Jean Wu, professor of American Studies and educational director of the Office of Diversity at Tufts University, told me recently, "a Korean international student who just arrived to campus and the third-generation Asian American are both subject to being called a 'chink.' As long as it's an 'East Asian' featured face in America, regardless of paper and political status, that person can and will have an Asian American experience."

In short, the day-to-day experiences of many Asian and Asian American students are riddled with complex issues that they must address, yet that are often not recognized or acknowledged by the school community.

---

[2] "Banana" and "twinkie" are derogatory terms used primarily by Asian and Asian Americans to describe an Asian or Asian American who in their mind has made a decision to ignore their Asian heritage and all things Asian and to subscribe to white values/culture and hence they are "white on the inside, yellow on the outside." A FOB, on the other hand, is a derogatory term used to describe a new Asian immigrant.

Examples of Programs, Speakers, and Performers at Phillips Academy

2011: Asian and Asian American High School Conference, hosted by Phillips Academy

2011: Lisa See, author of *Snow Flower and the Secret Fan*, *Shanghai Girls*, and O*n Gold Mountain: The One-Hundred-Year Odyssey of My Chinese-American Family* — Asian Arts Festival keynote speaker

2010: Empowerment workshops for Asian and Asian American students conducted by the Asian American Resource Workshop

2010: Yoon Byun, photojournalist and staff photographer for *The Boston Globe*

2009: Lela Lee — artist and creator of *Angry Little Asian Girl* — Asian Arts Festival Keynote Speaker

2008: Socheata Poeuv — filmmaker and director of *New Year Baby*

2008: Vivian Toy — journalist for *The New York Times* — Phillips Academy Alumni Event in NYC

2008: Phillips Academy Asian and Asian American Alumni Reunion and Student Gathering

2008: Vivian S. Louie, professor and author Compelled to *Excel: Immigration, Education, and Opportunity among Chinese Americans* — student workshop and faculty development workshop, MLK, Jr. Day programming

2007: Kenji Yoshino, professor and author of *Covering: The Hidden Assault on Our Civil Rights* — student workshop and faculty development workshop for MLK, Jr. Day programming

2005: Chang-rae Lee, professor and author of *A Gesture Life*, *Native Speaker*, *Aloft*, and *The Surrendered*.

2004: Frank H. Wu, professor and author of *Yellow: Race in America Beyond Black and White* — Asian Arts keynote speaker

2003: Ronald Takaki, scholar — Asian Arts Festival keynote speaker

2003: Ming Tsai, celebrity chef — Asian Arts kick-off event

2003: David Ho, AIDS researcher - *Time Magazine* Man of the Year 1996

2003: Empowerment workshop for Asian and Asian American students conducted by the Asian American Resource Workshop

2002: Eric Liu, author of *The Accidental Asian: Notes of a Native Speaker* — Asian Arts Festival keynote speaker

2000: B.D. Wong, actor — Asian Arts Festival keynote speaker

2000: Follow-up workshop based on the 1999 program offered

1999: Faculty development workshop addressing issues facing Asian and Asian American students at Phillips Academy conducted by Jean Wu, professor, Tufts University

1999: Renee Tajima-Pena, filmmaker and director of *My America... or Honk if You Love Buddha*

1999: Nanda Shewmangal, director of the Asian Task Force Against Domestic Violence (Boston) to present "Domestic Violence in the Asian Community: Cultural Barriers Affecting Battered Women"

SUPPORTING ASIAN AND ASIAN AMERICAN STUDENTS

To attend a boarding school such as Phillips Academy, students come from across the United States and around the world. Our Asian and Asian American student population, which includes mixed-heritage Asian students and transracial and transnational adoptees, is approximately 24 percent of our total enrollment. Depending on their prior living circumstances, they may land at Phillips Academy and feel what it is like to be a minority for the first time, or for others who were the only Asian American in their previous school, they are thrilled to be a part of a significant critical mass. All are adolescents who are grappling with a developing sense of identity and learning and acknowledging what role being Asian is in who they are. These are considerable issues to tackle, and to do so in a vacuum is challenging and isolating.

The brief sampling of issues outlined above clearly elucidates the fact that Asian and Asian American students confront a variety of unique challenges. It also highlights the clear need for our schools to recognize and address these challenges. With limited resources, however, it is easy for schools to cast an eye over this specific constituency and feel that these students are "doing fine" (e.g., performing well academically and out of disciplinary trouble) and that scarce resources are better directed elsewhere. Of course, I strongly disagree and urge schools to dig deeper and recognize that, as with an iceberg, much more is below the surface.

All students need to feel affirmed, and there are significant ways schools can make sure their Asian and Asian American students feel that they are an integral part of the community rather than an invisible minority relegated to the periphery. Such affirmation comes in various forms but here are some specific steps schools can take:

1. **Create an advisor position if one does not exist.**

   This role should be filled with someone who identifies as an Asian American and has knowledge about the complexities of what it means to be Asian in America.

2. **Hire both Asian and Asian American faculty who will be involved with the Asian and Asian American students, serving as active role models and mentors to this constituency specifically and to all students generally.**

   It is not enough to have the "faces"; schools must hire Asian and Asian American faculty who identify as such and are interested and sensitive to the complexity of the Asian and Asian American experience and who are willing to support students regardless of their own personal perspective and experience.

   First and foremost, students need role models and mentors they can relate to and with whom they feel comfortable. All faculty members should be available to serve in this role. However, some students will more likely gravitate toward and open up to someone with whom they feel they share a kinship; therefore, it is important for schools to hire engaged and involved Asian and Asian American faculty. In the words of one of my former students: "Coming all the way from Japan, I was super nervous about [the school] — you helped make this place my second home. For the times I was homesick, scared, frustrated, confused, and lonely — for the times I felt proud, excited, encouraged, optimistic, and challenged — thank you for the constant, comforting support."

3. **Evaluate your programming to ensure that the Asian and Asian American experience is represented in your school's outside speakers, campus events such as Martin Luther King, Jr. Day, and in your curriculum.**

Regarding the latter issue, it is important to distinguish between Asian curriculum and Asian American curriculum. Conflating the two is problematic and detrimental to students — not just to Asian and Asian American students, but to all students. An Asian American curriculum is not just some rarified curriculum incorporated to make the Asian and Asian American students feel good, but it is essential for all students' education — as it is often a missing but critical piece of American history and experience.

Through my work at Phillips Academy, I collaborate with departments, I apply for grants, and I work with the administration to bring a wide range of Asian and Asian American speakers/performers to campus. (See sidebar on page 136.) Sometimes, such visitors provide specific insight and information regarding the Asian American experience (e.g., writer and law professor Frank Wu and the late scholar Ronald Takaki) while other guests share their particular craft (e.g., writer Chang-rae Lee, actor B.D. Wong, comedian Jo Koy, and artist Lela Lee). These guests are important in affirming the experiences of our Asian and Asian American students while also providing them with myriad role models. Such outside speakers are important not just for the Asian and Asian American students, but also for the school community at large.

Since budgets are tight, we must think more creatively about how to provide such opportunities. One suggestion is to turn to local organizations, since their honoraria are quite reasonable; sometimes a speaker will come in gratis. Examples include local print and news media sources, Asian organizations, and politicians. Another suggestion is to tap into your alumni base and current parent network.

Examining your internal programming and curriculum is also crucial. Do your Asian and Asian American students see and hear themselves in what is presented and what is taught? If not, it is vital to take the time to explore ways to incorporate their experiences in all aspects of school life. "Extracurricular programming is not enough," Jean Wu says. "The formal curriculum represents what all students are expected to know and be able to utilize in their lives, their continuing analysis and production of knowledge, and their interpersonal ethics and relationships. It is particularly important to recognize that teaching and learning about Asian America is not 'just for' Asian and Asian American students. Knowledge about Asian America is critical knowledge for all."

4. **Dedicate time and resources for faculty development aimed at addressing issues specific to Asian and Asian American students.**

Whether it is required reading, off-campus workshop opportunities, or a mandated faculty meeting, faculty members need to better understand the complex issues Asian and Asian American students confront so that they can best serve and support these students.

5. **Provide opportunities for Asian and Asian American students to discuss topics of interest and concern; also offer them occasions to share with the greater community their traditions, history, and culture.**

At Phillips Academy, we achieved this through a variety of clubs, which are open to anyone in the school, regardless of race or ethnicity. The Asian Society, for example, meets weekly, and its activities range from social endeavors like K-Pop karaoke and Chinese take-out to discussions on subjects such as Asian vs. American standards of beauty or the phenomenon of "yellow fever." Additionally, I established the Asian Girls Forum (AGF) — an affinity group to exclusively serve Asian, Asian American, and Mixed-Heritage Asian girls. AGF meetings offer these girls the opportunity to share, express, unload, celebrate, and support one another in their common experiences as Asian females in a setting that feels safe and without judgment.

It is also important to allow students opportunities to share their cultures. In the dorms, for instance, students can prepare snacks native to their heritage to share with dormmates. Throughout the year, the school can recognize and celebrate particular holidays — for example, our dining hall prepares a special schoolwide dinner for Lunar New Year. Additionally, I work with students organizing a large-scale event in celebration of Asian Pacific American Heritage Month in May.

I also see my role as keeping my finger on the pulse of opportunities available outside of campus, such as book readings and events in Boston or conferences. Yale University and Columbia University both host conferences free of charge for Asian and Asian American high school students, and local chapters such as the Association of Independent Schools in New England host an annual high school conference for students of color. As one of my students wrote to me this spring: "This year has been great and a real eye-opener for me in the Asian/Asian American front. All the conferences and workshops were so important to me. I feel like (cheesy line coming up) I discovered a big part of my identity. I am so grateful to you because you were really the one who allowed me to learn so much about my culture and its history."

6. **Finally, we all need to get to know our Asian and Asian American students as individuals rather than relegate them to a homogenous population.**

It is crucial to be aware of the various racial and ethnic stereotypes and assumptions we make about Asians and check those stereotypes and assumptions at the door. This requires that one familiarize oneself with the history and contemporary realities that create and sustain such stereotypes and assumptions. At boarding schools, in particular, our Asian and Asian American students represent an incredible breadth and depth of perspectives and experiences — from the international student who has never been to the United States before, to the third-generation Asian American from California, to the transracially adopted child raised in an all-white community, to the "TCK" (third culture kid) who was born in Korea yet raised in various other countries, to students whose parents came to America under very different circumstances (scholars and refugees). Our Asian and Asian American students want to be seen and known as individuals and not presumed to be "all the same."

A recent graduate sent me a letter in which, among other things, he wrote, "You were the very first faculty member and the very first mentor I felt a connection with. You were the very first person on campus to really reach out to me. Coming from Hong Kong where I was part of the Asian majority, to being part of a minority at Andover, you can say that I was a little lost and confused. It was you who really sparked my interest in Asian Studies, bringing me into Andover Korean Society and getting me involved in Asian Society. I know that I will carry on this interest of mine for the rest of life, and it is thanks to you that I have developed such a curiosity and passion for Asian culture and language."

In the end, my job is sometimes difficult to explain and in some cases justify, but when I receive letters from students, I stand tall knowing that what I do is important and makes a lasting impact on the lives of my Asian and Asian American students.

Aya Murata serves as a dean and as the advisor to Asian and Asian American students at Phillips Academy (Massachusetts). She thanks Jean Wu, professor of American Studies and educational director of the Office of Diversity at Tufts University and co-editor of *Asian American Studies Now: A Critical Reader* (2010), for her role as reader and advisor to this article, and Linda Griffith, dean of community and multicultural development at Phillips Academy, for her continued support and encouragement of her work. This article first appeared in the Winter 2011 issue of *Independent School*.

RECOMMENDED READING

Angelo Ancheta, *Race, Rights, and the Asian American Experience* (Rutgers, NJ: Rutgers University Press, 2001).

Ronald Takaki, *Strangers from a Different Shore: A History of Asian Americans* (New York: Little, Brown and Company, 1998).

Frank Wu, *Yellow: Race in America Beyond Black and White* (New York: Basic Books, 2002).

Jean Wu and Thomas Chen, *Asian American Studies Now: A Critical Reader* (Rutgers, NJ: Rutgers University Press, 2010).

Jean Wu and Min Song, *Asian American Studies: A Reader* (Rutgers, NJ: Rutgers University Press, 2000).

Helen Zia, *Asian American Dreams: The Emergence of an American People* (New York: Farrar, Straus and Giroux, 2000).

'Children in multiracial families face a great deal of undue attention in their day-to-day lives.'

Conspicuously Mixed

The Experience of Multiracial Youth in Independent Schools

::

BY MATT KELLEY

You probably know that U.S. Senator and Presidential-hopeful Barack Obama is the son of a black Kenyan father and a white mother from Kansas. You may also know that he was born in Hawai'i and lived in Indonesia for a time.

Senator Obama discusses his multicultural heritage in his best-selling memoir, *Dreams from My Father: A Story of Race and Inheritance*, but, even for those of us who haven't read his book, the story of his racially mixed heritage and how his parents met has been repeated thousands of times in articles and on blogs. But I don't know the specific ethnic roots of the other candidates, much less how their parents met. Do you?

I'm confident that we know this information about Senator Obama because he is multiracial. I'm also confident that, like me and most multiracial Americans, he is all

Editor's Note: This article was written in the summer of 2007, when Barack Obama was a U.S. Senator from Illinois and a candidate for U.S. President. To this day, the news media continues to refer to him, not as the first multiracial President, but as the first black President of the United States.

too familiar with the litany of questions directed at the multiracial population. "What are you?" "Where are you from?" "How did your parents meet?"

Multiracial people are more present in the public eye than ever before. Certainly, the list of media-hyped, self-identified multiracial celebrities (such as Tiger Woods, Alicia Keyes, and Keanu Reeves) and multiracial adoptive families (the Angelina Jolie-Brad Pitt brood) serves to bring mixed heritage people and families into the mainstream. But, to put it bluntly, to be multiracial in the United States at the start of the 21st century is still to be a curiosity.

"Children in multiracial families face a great deal of undue attention in their day-to-day lives," says Donna Jackson Nakazawa, a speaker on multiraciality and the author of *Does Anybody Else Look Like Me?: A Parent's Guide to Raising Multiracial Children*. Nakazawa, who is white, has two young children with her husband, a Japanese-American man. Their kids attend independent schools in Maryland. She explains, "It's the combination of inquisitive looks, longer than passing glances, and comments of surprise, along with nonverbal communication, that convey to the [children] that… they are seen to be different, [which] is undesirable or wrong."

For independent school educators, it's important to know all this. Why? Because multiracial and transracially adopted youth are the fastest-growing racial/ethnic group at independent schools. And the experiences of these students, obviously, should be as affirming as that of any other student — for everyone's sake.

THEN AND NOW

The aggressive curiosity that confronts many multiracial people and families suggests that their lives and experiences stand out — that their stories must somehow be extraordinary. While we all want a certain level of attention, this added attention can be especially unwelcome to young people who are eager to fit into their peer group. A 2003 study published in the *American Journal of Public Health* found that mixed race teens suffered from higher rates of poor general health and feelings of depression than other teens. They also skip school more often. The authors hypothesized that the cause might be stress associated with their mixed heritage.

Although multiracial people have been in the United States since the early days of the Republic — from the offspring of slaves who were raped by slave masters to legally-sanctioned interracial couples and their children — sex and marriage across racial lines remained illegal in many states until the 1967 Supreme Court decision, *Loving v. Virginia*. Although it was overruled by the *Loving* decision, Alabama's constitution technically still forbade interracial marriage until 2000. Furthermore, it was only in Census 2000 that seven million Americans were given the option of officially claiming multiple races as their racial description. After three centuries of laws designed to keep people of different races apart, it is no wonder that "mixed" people and families still generate curiosity and confusion.

But times are obviously changing. Today in Seattle and San Antonio, one in six babies are mixed race. The rate is much higher in Sacramento and Honolulu. It is also increasingly common for individuals and couples to adopt across racial lines. These trends, as noted, are even more pronounced at independent schools. Data from the National Association of Independent Schools (NAIS) indicate that multiracial students are the fastest growing racial/ethnic group at its member institutions. Between 2001 and 2007, their percentage increased from 2.6 to 4.1 percent. (NAIS does not track adoption statistics.) I have heard from some schools who say that the majority of their students of color are, in fact, multiracial or transracially adopted.

Schools would do well to consider the comments of Tara Pham, a senior at an independent school in California, who is both Vietnamese and Caucasian. "I think [people] don't know how to treat me because either they cannot tell what ethnicity I am," she says, "or they want to treat me as one ethnicity that I do not completely identify with." Pham adds that, while it is human nature to treat people based on their appearance, racially ambiguous faces like hers complicate the impulse for simple categorization.

With the growing number of multiracial students and transracially adopted youth, it only makes sense that independent schools, concerned with developing healthy inclusive communities, would learn how to support students like Pham so they don't feel like curiosities.

RESOURCES IN ACTION

As the numbers grow, parents and schools are increasingly in need of resources to help them better understand the experiences of racially mixed young people. Thankfully, unlike 10 years ago, a wide array of resources is available today. In addition to hundreds of children's books, memoirs, parenting advice and academic anthologies, there are social groups, a preschool teacher-training curriculum, and even a summer art camp just for multiracial youth.

Yet, while great resources exist, it is clear that many parents and educators are not using them. A 2004 study by the MAVIN Foundation, a mixed heritage foundation found that 40 percent of multiracial respondents felt that multiracial issues were "never" or "rarely" discussed at home. (Only 8 percent of parents felt the same way.) Parents who hope that their children's excellent independent schools are picking up the slack will be disappointed to learn that the same study found that 81 percent of multiracial respondents reported that mixed race issues were "never" or "rarely" discussed in their schools.

Some schools, however, are taking action. After several multiracial students at Phillips Academy (Massachusetts) said they wanted to create an affinity group to talk about their experiences, two members of the school's Community and Multicultural Development (CAMD) office worked with them to make it happen.

After my workshops on multiracial youth at the 2006 NAIS People of Color Conference in Seattle, I met Linda Carter Griffith, dean of CAMD and advisor to the Black and Latino students at Phillips Academy, and Aya Murata, the advisor to the school's Asian and Asian-American students. While working with students on the nuts and bolts of starting the group, called MOSAIC, they invited me to campus to speak at the school's faculty development day. The next day, I had an informal dinner with approximately 40 students. During our two-hour, lively discussion, we talked about a broad range of issues. Many of the topics were generally shared concerns: about the way so many people assume that they were "just black" or about the constant debates over who can claim a multiethnic heritage. Some were personal, like the one biracial young woman who told us that her white adoptive parents discouraged her from attending a local black arts festival. (I also learned about the school's "Halfies are hot!" phenomenon.)

Although their stories highlighted some lingering identity confusion or a sense of isolation due, in some measure, to a lack of support and resources, the openness of these students told me that they felt as if they were in a safe place. Overall, it seemed to me that Phillips Academy was on the right track with these students — offering faculty support, backed financially and logistically by the administration. Griffith and Murata said that the MOSAIC group is moving forward. Before breaking for this past summer, for instance, the group was considering a film screening and campus discussion the coming academic year. One of their members also received support to conduct a summer research project about the experiences of biracial adolescents.

MULTIRACIAL: ENHANCING DIVERSITY

Several Phillips Academy students told me that, while they may look like people of color, they didn't always perceive themselves that way and wanted people to acknowledge that they weren't "just" Latino/a or "just" Asian or "just" black. One young woman described being told by a white friend that she was the "whitest black person she had ever met."

Like many multiracial and transracially adopted students that I have met at independent schools, many of the Phillips Academy students were raised in white families and/or in almost exclusively white communities. Although many of them are viewed as "minorities," they often do not have strong cultural ties to any particular community of color. Psychologist and multiracial scholar Maria P. P. Root calls this racial identity, "White with symbolic [non-white] identity."

Lisette Austin is a Seattle-based writer and speaker on multiraciality. Of African-American and Italian heritage, she was raised by a black/French-Canadian couple but grew up without extensive ties to the black community. She began attending Lakeside School (Washington) in the fifth grade, but dropped out early in her 11th-grade year. Austin was one of only four students of African descent in her class, and she felt unnecessarily targeted by teachers and administrators because of the way she looked. But when she left Lakeside to attend a more diverse public school, she realized that she didn't fit in there either. Lakeside, she felt, had managed to reinforce her cultural distance from the black community while never making her feel welcome in its predominately white institution.

"I felt caught in a "Catch 22" — I wanted to branch out and learn more about 'my people' but because I hadn't been around them, I was intimidated. [The other students] were right in a way: I had become an 'Oreo,' but not because I wanted to be."

Today, Austin feels much more comfortable with her racial identity as a mixed race woman of color. As someone who advocates on behalf of mixed heritage people on a national level, she encourages independent schools to allow their students to explore different racial identities, both mono-and multi-racially. She also implores schools to be a positive environment for all students who wish to maintain and develop cultural ties to different communities outside the institution.

GROW AND PROSPER

Mixed heritage people are a conspicuous addition to the always changing face of multiculturalism. While today I am grateful for the experience, I wished that I wasn't mixed countless times during my youth. It didn't really matter "what" I was, I just wanted nine out of 10 people to reach consensus about my race. No more invisibility on school enrollment, health, or job forms, and no hypervisibility to the strangers who inevitably popped up to ask me weird questions, like, "What are you?" While life in the racial borderlands remains exhausting for many multiracial and transracially adopted youth, there is growing consensus about what parents and educators can do to cultivate healthy identities for their kids. Indeed, these are increasingly important skills for everyone — not just multiracial people — to learn in our increasingly multicultural communities.

Senator Obama is a compelling example of a man who appears to have a strong sense of his multicultural identity. His alma mater, the Punahou School (Hawai'i), should be proud. Shortly after his landslide Senatorial victory, the Senator-elect returned to Hawai'i and spoke there, explaining to the capacity crowd, "There was something about this school that embraced me, gave me support and encouragement, and allowed me to grow and prosper. I am extraordinarily grateful."

From the students, teachers, and experts I have spoken with, the best way to help mixed heritage youth grow and prosper is to provide choices. For example, the Korean/Guatemalan youngster will have greater ability to integrate himself into the Korean American and/or Latino communities now or later in life if he is culturally and linguistically fluent, especially since his appearance may visually separate him. Furthermore, student and faculty bodies with a "critical mass" of people of color provide compelling examples of individual and collective diversity. Instead of being the "only Native American kid" or "the black teacher" in a diverse environment, the mixed heritage person is more able to express her or his individuality, including explicitly choosing to identify with more than one race or culture.

Multiracial and transracially adopted students should also have the choice of embracing a monoracial identity, which is best explored when they have peers and faculty who identify this way in a school culture that isn't hostile or otherwise confusing to people of color. Over the past few years, I've noticed an interesting and problematic trend. Some of the same independent schools that are enrolling growing numbers of multiracial and transracially adopted students are accepting fewer children from same-race backgrounds. While there may be an overall increase in their number of "non-white" students, is there a net loss of cultural diversity? While trying to find a "good fit" for independent schools, are schools enrolling students who, because of their family composition and cultural upbringing, are best able to assimilate into a stubbornly white and affluent school culture?

Multiracial people shouldn't be "minority" replacements for a broad spectrum of diversity. To enhance other quantitative and qualitative data, schools should collect detailed racial/ethnic data on their students and faculty (using self-identified groups), and examine enrollment and retention trends to critically examine their cultural climate. If data suggest a hostile environment for people of color, schools must be willing to make structural changes if they are truly committed to giving all students the opportunity to "grow and prosper."

Ultimately, independent schools benefit their students — white, nonwhite, and mixed race, alike — when they refuse to put students of color at odds with their birth cultures and communities. This is achieved through environments that sincerely embrace diversity. One of the best outcomes of growing up at the intersection of different cultures is the ability to relate to, and feel comfortable among, different groups of people. Being sensitive to cultural nuance and knowing when to make slight changes in verbal cadence or body language eases access into groups and helps to avoid conflict. These are vital skills in our multicultural society, and there is a large and growing body of mixed heritage young people who possess this potential. By encouraging multiracial students to integrate the cultural capital of their heritages with the immense resources and privileges of the independent school community, America's private schools can prepare the next generation of multicultural leaders.

Matt Kelley is an alumnus of the Lakeside School (1997) in Seattle. As a 19-year-old college freshman, he founded the MAVIN Foundation, the nation's leading mixed heritage organization. He is a writer and consultant based in Seattle and Seoul, Korea. This article first appeared in the Fall 2007 issue of *Independent School*.

Schools inadvertently create **uniquely awkward** or painful situations when lessons of Asian history or culture are not facilitated with proper sensitivity.

Same and Different
Supporting Transracially Adopted Asian Americans

::

BY ROSETTA EUN RYONG LEE

"Transracial adoption is a reality of contemporary American life," note the authors of a recent landmark study. "Since 1971, parents in this country have adopted nearly a half-million children from other countries, the vast majority of them from orphanages throughout Asia, South America, and, most recently, Africa.

Additional tens of thousands of multiracial families have been formed during this period with boys and girls adopted from foster care, with the rate of such adoptions from the domestic system growing from 10.8 percent in 1995, when there were about 20,000 total adoptions, to 15 percent in 2001, when there were over 50,000. In the vast majority of these cases — domestic and international — children of color have been adopted by Caucasian parents."

Given these numbers, it's no surprise that a significant and increasing number of transracially adopted children are enrolled in independent schools. And yet, there is very little in the research and literature that specifically addresses how schools can help the students form a positive identity. Of particular concern is how schools work to support children adopted from Asian countries. Since nearly half of all foreign-born adopted children in 2009 are from Asia, and one in 10 Korean American citizens

entered the United States through adoption, transracial adoption is an increasingly significant Asian American issue.

In 2009, the Evan B. Donaldson Adoption Institute published its study of identity development in adults who were adopted as children. Previous research involving identity development of adopted individuals focused primarily on the experiences
of children and youth. The institute's study offers us a more complete perspective of
how these adults have integrated "adoptedness" and race/ethnicity into the whole that
comprises their sense of identity. The study included 468 adults — 179 of whom were
born in South Korea and adopted by white parents, and 156 of whom were U.S.-born
whites adopted by white parents. Comparing the responses of the two groups resulted
in important findings and recommendations that specifically address the challenges
and opportunities faced by individuals transracially adopted from Asia — and included
some clear lessons for schools.

THE SCHOOL EXPERIENCE OF TRANSRACIALLY ADOPTED CHILDREN FROM ASIA

The central findings of the Donaldson Adoption Institute's study add macroscopic
understanding to existing research and literature about racial/ ethnic identity development and transracial adoption. These resources combined provide a significant window
into the struggles transracially adopted students of Asian origin face in school.

**Adoption is an increasingly significant aspect of identity
for adopted people as they grow up and remains significant
even when they are adults.**

Regarding their adoption status, Asian-born students who have white parents don't
have the same privilege of invisibility as white students who are adopted. Rather, they
face an immediate reminder of their adopted status every time they enter a new school
or new environment within a school. Peers, and even teachers, often ask questions that
have a profound impact on these students. The questions — such as, Are you adopted?
Is that your real mom/dad? Where are you from? What are you? How do you speak
English so well? — may be asked out of a sense of innocent curiosity. But for transracially adopted children, they are more often than not injurious.

These micro-aggressions are brief and commonplace verbal, behavioral, or environmental indignities that communicate hostile, derogatory, or negative slights and
insults, whether intentional or unintentional. They serve to remind youth that they are
adopted and foreign-born, and they imply that such students' relationship to their parents may not be legitimate.

In addition to the impact of innocent but damaging questions, transracially adopted students of Asian origin face a host of other school-related issues. For instance, they are more often than not subject to unfairly high academic and social expectations stemming from the myth of the model minority and the quiet and submissive Asian. At some point in their school careers, they are given assignments that require background information and connection to biological roots (family tree, ancestors, genetics, baby pictures, etc.). In addition, in independent schools, they are subject to admissions materials that presume the same race of parents and children.

Race/ethnicity is an increasingly significant aspect of identity for those adopted across race and culture.

Although the Korean-born participants in the Donaldson Adoption Institute study reported a stronger sense of ethnic identity than their white counterparts, they were also less likely to have a strong sense of belonging to their ethnic group. Other research describes the "between two worlds" status of many transracially adopted Asians. Many report not feeling a part of the white world as a result of the physical attributes that make them stand out as different, and thus they are compelled to connect with their "Asianness." And yet, many also report not being part of the Asian world because they do not have the same language and cultural knowledge necessary to feel a full sense of belonging or worth. Indeed, many transracially adopted individuals report feeling a full sense of belonging only with other transracially adopted people.

Schools inadvertently create uniquely awkward or painful situations when lessons of Asian history or culture are not facilitated with proper sensitivity. Transracially adopted students of Asian origin report feeling "stared at" by peers or asked to corroborate or refute "the Asian perspective." As a young woman in one study stated: "It's always when they're talking about Korea. If [classmates] say something wrong, they would ask 'Michelle, is that right?' And I'd answer, 'I don't know.' It's like I'm ashamed…. I'm Korean [by birth], but I grew up in this white society…. I just feel really ashamed that I can't answer their questions."

The all-too-common stress of isolation and difference compounded by the burden of being a "spokesperson" for one's group is difficult for any student of color. When the student shares little to no cultural, historical, or language background with his or her racial/ethnic group, there are additional feelings of inadequacy and shame.

Coping with discrimination is an important aspect of coming to terms with racial/ethnic identity for adoptees of color.

In the Institute study, 80 percent of Korean-born respondents reported racial discrimination from strangers; 75 percent reported racism from classmates; 48 percent reported negative racial experiences due to interactions with childhood friends; and, sadly, 39 percent reported race-based discrimination from teachers.

Quite often, especially when transracially adopted youth live in mostly white communities, much of the racial discrimination isn't directed toward the individuals. Nonetheless, the individuals experience negative self-construal as a result. Sometimes, negative stereotypes and jokes arise about Asians in general or other people of color. When people protest or express discomfort, perpetrators often explain, "It's not directed towards you. We're just talking about Asians." Although the intention of these responses is to profess to seeing the person as an individual, to transracially adopted youth, such comments are an affirmation of two debilitating facts: They do not fully belong to their racial/ethnic group, and the community around them believes the same negative racial stereotypes portrayed by much of the media.

An additional problem is that transracially adopted youth often find little comfort or training in how to cope with such racial assaults from their white parents, teachers, or peers. Most parents of color train their children to recognize, cope with, and respond to racial stereotypes and harassment. At the very least, these parents can speak from experience about what racial encounters are like, thus giving legitimacy to the strategies they suggest to their children. But white parents, teachers, and peers attempting to help adopted children in such situations generally don't have the resources or experience to be of help. In fact, the typical approach to comforting transracially adopted youth in such situations — saying, for instance, "Just ignore them," or "I totally understand what you're going through" — tends to silence youth into thinking racial discrimination is something to be dealt with on one's own — and thus further increases the feelings of difference and isolation.

WHAT SCHOOLS CAN DO TO HELP

These basic findings make it clear that transracially adopted children need our concerted effort in order to thrive in schools. Schools can take many steps, including the following.

Acknowledge the realities of adoption.

As with any important issue in school, the first step is to acknowledge the issue. To this end, schools need to help teachers, administrators, parents, and students understand the realities of adoption — for all adopted children, but especially for transracially adopted children. The next step is to work together as a community to erase stigmas and

stereotypes, minimize discrimination, and provide adopted children with more opportunities for positive development.

Consciously support the positive racial/ethnic identity of students.

In particular, the Donaldson Adoption Institute study highlights how, for transracially
adopted children, "positive racial/ethnic identity development is most effectively facilitated by 'lived' experiences such as travel to [their] native country, attending racially
diverse schools, and having role models of their own race/ethnicity." The study's
respondents appreciated cultural celebrations and other opportunities to learn about
their racial and ethnic heritage, but these are singular events and do not offer a whole-
sale solution to the struggles transracially adopted people face.

As one youth states in a different study: "What's hard for me is that [Korean Culture Camp] takes place only once a year! I finally get to go to a place where I feel safe,
where I feel comfortable, where I feel like I'm around people who understand me…. If I
had been able to grow up that way, and if I always had those role models to say, 'You're
Korean — be proud of yourself,' instead of always feeling 'I'm American — I don't
know what that means,' I think I would be a little more confident."

Identify and confront micro-aggressions.

All educators need to understand that transracially adopted students constantly face
micro-aggressions. Since the research reveals that most adults and students in school are
not even aware of this fact, it behooves schools to raise awareness. For instance, teachers
can be trained on the accumulated impact created when students are repeatedly asked
to represent "their group" in the classroom. They can also be trained to facilitate the
conversations that arise when peers ask a student to speak as a representative of his or
her group.

The goal is not only to help reduce these micro-aggressions, but also to help transracially adopted students deal with them. In addition, such students need support as
they seek to negotiate difficult situations in schools so that their identity as an adopted
person is neither ignored nor highlighted as a deficit.

Psychologist April Harris-Britt describes training to deal with the realities of race
and racism as "Parental Race Socialization." Schools can augment this parental effort
by providing "School Race Socialization." Harris-Britt's studies suggest that a certain
amount of this training is necessary to ensure resilience through painful encounters
of prejudice and discrimination. At the same time, her research also suggests that too
much of this training — defensive by definition — could result in youth approaching life

in a white-majority society with fatalism and suspicion. Racial pride, on the other hand, is something that can be taught in abundance without negative side effects. Whether by parents or role models of the same race/ethnicity, this socialization is clearly a necessity in the transracially adopted youth's life.

Provide affinity group space that's welcoming to transracially adopted students.

As diversity in schools increases, more and more schools find value in offering affinity groups for students. Students adopted from Asian countries can benefit from an Asian American affinity group. It is also important to ensure that such a group welcomes everyone, regardless of cultural or language knowledge or access to a parent with such knowledge. Better yet, schools can provide a space specifically for students who are transracially adopted.

Focus on developing a welcoming, diverse culture in the school.

Schools can — and should — provide support, role models, information, and the understanding that, when it comes to race/ethnicity and discrimination, they need to supplement parental efforts and provide a safer climate for all. A diverse student body and faculty/ staff population can present mirrors of experience and positive role models for transracially adopted students. Affinity groups can offer a space where experiences and strategies are shared and discussed.

Beyond diversity and safe spaces, however, schools must help raise the critical consciousness for all. The discussion must go beyond how people of color can cope with prejudice and discrimination and venture into what such acts of prejudice and discrimination are and how so many of us perpetrate them overtly or implicitly. When there is a common community understanding and commitment to undo bias, transracially adopted students no longer carry alone the burden of needing to know how to recognize and combat acts of racial/ethnic aggression. Rather, these actions become a community charge.

Consider school publications from the perspective of adopted students.

Admission brochures and other school publications are designed to accurately put forth the best possible image of the school. But if they contain no images of or references to transracially adopted children, an unintended message of indifference is sent to such students and their families.

ONE EDUCATOR'S PERSPECTIVE

I am a teacher and Asian and Pacific Island Affinity Group co-facilitator at Seattle Girls' School (Washington). We have 117 girls, over 40 percent of whom are girls of color, and many of whom are Asian American. A vast majority of these Asian American students are multiracial or transracially adopted. As a Korean-born immigrant with two Korean parents, I attempt to provide students with a positive role model, create a safe space where they can openly discuss challenges, and teach them a little about what it is to be a confident Asian woman in a society that does not always make it easy. I will never know what it's like to have white parents and navigate the world with this compass, but I can show them full acceptance for exactly who they are: Asian, adopted, culturally white, and more. With the school's anti-bias core belief that "it is fundamental to understand and address issues of difference and oppression," we attempt to have dialogue in the classroom and as a whole school about the realities of the world as well as provide students critical thinking skills and practical tools to change the world for the better.

Given this context and the location of Seattle — a racially diverse city with a large transracial adoption community — the transracially adopted students at my school have a better shot at establishing a positive self-identity. As one of my students said to me, "I like it here — you don't get stereotyped.… I like being Asian, and I like being adopted.… I like that my parents aren't the same race as me, because it's like we're special."

Not every transracially adopted student will attain this enlightened state of self-awareness, and the school and I will continue to stumble and make mistakes as we try to support these girls well. However, doing right by them is a critical challenge and opportunity we welcome. I invite your schools to continue to do great work as you open your approach and practices to include as fully as possible these vibrant, truly multicultural, multiethnic, and multiracial families that constitute a growing part of the norm of the American family.

Rosetta Eun Ryong Lee is a teacher, professional outreach specialist, and Asian and Pacific Island Affinity Group co-facilitator at Seattle Girls' School (Washington). This article first appeared in the Winter 2011 issue of *Independent School*.

REFERENCES

Geneva Gay, "Ethnic Identity Development and Multicultural Education," in Rosa H. Sheets, Etta R. Hollins (Eds.). *Racial and Ethnic Identity in School Practices: Aspects of Human Development* (Mahwah, NJ: Lawrence Erlbaum Associates, 1999).

April Harris-Britt, Cecilia R. Valrie, Beth Kurtz-Costes, and Stephanie J. Rowley, "Perceived Racial Discrimination and Self-Esteem in African American Youth: Racial Socialization as a Protective Factor," *Journal of Research on Adolescence* (2001): 17.

Jean Kim, "Processes of Asian American Identity Development: A Study of Japanese American Women's Perceptions of Their Struggle to Achieve Positive Identities as Americans of Asian Ancestry" (Unpublished doctoral dissertation, University of Massachusetts, 1981).

Stacey J. Lee, *Unraveling the "Model Minority" Stereotype: Listening to Asian American Youth* (New York: Teachers College Press, 1996).

Mary Mullen, "Identity Development of Korean Adoptees," in *Reviewing Asian America: Locating Diversity,* ed. Wendy L. Ng, Soo-Young Chin, James S. Moy, and Gary Y. Okihiro (Pullman, WA: Washington State University Press, 1995).

John D. Palmer, "Korean Adopted Young Women: Gender Bias, Racial Issues, and Educational Implications," in *Research on the Education of Asian Pacific Americans,* ed. Clara C. Park, A. Lin Goodwin, and Stacey J. Lee (Greenwich, CT: Information Age Publishing Inc., 2001).

Hollee McGinnis et al., *Beyond Culture Camp: Promoting Healthy Identity Formation in Adoption* (New York: Evan B. Donaldson Adoption Institute, November 2009).

"Adoption Statistics," Child Welfare Information Gateway, September 10, 2010, *www.childwelfare.gov/systemwide/statistics/adoption.cfm#inter.*

The trends in the U.S. show that economic advances are more evident in those occupations requiring higher levels of education.

A Space at the Table

::

BY D. SCOTT LOONEY

In a speech at the American Council on Education, then-president of Harvard University, Lawrence H. Summers, said this regarding socioeconomic diversity in higher education: "In the United States today, a student from the top income quartile is more than six times as likely as a student from the bottom quartile to graduate with a B.A. within five years of leaving high school.

And in the most selective colleges and universities, only 3 percent of students come from the bottom income quartile and only 10 percent come from the bottom half of the income scale…. These differences cannot be fully accounted for by native ability or academic preparation. Indeed, a student from the highest income quartile and the lowest aptitude quartile is as likely to be enrolled in college as a student from the lowest income quartile and the highest aptitude quartile."

Anthony P. Carnevale, vice president of the Educational Testing Service and a coauthor of a new study on socioeconomic diversity at the 146 most selective colleges and universities,[1] underscored this point: "There is even less socioeconomic diversity

---

Editor's Note: The statistics in this article represent a snapshot of the American society and independent schools at the first decade of the 21st century. While the numbers regarding the socioeconomic divide in high education and independent schools have changed, the percentages remain similar, if not worse — and the argument for greater socioeconomic diversity in schools still stands.

[1] Anthony P. Carnevale is now the director of the Georgetown University Center on Education and the Workforce.

than racial or ethnic diversity at the most selective colleges. There are four times as many African-American and Hispanic students as there are students from the lowest [socioeconomic status] quartile."[2] While there is considerable debate about the merits of affirmative action programs, they have been at least partially responsible for significant diversification of the college population by race. Corresponding diversification by socio-economic class in higher education has not been achieved.

The statistics for independent schools appear to be remarkably similar to those for the top colleges. The percentage of students of color at NAIS member schools in 2004–2005 was 21.1 percent, up from 16.8 percent in 1994–1995. The U.S. Census bureau estimates the percentage of the non-white population of the United States in 2004 at 25 percent. While the racial diversity of independent schools is not yet equal to that of the United States, the gap is closing and is not nearly as great as the socioeconomic gap. The estimated median household income in the United States in 2004 was $45,660. The median tuition for a NAIS member school was $13,639. According to the financial aid algorithm used by the NAIS School and Student Service for Financial Aid (SSS) to calculate need-based financial aid, a family of four at the national median income would qualify for a full scholarship. The NAIS average percentage of students receiving full need-based scholarships was 9.6 percent. It stands to reason, then, that students from families in the bottom 50 percent of household incomes represented less than 10 percent of the enrollments for typical NAIS member schools.

So it is clear that students from families in the bottom 50 percent of household incomes represented less than 10 percent of the enrollments for typical independent schools. Since many schools only meet 80 to 90 percent of the demonstrated financial need, the percentage of students from the bottom half of household incomes is probably well below 9 percent. It is clear that NAIS member schools, on average, have made far more progress on racial diversification than socioeconomic. The difference between the NAIS and national averages for non-white population is only 4 percentage points and closing, while the representation at NAIS member schools from the bottom half of incomes in the United States is less than 9 percent, a 41-point gap that is getting larger.

Given that the average percentage of students receiving financial aid at NAIS member schools was 17.2 percent, approximately 83 percent of the families in these schools are paying full tuition. Using the SSS formula for financial aid calculation, a family with only one child must have a household income of $86,000 or more to afford (not qualify for any financial assistance) the NAIS average full tuition. For a family to afford to have

---

[2] David G. Savage, "Ranks of Poor Are Thin at Top Colleges," *The Los Angeles Times*, April 7, 2004.

The Inclusive School
A Selection of Writing on Diversity Issues in Independent Schools

two children in a school at the NAIS median tuition, the income must be over $139,000. For schools with tuitions greater than the NAIS average, a day school charging a tuition of $20,000, for example, the income needed for one child would be over $100,000, and, for two children, over $180,000. With the exception of independent schools where the tuition is under the NAIS median, the realistic household income necessary to support tuition for one child would be $100,000 or more and for two children above $150,000. According to U.S. Census Bureau estimates for 2005, 16 percent of American households have incomes over $100,000, while only 6 percent have household incomes over $150,000. These figures reveal an undeniable truth: Independent schools are still primarily attended by children from affluent families.

THE GAP WIDENS

Since the 1970s, the U.S. economy has gone through three important changes:

- Economic restructuring characterized by a decline in manufacturing jobs and growth in service jobs, coupled with the increasing use of part-time and temporary workers;
- A shift from a material economy to one based primarily on information and service; and
- A growing concentration of wealth and income among the top 20 percent of the population and a diminution in wealth and income among the lower quartiles.[3]

These changes have dramatically increased the gap between the "haves" and "have-nots" in America. This gap can be measured in income, educational attainment, social engagement, political participation, knowledge, job skills, and opportunities.

In 1912, an Italian statistician and demographer named Corrado Gini developed a statistical measurement for inequality, now called the Gini coefficient. The Gini coefficient is used throughout the world to measure the relative level of income and wealth polarization of a society. The Gini coefficient is a number between 0 and 1, where 0 corresponds with perfect equality (where everyone has the same income) and 1 corresponds with perfect inequality (where one person has all the income, and everyone else has zero income). In 1970, the Gini coefficient in the United States was .394 and in 2000 it was .462. Inequality has increased 17 percent in the last 30 years. In a list of the 124 most industrialized countries in the world, the United States ranks 74th in equality, with Denmark ranking first as the country with the most equality and Namibia 124th as the country with the least equality. So the United States' income polarization is worse than

---

[3] "A Central Focus: Economic Opportunities in Central Cities," Towson University Institute for Teaching and Research on Women website, *http://pages.towson.edu/itrow/research/current percent20research percent20projects/ economic_opportunity_structure.htm.*

that of Cambodia, Turkey, Vietnam, Nepal, Moldova, Jordan, Mauritania, Tanzania, and 68 other countries.

From the late 1940s through the 1970s, it was possible to be solidly middle class while working in jobs that did not require a college degree. That is not true today; the trend since the early 1980s has favored those with more education. As the Information Age displaces the Industrial Age, world economies become more dependent upon information, service, and technology — and successful participation in these economies becomes more dependent upon education. The trends in the U.S. show that economic advances are more evident in those occupations requiring higher levels of education. Between 1982 and 1997, the incomes for professional/executives and occupations in the technology field rose 7 percent and 5 percent, respectively, in real dollars (1997 inflation-adjusted dollars), while those in the fields of production/ craft/repair and those in operators/fabricators/laborers saw their earnings in real dollars drop by 10 percent and 9 percent respectively.

As David Brooks points out in an op-ed piece for *The New York Times*, there is also a widening gap in behavioral differences between the "haves" and the "have nots":

> Divorce rates for college grads are plummeting, but… the divorce rate for high school grads is now twice as high as that of college grads…. High school grads are twice as likely to smoke as college grads. They are much less likely to exercise. College grads are nearly twice as likely to vote. They are more than twice as likely to do voluntary work. They are much more likely to give blood. These behavioral gaps are widening.[4]

THE AMERICAN CASTE SYSTEM

According to one source, the American Dream is "the widespread aspiration of Americans to live better than their parents did."[5] Another source defines the American Dream as "an American social ideal that stresses egalitarianism and especially material prosperity."[6] A third source defines the American Dream as "the idea (often associated with the Protestant work ethic) held by many in the United States that through hard work, courage, and determination one can achieve prosperity."[7]

Specifics aside, the American Dream is a pervasive belief that society rewards effort and determination and those who attain material success do so largely through their efforts, rather than through an inherited birthright. The United States was founded

---

[4] David Brooks, "The Education Gap," *New York Times*, September 25, 2005.

[5] WordNet ® 2.0, 2003 Princeton University.

[6] Merriam-Webster Dictionary, 2005.

[7] *Wikipedia.com*, 2005.

with an intentional opposition to the hereditary aristocracy of the Old World. That founding ideal is still widely held by most Americans and is the basis for a large number of political and social policies. So, several hundred years after the founding of America, how is the American Dream faring? The data suggests not so well.

In households where even one parent did not complete a high school education, the children have less than a 30 percent chance of even starting college of any kind, including two-year colleges. Those same children, even if they do begin college, have less than a 30-percent chance of achieving a bachelor's degree.[8] Conversely, in those households where at least one parent achieved a bachelor's degree or higher, the children have over an 80-percent chance of beginning college, and over a 75-percent chance of completing a bachelor's degree. This situation has not changed for the last 20 years. Children born into well-educated families stand a good chance of becoming well educated; children born to less educated parents have slim chances of attaining a college degree.

According to the 2000 census, the average family income for households headed by a high school dropout was $32,948. For a high school graduate, it was $46,523; for a college graduate, it was $81,026; for someone with a master's degree, it was $96,519; and for a professional degree, it was $144,709. There is an exponential relationship between level of education and income attainment. Conversely, there is also a powerful relationship between income and educational attainment. "Only about one in 17 young people from the nation's poorest families, those earning less than $35,377 a year, can expect to earn a bachelor's degree by age 24. For those from the nation's wealthiest families, those who earn about $85,000 or higher, it's better than one in two."[9] In America today, those with education achieve affluence; those with affluence can attain education for their children. What chance do the children of parents without college degrees have to participate in the American Dream? Are their dreams going to be perpetually deferred?

A SPACE AT THE TABLE

The extraordinary generosity of Americans in response to the Hurricane Katrina disaster reminds us all of one of the greatest of American virtues: We can always make room for one more hungry neighbor for dinner. NAIS member schools from all parts of the nation have made extraordinary gestures to the families of those affected by the hurricane. Hundreds of NAIS member schools have allowed displaced students from the independent schools of the Gulf region to join their schools for little or no tuition.

---

[8] *Raising the Graduation Rates of Low Income College Students: A Report by the Pell Institute for Study of Opportunity in Higher Education*, December 2004.

[9] Greg Toppo and Anthony DeBarros, "Reality Weighs Down Dreams of College," *USA Today*, February 2, 2005.

Hundreds of other schools mobilized their students, parents, and faculty to gather and distribute hundreds of thousands — perhaps more than a million — dollars worth of relief in the form of materials or funding. Episcopal High School in Houston found a place for 47 students who had been displaced from their schools in the New Orleans area. When an additional 60 students were still without placement, Episcopal worked out an arrangement with the leadership and faculty from three NAIS member schools in New Orleans — Isidore Newman School, Louise S. McGehee School, and Metairie Park Country Day School. Episcopal then offered extra classroom space to provide enrollment for these students, and welcomed faculty and staff from the displaced schools to teach and help out all the newly enrolled students. This type of response to Hurricane Katrina stands as a tangible example of the generosity and resources that NAIS member schools can offer to the less fortunate.

But in every one of those cities where the additional enrollment spaces have been offered to children affected by Katrina, there are already children, capable children, who are from lower-income families and receiving a poor education. What if each independent school were to make a space at the table for a child from the bottom half of the socioeconomic spectrum in each section of each grade of its school? If a K–12 school with three sections per grade and 14 grades makes a space at the table for one additional child per section, 42 poor children would have the opportunity to attend a good school. What are the real costs of this extraordinary act? Using traditional financial aid accounting, which assumes that the opportunity cost of having students not paying the full tuition is real money lost, the cost would be about $572,838 (42 students X $13,639 — the average NAIS tuition). Given that the average cost of educating a child in an independent school is above the cost of the tuition, that total expenditure could be estimated at closer to $650,000.

However, there is another way of thinking about this. The vast majority of the costs to run a school are fixed costs — such as staff salaries and benefits, physical plant maintenance, and insurance — that do not go up or down based on adding or subtracting a small number of students. So those additional 42 students would actually cost the school only a relatively small amount (lunch, classroom supplies, etc.) and teacher time. Given the exceptionally caring nature of independent school teachers, it is reasonable to assume that they would be willing to contribute their time to teach a few additional students — in this model, about four additional students per teacher — if they knew that those additional students were the most underprivileged. For a school with a balanced budget, these students actually represent little threat to the budget's alignment.

The Inclusive School
A Selection of Writing on Diversity Issues in Independent Schools

For schools that do not have surplus enrollment demand, the financial implications are simple and few. If it is unlikely that a full-paying or high-partial-paying family will fill an empty enrollment space, then making the school more affordable to an economically disadvantaged student does not represent any opportunity cost, only the small marginal costs like lunch and supplies. However, for schools in markets with exceptionally high enrollment demand (measured by full-paying students on the waiting lists) the opportunity cost of filling those spaces with economically disadvantaged students is real.

These schools have access to and myriad uses for the income that could be generated by additional paying enrollments. In schools with strong enrollment demand, then, the case for greater socioeconomic diversity must be one of mission and philosophy. Most independent school mission statements include some reference to the value of diversity. Given that the most underrepresented group in independent schools is the socioeconomically disadvantaged, any serious movement towards greater diversity and inclusion must begin by directing additional resources to this end.

There are a host of modifications to this type of model that might be more palatable to some schools. For example, instead of full scholarships, perhaps a school could offer spaces for only $1,000 to $2,000. That would still allow a student from an underrepresented socioeconomic group to attend the school, while also covering those small, per-student, incremental costs. A school with strong enrollment demand might decide to expand each of the three sections by one student, filling two of the three spaces with full-paying students and the third space with a student on full scholarship. In this scenario, the school would actually generate an additional $381,982 in tuition revenue while also allowing 14 more economically disadvantaged students to attend. That additional revenue could easily cover the incremental costs of the extra 42 students as well as the cost of increasing faculty compensation to recognize the increased workload.

But what about the reaction from the families who pay the full tuition? It is easy to imagine them saying, "Hey, wait a minute. I am paying full tuition, and the school is just giving away spaces!" The response to this lies in a school educating its constituents about the value and purpose of a financial aid program. Since most schools currently offer need-based financial aid, the rationale for making "a space at the table" for additional students would be an extension of the education and communication that should already be happening.

Most parents who send their children to independent schools want their children to be broadly and vigorously educated so that they can gain entrance to a good college and find happiness and success in the adult world. The benefits of having the broadest possible exposure to students from other backgrounds and races, and with different ideas and experiences, must be part of that education — and it must include children from families in the bottom 50 percent of the socioeconomic tier. It is a common confusion among families who pay independent school tuition that some of their tuition dollars are being used to fund the need-based aid program. Some families are happy to think they are helping the less fortunate; some resent having to "subsidize" the education of other people's children. The reality is that the additional spaces at the table can be made without increasing the specific cost for any other family.

What about class size? Public opinion research suggests that the small class size that independent schools offer plays a significant factor in creating enrollment demand for private schools.[10] However, looking at class-size research a little more deeply, it appears that it is not class size, per se, that is the key to the success of independent schools; it is the delivery of individual attention and small school size that make the difference.[11] Many independent schools could afford to add one student per section without notably changing the delivery of individualized attention or growing the size of the school significantly.

What if all independent schools from a geographic region or city were all to agree to make additional space at their tables? What if all independent schools were to launch a collective initiative? It would almost certainly mean greater, more representative socioeconomic diversity, a reduction of the pervasive belief that independent schools are elitist, the creation of a new ethic for our school communities to rally around, and opportunities for students in independent schools to learn from people from across the socioeconomic spectrum.

The practical realities of school operations, parent/community relations, school finance, and the exceptionally independent nature of independent schools mean the aforementioned "what ifs" are not likely to come to fruition. But if independent schools hope to truly educate children in a way that will prepare them best for the future, the schools should provide their current students with more classmates from the bottom half of the American socioeconomic tier.

Although the law does not codify the hereditary aristocracy in the United States, stultifying socioeconomic stratification produces the same result. Until the funding for public elementary and secondary schools is no longer tied to the local tax base, until the public funding for public colleges and universities allows for a much lower tuition, and until private educational institutions find mechanisms to provide broader

---

[10] 1999 NAIS Public Opinion Poll.

[11] H. Peter Aitken, Vivian Anthony, William Keator, and Ann Tottenham, *Access and Affordability: Strategic Planning Perspectives for Independent Schools* (Washington: National Association of Independent Schools, 1994).

socioeconomic representation, the socioeconomic class into which people are born will continue to determine the socioeconomic class of their children. The irony is painful. The education industry, largely made up of people who themselves are making significant material sacrifice to better the lives of others, is the central engine perpetuating economic inequality. The generous spirit of those people within the independent school world suggests that we should find a way to make room for a few more needy students at our table.

At the time this article was written, **D. Scott Looney** was the assistant director of schools, Cranbrook Schools (Michigan). He is now head of school at Hawken School (Ohio). This article first appeared in the Winter 2006 issue of *Independent School*.

The students in our schools get so much, and yet if you are in an urban area there are probably other children within a mile or two of you who get so little.

School Head, Know Thy Neighbor

Why You Should Get Out of the Office and Meet Your Neighboring Non-Independent School Colleagues

::

BY ROGER WEAVER

In the early 1980s, Paul Cummins, the founding headmaster of Crossroads School for Arts and Sciences, a K–12 independent school in Santa Monica, California, did something simultaneously counterintuitive and completely obvious: He took out the Yellow Pages, started calling the principals of nearby public schools, and arranged to visit them, one after another.

Today, a direct result of Paul's conversations with local principals is that more than 11,000 students in underserved public schools in the Los Angeles area and California's central valley annually receive fully funded, year-long, hands-on, in-school arts programs delivered by professional teaching artists.

About a decade later, I became headmaster of Crossroads after serving for 10 years as assistant headmaster to Paul. For many years, our school's community involvement continued to focus on strengthening and growing the public school arts education program we had initiated. But one day, having learned from Paul the value of reaching out to neighboring schools, I decided to visit a small Catholic K–8 school two blocks away from Crossroads that I had been driving by for years but knew absolutely nothing about. The direct result of that visit is that today volunteers from a consortium of area independent schools have quite literally saved this school from closure, and the 175 children enrolled there, 70 percent of whom are living below the federal poverty index, have a sustainable educational community in which to learn and grow.

Paul's decision to find out what was going on in the public schools around him and my decision to visit a neighboring Catholic school were not based on either of us looking for ways to fill vast colonnades of leisure time in our schedules or from a lack of things on our to-do lists. Nor were they based on a perception that Crossroads had an excess of resources to meet the needs of our own young and growing school.

Independent schools are increasingly placing significant priority on community service. They understand the important messages about social and personal responsibility that these programs convey to our students, along with the invaluable hands-on, real-world experience that students get from community service work. And while student community service is certainly an important part of what goes on in independent schools, if we are truly going to walk our talk with respect to the importance of community service, we need to do something more, something that students and parents can see as evidence of our institutional commitment in this area.

THE ART OF CONNECTION

One of the things that commonly make independent school heads bridle is the fact that, in the news media, the words "independent school" (or more commonly "private school") are almost without exception preceded by either the word "elite" and "exclusive." The problem with these epithets, of course, is not that they were conferred out of malice, but that, historically, they have been earned. If we don't like them, then we should actually do something about it. Institutional community service is one of the things that we can do about it. Having our students go out and do community service work is good and appropriate and a valuable teaching tool, but it is not enough. Urban independent schools in particular have extraordinary networks of people and other resources that enable them to be part of a bigger picture of education — part of a solution to the pervasive educational affliction of under-funded, undervalued, overloaded, and chronically struggling schools, of which there are far too many.

When Paul Cummins started visiting the public schools around Crossroads, he was the first independent school head any of the principals had ever met, and certainly the first to set foot on any of their campuses. He initiated these visits because he felt woefully ignorant about his educational neighbors, and he was interested in seeing if Crossroads and these schools could collaborate in any way to each of their benefits. When he started down this path, he did not have a destination in mind, but where it led him and the schools that ultimately became involved in his initiative is an interesting example of the power of exploring possibilities when impulse, opportunity, and some good fortune align.

In learning about his neighboring public schools, Paul was immediately struck by two things: how segregated they were and the virtually complete absence of the arts. Since Paul was the founder of a school with diversity and the arts as two of its five founding core values, that made an impression on him. He realized that he couldn't do much about their enrollment profile, but when he learned in one elementary school that its choral teacher's funding had been cut (the school's only arts program), he offered to "lend" the school the Crossroads choral teacher for an after-school program. Eighty kids showed up. The principal subsequently asked if the program could be offered during the day, and, at that point, Paul had the Crossroads development office pursue and secure a small grant from the American Express Foundation to fund a part-time choral instructor during the regular school day.

Shortly afterwards, Paul was at a Crossroads potluck dinner for new families and got into a conversation with a group of parents about the dire state of the arts in public schools. He told the story of the choral teacher in the public elementary school, and one of the new parents took him aside later in the evening and asked if a substantial grant would enable a comprehensive music, dance, drama, and visual arts program to be put into the school. That parent was musician Herb Alpert, who made an initial "life changing" gift. He subsequently provided additional strong support to what became the Crossroads Community Outreach Foundation, and its major project, which is now its own independent 501(c)3 known as PS Arts. Currently in its 20th year, PS Arts annually provides fully funded arts programs to over 11,000 students in two dozen Title I public schools. Its more than $2-million annual operating budget comes entirely from contributed funds.

Because Crossroads has service to the greater community as one of its five founding core values, it made sense to create a legally separate nonprofit entity to seek funding for our public outreach work. Among other things, this enabled us to seek grants from individuals, corporations, and foundations that would not support an independent school or whose charters excluded directly supporting precollegiate education.

SUPPORT BY CONSORTIUM

When I became headmaster of Crossroads, I was committed to carrying on the out-reach work of the Crossroads Community Outreach Foundation (CCOF), and particularly interested in finding a way to engage other schools in the area in the effort. I found that way a few blocks from the Crossroads campus. Saint Anne School was founded in 1908 with a commitment to "exercising a preferential option for the poor" by providing affordable quality education regardless of a family's capacity to pay tuition. In the early years of the K–8 school, migrant farm workers from Mexico worked side-by-side with those from Oklahoma and the Southern states as their children studied together in the school.

Today the school has a population of 175 students — a mix of Latino, African-American, Asian-American, and white students. I was surprised to discover that even though Saint Anne is a Catholic school, it receives very little funding from the Los Angeles Archdiocese. The formula used to allocate financial support to diocesan schools is based on the median income of the community where the school is located. Because Santa Monica's median income is relatively high, Saint Anne gets minimal funding from the archdiocese.

The result is that Saint Anne is the only nonpublic Title I school in Santa Monica, and an average of 70 percent of its students qualify for federal food programs under the poverty index criteria. Its financial picture is made even more challenging because the founding philosophy of the school requires that flexible, affordable tuition means reduced payment obligations for families with multiple children. The consequence, of course, is that the larger the number of students from a single family, the smaller the income per student. The already minimal fee structure of $3,400 per year for one student decreases with each family member to $2,300 per year per student for a family with four children attending. In short, Saint Anne School is under the most severe financial circumstances of any educational institution in our community and in far worse shape financially than even the most severely under-funded public schools.

The reality of Saint Anne was quite an eye-opener for me, and I immediately saw its situation as an obvious one around which to attempt to rally support from a group of neighboring independent schools. I began calling my friends and colleagues in surrounding independent schools, explaining the circumstances of Saint Anne School and asking if they would join a group effort to support this at-risk community resource. I had learned that Saint Anne at that time was looking at a $60,000 annual operating budget deficit. I purposefully did not ask for money; instead, I asked each school to "contribute a person" — either a trustee, parent, staff member, or friend of the school — who would be willing to sit on the Saint Anne development advisory group with the specific goal of using their contacts, connections, and personal network to raise $60,000 a year in support of the school. I argued that some focused, thoughtful, volunteer assistance would have a reasonable chance of raising that relatively modest amount annually to support the operations of this extraordinary educational institution. Nine schools and a local hospital that heard about the idea agreed to join the effort, and the Saint Anne Support Council was born.

Initially, the Saint Anne Support Council received guidance and support from CCOF. Now the Support Council operates independently, and when its members actually came to understand the school and see what it was doing with its students and families, they became so committed and passionate about the work that they far exceeded anyone's wildest hopes for what they could achieve. In the last four years, for example, the Saint Anne Support Council has raised over $760,000 for the school. Michael Browning, the incredibly dedicated principal of Saint Anne School said recently, "The impact of the Support Council has been immeasurable; it is the single biggest reason the school is in existence today. Without it, the school would have closed two years ago."

THE BENEFITS OF OUTREACH

There also turned out to be an unanticipated but significant benefit to Crossroads as a result of the various community initiatives we have undertaken. During my tenure as headmaster, we were able to purchase land and develop an elementary school campus and K–12 sports center two blocks from our main campus. The fund-raising portion of that project totaled $14 million. As the primary fund-raiser in that effort, I was very interested to see that, without exception, every major gift we received in that campaign was accompanied by some version of "I am happy to support this project, but I want you to know that I would not be making this level of commitment if you were not doing what you are out in the community."

Independent schools have many good reasons to get directly involved with the educational environment around them. It is good modeling for students, there is an enlightened self-interest return on the effort invested, and, most important, it is the right thing to do. And when independent schools begin to develop a reputation for community engagement, a subtle but important shift begins to occur in three key areas: admissions, hiring, and board recruitment. As that plays out, the understanding of and support for a public purpose commitment increases among families in the school, the professional staff, and the board of trustees. Now the school is moving toward an interesting paradigm shift in the purposes and purviews of independent education.

The students in our schools get so much, and yet if you are in an urban area there are probably other children within a mile or two of you who get so little. If you have read Jonathan Kozol's *Savage Inequalities*, this is not news to you. (And if you haven't read it, you need to.) Independent schools cannot undo all the social, economic, and political reasons that education is failing so many of our young people, but we do not have to be part of the problem. Quality education is a social justice issue, and we all need to take measure of our institutions and ask ourselves what we can do to be part of the solution. The schools around you probably won't reach out to you. They assume you don't care. Prove them wrong.

Roger Weaver, the former headmaster of Crossroads School for Arts and Sciences (California), is the president of The Weaver Group, a consulting firm for organizations and leaders. This article first appeared in the Spring 2011 issue of *Independent School*.

The Inclusive School
A Selection of Writing on Diversity Issues in Independent Schools

…well-to-do adults who were raising their sons in secure surroundings were nevertheless **a bit jumpy** about boys.

Are We Afraid of Our Boys?

::

BY MICHAEL THOMPSON

In 1999, my life dramatically changed. I wrote a book about boys — and it was published a week before the shootings at Columbine High School. Before the disaster in Littleton, Colorado, I didn't consider myself a national expert on boys. I was a local psychologist with a private practice in the Boston area. In addition, I had worked as a psychologist at four coeducational schools over a period of 12 years. As with many counselors, a majority of my customers were girls who came to my office on their own initiative.

When I went to work as the consulting psychologist at the Belmont Hill School, an all-boys independent school with 400 students in grades seven through 12, my patients (obviously) were boys. They almost never referred themselves to the psychologist. In fact, of the 41 boys I evaluated there last year, only one came to see me voluntarily. All the others had to be pushed to talk to me by their advisors, or by the dean, or by the trouble they had gotten themselves into. Tenth-grade boys don't say to their friends, "Gee, guys,

Editor's Note: A version of the following article was first presented at the American Library Association meeting in Toronto in 2003 and appeared in the June 2004 issue of *Children and Libraries*. It is reprinted with permission of the author.

I've got to go see the psychologist to talk over some emotional problems I've been having." I like to joke that if it were not for the dean and the disciplinary process, a psychologist at an all-boys school would be like the Maytag repairman.

Over the years of my work at a boys' school, I saw boys and more boys for evaluation and therapy. Interestingly, my experience mirrored a trend in my private practice: My patient list grew to be 70 percent boys and men. (This was unusual, as women are the traditional consumers of psychotherapy services.) The experience of talking to lots of boys who were sad, disappointed, and ashamed, but who expressed their hurt through anger and irrationality, made me want to write about them.

A similar set of experiences at another boys' school moved my coauthor, psychologist Dan Kindlon, to suggest that we write a book about boys. The result was *Raising Cain*. A week after publication came the carnage at Columbine High School. During the next three weeks, Dan and I appeared on *The Today Show* three times, and I did television and radio interviews for months thereafter.

The journalists I met all tended to ask the same predictable questions about boy violence and school shootings. But after the microphones, cameras, and lights were turned off, something more interesting happened. At the end of the interview, the anchor or camera operator would ask me, "How do I know if my son is violent? He doesn't talk to me. I don't know what's going on inside him. How would I know if he were going to hurt someone?" These kinds of questions came more often from women than from men, but the fear that boys are mysterious and potentially violent was visible in many people.

I was startled, because I have worked with and known boys all my life, and I have rarely experienced them as threatening or potentially violent.

Of course, I am not a police officer, nor do I work in corrections or violence prevention. Though I originally trained on the South Side of Chicago with a largely poor and African-American population, for the last two decades I have worked in a suburban setting with middle class and upper-middle class children, with their parents, and with their teachers. What I found was that many thoughtful, well-to-do adults who were raising their sons in secure surroundings were nevertheless a bit jumpy about boys. Or, if they were not scared of their own sons, they were scared of other people's. I visit about 30 schools each year, and I have witnessed, unmistakably, this same subtle fear in all of them. And I believe this fear has an impact on the lives of boys.

Let me give you some examples of what I mean:

A couple of years ago, I arranged for a local TV anchorwoman in Boston to meet with five eighth-grade boys. She wanted to interview them alone, and she did. After spending half an hour with them she came back to me and said, with embarrassment in her voice, "I know this sounds stupid, but they were really very nice." Implicit in her tone was something like, "I am genuinely surprised. I had half expected that they would be awful, rude, or aggressive."

More recently, I received a phone message from a mother saying that her four-year-old son was making his Legos into a gun and it was very upsetting to her, her husband, and her daughter. What could she do to stop him from doing that?

Then I received an email from the mother of a five-year-old boy who had been suspended from kindergarten for hitting his teacher with a stick. The school had told her that if it happened again, the police would be summoned and her little boy would be charged with assault and sent to juvenile court.

I recently received a call from an educator in New York City who is starting a new all-boys school on the Lower East Side. "What," he asked me, "is the one most important thing I should look for in starting out?" I told him, "Hire people who are not afraid of boys, because adults who are frightened of boys are of no use to them."

CONNECTING WITH BOYS

When we sat down to write *Raising Cain*, Dan and I had some central concerns. As a professor at the Harvard School of Public Health, Dan was worried that boys were at risk from a public health point of view. Twice as many boys die from accidental death in their teenage years than do girls, and boys are at a vastly higher risk of suicide. Eighty-five percent of completed teen suicides are boys. There had been a rising tide of male violence between 1975 and 1994, making the United States the most murderous and rape-prone country in the industrialized world. There are 23,000 homicides in the country every year, and 10 percent of them are committed by males under the age of 25.

Since 1994, boy violence in this country has dropped dramatically as inner-city communities have come to grips with drug problems. There is better policing, and the black community has risen up to save its sons. What we are seeing now is that white suburban and rural America is coming to understand that the problems of the inner city were not specific to blacks and Hispanics, or even to crack cocaine. We have seen a spike in suburban and rural violence among white boys that has finally aroused Americans to an awareness that perhaps we have been raising our sons wrong.

As we worked, Dan and I focused on the fact that, in American culture, we raise boys in a way that leaves them emotionally uneducated and inarticulate about their psychological pain. In an effort to make our sons masculine, our culture has forgotten what boys need psychologically. We have lost touch with the work and rituals that connect boys to the adult world and meaningful adult manhood. We often take them at face value and react only to their obnoxious behavior and not to their inner lives. We either treat them like wild animals who need to be controlled or as entitled princes of whom we cannot ask very much on a moral basis. We seem to think they are too *something* — too immature, or morally backward, or fragile, or homophobic, or masculine.

Dan and I felt that boys were emotionally illiterate, burdened by a conception of masculinity that narrowed their lives. They were unable to express their pain, their sense of shame, their sadness and inadequacy, except through anger. Eighty percent of depressed teenage boys manifest irritability as their leading symptom because they do not feel that they are able to say they are sad. That would be a strike against their masculinity. *Raising Cain* was a complaint against the American concept of masculinity that narrows what a boy can say and reveal about his inner life.

THE EDUCATION GAP

If you go into any kindergarten class in the country at "Circle Time" you will see a group of girls patiently waiting for the reading or discussion to begin. But several boys will be wandering around the classroom. "Come on guys," the teacher will say. "We're ready to start." Or, exasperated, she may say, "Come on guys! The girls have been ready for a long time now."

Girls outperform boys in elementary school, middle school, high school, and college. At present, 56 percent of college degrees go to women; 55 percent of graduate degrees go to women, and that trend is accelerating. One actuarial statistician took the present trend out to its absurd conclusion and found that the last man in the United States to get a bachelor's degree would do so in 2068.

Twenty years ago, there was a significant gap between boys and girls in science and math — with boys ahead. Feminists and dedicated teachers worked with girls over the years to overcome their math phobias and their belief that science wasn't "feminine." And it worked. The gap has closed almost all the way. There is still a gap between boys and girls in math concepts, but it is now quite small. But — according to a meta-analysis of 15 different academic assessments, including the National Assessment of Academic Progress — the gap between girls and boys, with girls in the lead, is six times greater than the gap between boys and girls in math concepts. It is huge. And in writing, females outperform males by 25 points.

Many writers, including Tom Newkirk, a professor of English at the University of New Hampshire, and Christina Hoff Sommers, a resident scholar at the American Enterprise Institute and former philosophy professor, have drawn our attention to this gender gap in education. In the summer of 2003, *Businessweek* magazine reported that girls have achieved almost all of the educational gains of the last 30 years. We owe it to our boys to close these historic gaps.

FEAR OF BOYS

I believe the gender gap in writing and reading is at least partly attributable to the discomfort that normal, helpful teachers experience with boys. Against a backdrop of societal violence, 90 percent of which is male, those of us who work with children have to constantly make judgments about what is good or bad, about which kind of interventions will produce children of character, and about what the things that children are doing right now presage for their behavior as adults. This business of predicting how boys are going to turn out can be tricky if you extrapolate from their first grade or eighth grade behavior. I know. I was the class clown in my eighth grade! I am very sensitive to schools that have tolerance for boys, as well as to those that chronically seem to distrust them.

What it is about boys that disrupts our world and frightens us?

Boys are active and take more physical risks than girls. They break stuff. Their impulsivity and apparent lack of control scares us because it always threatens to "disrupt the learning environment." By school age, three-quarters of the boys in a class are more physically active, more impulsive, and more developmentally immature than girls the same age. Our average boy is also one to two years behind the average girl in his language development and reading. That's not news to anyone — but it does mean that he is going to find school a difficult fit. Think about school from the average boy's point of view. It seems to be a place that is all about sitting down and listening to women talk. And the girls have a decided advantage at that. The level of a boy's physical activity means that he is restrained more often, that he is spoken to more often, than the girls are.

I was once standing on a school playground with some kindergarten teachers who were supervising the children at recess. The boys did something loud and potentially disruptive, but the matter settled down quickly. One of the teachers turned to the other and said, "Oh, it's just the BBC." They laughed. Later I asked what BBC meant. You have probably already figured out that it stands for Bad Boys Club.

Here is a conversation recorded between kindergarten children by Vivian Paley in her brilliant book, *Boys and Girls: Superheroes in the Doll Corner*:

"Karen says: 'Girls are nicer than boys.'

Janie adds: 'Boys are bad. Some boys are.'

Paul then says: 'Not bad, pretend bad, like bad guys.'

Karen, undaunted, continues: 'My brother is really bad.'

Vivian Paley poses a question: 'Aren't girls ever bad?'

Paul answers: 'I don't think so. Not very much.'

Vivian Paley: 'Why not?'

Paul: 'Because they like to color so much. That's one thing I know. Boys have to practice running.'

Karen then adds: 'And they practice being silly.'"

If you ask third-grade boys whom teachers like better, they'll say, "The girls." If you ask third-grade girls whom the teachers like best, they'll say, "The girls." And, of course, they're both right. How would you react if you had to go to a place every day where you thought you were destined to be liked less well and where you would be less successful than the other half of the population? You would start to challenge the authority of the people who run the place.

Boys challenge us. Boys often seem to be proud of being bad, and there are moments when they have no use for our ideas of politeness. Boys in groups seem obsessed with things that are rude, crude, and antisocial. I don't know how many times I have heard an adult say that a particular boy doesn't seem to have a conscience.

Boys don't seem to value what we value, especially in literature. Boys value low-class literature; they value TV, comics, and video games. This makes us nervous. We often think this is because we are so moral and high-minded and interested in character. But it is often a matter of taste and educational elitism — and a wish for control. Rousseau, writing in 1762 about his son, Emile, said, "Emile ought to do only what he wants, but he ought to want only what you want him to do." We all have that problem. We all want our children to feel free — but not really.

I was talking with a teacher recently about a learning-disabled boy in her class — a boy who struggles with reading. He had read one of the *Captain Underpants* series and loved it. The teacher tried very hard to steer him away from reading any more of them. One was OK, she told me, because the boy wasn't a reader. But she was reluctant to have him read more because he was a bad speller, and there are many misspelled words in the book. Please! Do you really think this boy was in danger from *Captain Underpants?*

Last summer, my daughter's 17-year-old boyfriend told me, "I know I should read more," in the same tone of voice that people say, "I know I should lose weight. I shouldn't have this dessert." When we tell boys that reading is good for them, it sounds like self-improvement. It sounds like betterment. We do things to boys to suggest that we are going to improve them, and they resist us.

In his book, *Misreading Masculinity: Boys, Literacy and Popular Culture,* Tom Newkirk gives a detailed analysis about how teachers subtly discourage boys from reading, primarily by creating a hierarchy of good literature. He also says that we are never going to get boys to read unless they have the experience of reading as deep pleasure. But we make it like medicine.

Teachers have a "free-choice" reading period, for example, and if a boy wants to read comic books the teacher says, "Well, perhaps you should save those for home and read something worthwhile." Where's the free choice in that?

Newkirk provides another subtle example: A child picks a book on his own, and you say, "Oh, good choice." I've said that myself, and I've heard people say it many times. But Newkirk says no, don't do it. A "good" choice implies that there wasn't really a choice in the first place because there are good choices, and then, of course, there are bad choices. Any boy worth his salt can hear that undertone in what we intend as positive reinforcement. And any boy worth his salt will be tempted not to make a good choice the next time, precisely because he hears that the "good" part eclipses the "choice" part.

It is different to say to a boy, "Oh, I loved that book!" or "So many kids have loved that book." That is descriptive, not judgmental.

OUR WORST FEAR

The thing that really scares us, however, is a boy's potential for violence. That is the heart of the matter. That is why the Boston anchorwoman expected the eighth grade boys to be scary. That's why the mom worried about her son turning Legos into guns. That's why the kindergarten administrators threatened an impulsive five-year-old with the police.

Why does boys' play violence make us so nervous? It is because we believe that boys cannot make a distinction between play and reality. We believe that they will be pulled into violence against their will, that they won't be able to help themselves.

I believe we have never really faced the roots of violence in this society at the deepest level, so we spend our time on trivial stuff like stopping our children from making Legos into guns. But the truth is that's not the problem. If we think that making toy guns or playing violent video games is really the problem, and not broken homes or child abuse or the fact that we're spending 40 percent less time with our children than we did in 1965, then we are deluding ourselves. We're wringing our hands for no reason. And we're scapegoating boys.

The impact of our hand wringing is that we lose credibility with boys. They experience us as either excessively controlling and mean, or they consider us clueless. Or, worst of all, they see that we are afraid of them. When little boys think that adults are scared of them, they become truly terrified.

I believe that children who have been brutalized may find media violence is in tune with them, but I don't believe that children who come from loving, attentive homes are going to be induced unwittingly into violence.

I also know that boys can tell the difference between play and reality, between games and real violence. Violence is what happens when one person intends to hurt another person and succeeds. When that happens in a classroom, all the kids point to it. Violence is now what happens in movies; that is pretend violence and kids know it. Yet we act afraid of our boys. We talk as if we are afraid of them. We have to get over that fear. We have to conquer our assumptions and inhibitions if we are going to be truly helpful to our boys. I have five suggestions to get us started.

The Bettelheim Solution

The late Bruno Bettelheim was my professor at the University of Chicago, and when I was there in the early 1970s, he was working on *The Uses of Enchantment*, his great book about the meaning of fairy tales and the ways in which they help children master the most ferocious conflicts and developmental struggles of childhood. Through his book, Bettelheim asks us to come to grips with the dark side of human life. Now, that's the problem with boys. They often throw the dark side of life in our faces. They are too open about greediness, competitiveness, lust, murderous feelings, fury, perfectionism. They'd rather urinate on trees in the playground than use the bathroom — and they do that psychologically as well. We don't always want to deal with their powerful emotions in our quiet settings. We prefer the way girls protect us. It is not that girls aren't grappling with all the same conflicts. They are, but they make it easy on us. Bettelheim would tell us that the problem is with us. We have forgotten how ferocious childhood is. And we need to remember.

The Paley-Katch Solution

Teachers and writers Vivian Paley and Jane Katch talk to children. They let them dictate stories. They have them act out their deepest conflicts right there in the classroom. They are utterly fearless in what they let kids talk about. In her book, *Under Deadman's Skin: Discovering the Meaning of Children's Violent Play*, Jane Katch describes a discussion of the rules about talking about violence in the classroom. The original list was: (1) no excessive blood; (2) no chopping off of body parts; (3) no guts or other things that belong inside the body can come out. But one of the girls said it would be unfair to stop the boys from talking about these things every day. So they went to an alternate-day format. The kids had a wonderful, moral, democratic discussion about violence because Jane Katch trusted them. Be afraid of teachers and administrators who won't let you talk to kids this way.

The Newkirk Solution

Acknowledge the complexity of "violence" in art and literature. Keep asking whether it is really violence, or humor, that kids are after. Often, what they seek is a feeling of mastery of the violence. We should be able to see this in their choices. And, Tom Newkirk notes, we should allow cartooning as a serious business in the classroom. We should accept youth genres in which fiction becomes a way of assuming freedoms, powers, and competencies that the writer does not possess in real life. It is an act of wish fulfillment, not an accurate and realistic rendering of their experience. The writing is often extreme and exaggerated — and it's funny.

The Captain Underpants Solution

Dav Pilkey, the author of the Captain Underpants books, often issues ironic warnings. When Harold and George must confront two evil robots, Harold worries, "We're not going to have to resort to extreme graphic violence, are we?" George replies that he hopes not. The next chapter is titled "The Extremely Graphic Violence Chapter" and it begins with a label: "WARNING: The following chapter contains graphic scenes showing two boys beating the tar out of a couple of robots. If you have high blood pressure, or faint at the sight of motor oil, we strongly encourage you to take better care of yourself and stop being such a baby."

The Thompson Solution

Now, here's mine: Every time you start to worry about boy behavior, think of a man you love — your father, your brother, your cousin, your husband, or your own son. And then talk to him. Get in touch with his inner life. Put away your fear.

Michael Thompson's books include *Raising Cain: Protecting the Emotional Lives of Boys; Best Friends, Worst Enemies: Understanding the Emotional Lives of Children* and *The Pressured Child*. This article appeared in the Summer 2004 issue of *Independent School*.

In essence, the more she tries to please, the more she **negates her other needs,** and the worse she feels.

Parents, Girls, and the "Tyranny Of Nice"

BY JOANN DEAK

Carol Gilligan, author and feminist scholar, was the first to coin the phrase "tyranny of nice." Afterwards, Oprah Winfrey popularized the phrase by making it almost her public mantra.

Regardless of the attention it has received in Oprah's magazine, *O*, the "tyranny of nice" — in essence, over-pleasing or being too nice — has not been widely discussed in terms of how such fawning behavior can inhibit the healthy growth of girls. Indeed, there is no consistent research on such a hard-to-define issue.

But what's so bad about wanting to be good? Most of us would rather be liked than not liked. It's normal to seek the approval of those you respect, isn't it? Don't you want your daughter to care about other people? Don't we feel happier when we care about others? Wouldn't the world be a better place if everyone tried a little harder to be pleasing?

To the latter questions, the answer is "Of course." But the people who do it most predictably to excess are girls, and the problem is that when a girl invests too much of her emotional energy in pleasing others, she loses strength as an individual. For such a girl, being "just" herself isn't good enough. A girl who feels the need to please will sacrifice a lot of herself — her feelings, her intuition, her judgment, her ambitions, and her dreams — to keep others happy.

Self-esteem is an important piece in a girl's emotional life. In the pleaser's life it is a twisted piece. A girl builds self-esteem by doing things that lead her to feel confident, competent, and emotionally connected. These three ingredients — confidence, competence, and connectedness — need to be fairly equal for emotional growth. The problem with the overpleasing girl is that she has too much connection, too much need to receive praise, to be liked, to be nice. This overabundance of connectedness stunts her ability to do the things that build confidence and competence.

It might seem like a pleaser would feel good about herself, raking in the compliments for her behavior, her helpfulness, her selflessness. And that may be true at the beginning, especially for young girls. But as a girl gets older, the opposite is true. Her self-esteem is often very low, and she can get caught in a cycle that won't allow her self-esteem to improve. In essence, the more she tries to please, the more she negates her other needs, and the worse she feels. The pleaser's self takes a steady drubbing while she routinely puts other peoples' feelings and desires ahead of her own. At the end of the day, she has marginalized herself in her effort to stay connected.

Talking about pleasing as a problem may come as a surprise if you've never thought of it as one. Most people don't. After all, girls who please are so nice, so compliant. They are easier to handle at home and at school. Girls who strive to please aren't often identified as girls with a problem because their behavior is so rarely problematic. They blend in, they smile, they agree. But it is a problem — a problem of short-term gain for long-term damage.

How do we help girls stay in the middle of the continuum between self and others? The first obvious response it that we have to stop giving them the constant messages that "you have to be nice." One of the things that upsets girls most is when, early on, their peers say something like, "you're mean" or a parent says, "you're not being nice." It is important for parents and teachers to alter their words and make the messages clearer. In many instances, we need to "rescript" how we talk to girls. Here are three examples:

1. "You're a bad girl."

   Rescript: "When you hit your little sister, it could hurt her and I can't allow that."

2. "I'm disappointed in you."

   Rescript: "I'd like to talk to you about why it's important for you to do your homework and not to lie to your teacher when she asks you about it."

3. "Wait until your father hears what you've done."

   Rescript: "Let's talk about how you're going to share with your father what happened today."

This is not merely a change of words, not merely "psychologizing." The first set of responses, consistently applied, over days and weeks and months of development, help

The Inclusive School
A Selection of Writing on Diversity Issues in Independent Schools

create a girl who not only wants to please, but has to please. She can become so tied to praise and acceptance that she has difficulty saying no (because it might upset someone), taking risks (because someone might disapprove), or becoming a leader or strong individual (both of which result in a great deal of conflict).

The problem of over-pleasing — the tyranny of niceness — is one of the most pervasive issues facing the development of strong, healthy, and successful females. Because of this, schools and parents must think about their words, about how they discipline girls, and about what overriding messages they are layering over time. It's an important, and often overlooked, step in helping to create thriving and striving girls.

JoAnn Deak is author of *How Girls Thrive* and *Girls Will Be Girls: Raising Confident and Courageous Daughters* (now in a new edition). A former school psychologist, Deak is now an independent school consultant specializing in gender issues in education. She can be reached at *www.DEAKgroup.com*. This article first appeared in the Spring 2002 issue of *Independent School*.

To truly break with the system of gender discrimination in independent schools, school leaders … need first to **acknowledge the problem** as a serious issue that undermines the quality of their schools.…

Independent School Leadership
A Gendered Experience

::

BY SUSAN FEIBELMAN AND MARTHA HAAKMAT

The National Association of Independent Schools' 2009 report on "The State of Independent School Leadership" notes that women currently make up 31 percent of school heads. It would be one thing if this number reflected the percentage of women in the independent school leadership pipeline, but the NAIS study makes it clear that there are plenty of talented women in administrative positions.

Of the 548 independent school heads who participated in the study, 74 percent were male and just 26 percent were female. But of the 514 other administrators who responded, 39 percent were male and 61 percent female.

Why aren't more women moving up the ranks of leadership in independent school communities to become school heads? As in all issues in education, the answer is not simple. But one overarching reason for this gender skew, no doubt, relates to gender biases and issues in the broader culture. In fact, the reason we don't have more women heads of school is eerily similar to the reasons why United States citizens have yet to elect a woman president. According to the Inter-Parliamentary Union, the United States is presently tied for 69th place among countries with the highest percentage of women elected to their national legislatures; women held only 16 percent of U.S. Congressional seats in 2010.

The low number of women leaders, it turns out, is directly connected to cultural attitudes toward women as leaders. According to Radford University professor Hilary Lips, gender-studies research has uncovered four key areas in which women's leadership, in comparison to that of men, draws out a different response from those around them:

- Women are expected to combine leadership with compassion and are disliked if they don't;
- People do not listen to or take direction from women as comfortably as they do from men;
- Women who promote themselves and their abilities reap disapproval; and
- Women require more external validation or endorsements than men do to be accepted as leaders in some contexts.

Many other studies echo Lips' findings. Even in an era when we should all know better, female leaders, compared to their male counterparts, are seen as different and deficient. *Wharton@Work*, an electronic newsletter for executive education by the Wharton School of business, notes that the greatest leadership challenge faced by women has nothing to do with their actual leadership skills. Rather, it is that the people around them treat women differently than they do men because of broadly held gender stereotypes.

The 2009 NAIS study indicates that such national gender-bias issues are alive and well within its membership. The report notes a clear "lack of willingness of some schools to hire a head who does not fit the traditional stereotype of what a head is supposed to be like." Indeed, when one looks around, it's not hard to see how leadership in independent schools continues to be shaped by the perception of a glass ceiling — a time-honored tradition of an old boys' network that promotes white males into leadership positions over women, coupled with a mentoring system that reinforces such barriers.

GENDER BIAS AND SCHOOL CULTURE

To truly break with the system of gender discrimination in independent schools, school leaders — administrators and boards — need first to acknowledge the problem as a serious issue that undermines the quality of their schools and their ability to fulfill their missions well. Next, they need to carefully examine the ways in which gender bias frames our conversations and relationships in schools, and, as a result, how it shapes the vision for our schools' futures.

Unfortunately, despite school efforts to become inclusive institutions that encourage awareness of social identifiers — socioeconomic class, religion, race, sexual orientation, gender, age, language, and ability — one has to look hard to find independent schools that work explicitly in their school communities on gender issues, especially in relationship to privilege, power, and identity. It appears that most of us in independent schools are unwilling to acknowledge that the system of oppression of women continues to exist. We are also not asking ourselves to look deeply into how we each support this system through our silence and unchallenged acceptance. As a result, not many schools teach or model for students (or adults, for that matter) how to confront sexism.

This is not an academic exercise. Sexism exists in our schools in both large and small ways. From our students' approach to informal games on the playground to packed bleachers for the boys' basketball team, from developing curriculum to conducting a search for a senior-level administrative position, gender bias informs much of our decision-making.

While we may be aware of this, we are more inclined to nibble at the edges of the problem. We react to gender-based teasing on the playground rather than proactively plan a curriculum that increases our students' gender awareness in their play. We shrug our shoulders when the boys' baseball team goes off for spring training trips while the girls' softball team stays home. We do not question why it is that the majority of protagonists in the books we teach in our upper school's English curriculum are male. We shake our heads and accept the "best man for the job" adage rather than explore the reasons why our community members gravitate toward male models of leadership, and we look the other way when female candidates are more heavily scrutinized because they might be mothers or may be nearing childbearing age.

As we think about who has access to leadership opportunities, who gets recognized and heard as leaders, who gets selected to be groomed for leadership, and how school leaders are evaluated, gender is a constant variable.

WOMEN LEADERS ON SCHOOL LEADERSHIP

How do we interrupt this boys' club culture and begin to create equal access for women to headships at independent schools across the nation? Where can women find mentors and see themselves reflected among the movers and shakers of independent schools? How can we level the playing field for ourselves and for the students we serve?

To find some answers to these questions, we began a dialogue with other women leaders from independent schools, hoping their stories would offer some fresh perspective. We asked 25 women in different leadership positions on the East and West coasts to define leadership and to reflect on the ways in which they have learned to be effective leaders, where they have faced challenges, and where they have found support. The responses were as varied as the women with whom we spoke. Nevertheless, several common themes emerged.

Training ground for leadership: family life

Many of the women we interviewed described familial roles from childhood that demanded that they learn how to use their voices to get what they wanted. At a young age, they learned to be self-advocates and internalized the importance of effective communication in order to be heard and supported. They also spoke of having strong female role models, both in their families and among the adults in their lives, who taught them organizational skills, how to think strategically, and how to rely on their intuition when faced with problems that needed to be solved.

Several women described their earnest desire to be at the table when family decisions were made, and they shared lessons learned about being supportive teammates and collaborators. For some women, being from larger families demanded an early knowledge of when to keep quiet, listen and learn, and when to interrupt and speak up in order to be heard.

Valuing effective communication skills

Many interview subjects identified as a key to their success their ability to be diplomatic, clear, and firm while also being authentic. Having a heightened awareness of other's social and emotional well-being was an important advantage when it came to communicating with constituents about tough topics. Others commented on the ways they used their understanding of people and social groups to help them work well with a wide variety of personalities.

Owning one's gravitas

Every woman commented on the assumptions that various members of their school community made about them. We heard stories about the double standard faced by young women who were given a narrow window of time to win the respect of those they were leading, while young male leaders in the same school were given a longer grace period and more chances to make mistakes. We heard female leaders talk about not knowing how much gender played a role in the way they were seen until disagreement occurred over a decision, eliciting comments about their being too emotional. The B-word came up often as women spoke about perceptions that spread across the school campuses when they needed to make a difficult or unpopular decision.

Challenging the double standards

Our conversations revealed that women as school leaders are too often expected to play the role of gracious hostess and nurturing mother, while making strategic decisions that impact the health and well-being of a school community. By contrast, their male counterparts are given both implicit and explicit permission to be rough around the edges, to use "shoot from the hip" type language frequently, and to pay less attention to the relational aspects of leadership.

Too often in independent school cultures, there is an assumption that male leaders are genetically predisposed to be tough and strategic, which often leads to a naïve sense of wonderment when school communities witness women displaying similar leadership qualities. We are often surprised that a female leader is equipped to do the hard parts of the job, like not renewing the contract of a beloved teacher whose classroom performance has been on a steady decline, or explaining to parents who have given generously to the school why their child is being expelled for a gross misuse of laptop privileges.

One person we interviewed spoke about learning to distance herself from her emotions in order to be taken seriously by her faculty, whether she was supporting a new initiative or fielding personal attacks about an administrative decision. However, these women also understood that displaying what are often termed "male leadership traits" (i.e., hard-edged, authoritative decision-making) could make them less effective if they were unable to also convey an appropriate degree of emotional availability.

Those we spoke with generally agreed that female leaders walk a fine line. If a female leader cries, it is a sure sign of weakness and considered to be unprofessional, while male counterparts who cry in public are more apt to be praised for their sensitivity. Another woman acknowledged that, as a female leader, she felt that she needed to limit the amount of time she spent sharing stories about her first baby so as not to be viewed as distracted or overly adoring. Meanwhile, her male colleague who was also a first-time parent unselfconsciously talked on and on about his new child — always at the ready with the latest pictures. To her dismay, this behavior only added to the list of admirable traits he possessed in the eyes of his peers.

Creating a supportive culture

According to women with whom we talked, the "culture of care" in independent schools, particularly in the lower grades, supported their desire to pursue various leadership roles. Working with younger children was often the path of least resistance for women seeking administrative opportunities. Yet these women consistently commented on the fact that lower school positions can be seen as just the kind of grunt work that men are typically not interested in pursuing — and by association devaluing the leadership skills necessary for working with our youngest learners.

GENDER EQUITY IN SCHOOLS OF THE FUTURE

If we want to interrupt the influence of gender bias in the leadership choices currently being made in independent schools, we will have to shine a light on the issues and patterns it raises. Schools will need to set up structures that promote the emergence of new leadership models, and there will have to be a culture shift away from business as usual to a more inclusive definition of an effective leader. The following four areas are a starting place:

1. **Unpacking privilege, naming sexism**

   As the face of leadership in independent schools changes in the coming years with the retirement of many long-tenured school heads, we will have to take a long, hard look at diversifying our pool of talented new hopefuls and plugging the leak in the leadership pipeline. Independent schools will have to think critically about living their missions to be inclusive and to graduate globally-minded and responsible women and men — and the modeling of leadership must be a part of this work. We need to name and define sexism within our institutions in order to give our students the tools for dismantling it in their lives. We need to call on our girls and boys to be more aware of how systems of privilege exist in schools to the benefit of one gender over another.

   This doesn't mean that schools shouldn't take into consideration gender differences. All the research makes it clear that boys and girls have different developmental needs at different stages of their school lives — and we need to support both genders appropriately. But we also need to provide explicit and sequential opportunities that allow our students to participate in an honest dialogue about gender, privilege, and sexism. In particular, we need to combat the boys' club mentality and the attitudes of those who think sexism is a thing of the past. We need to be more aware, not because women are being given less access to the same leadership development as men, but because our schools should be engaged in this work as they seek greater inclusivity.

2. **Managing and promoting talent**

   Studies on leadership development have proven that people in leadership positions gravitate toward protégés that remind them of themselves. It is no surprise then that a predominantly male group of independent school heads would overwhelmingly choose and groom successors who are also male. If we want to seriously work on increasing the numbers of female heads of school in our institutions, we will have to look at this problem squarely, study past patterns, and put systems in place that foster greater collaboration between experienced women leaders and those in the pipeline. We must invest in new ways to identify diverse leadership talent, work with women to build upon their leadership experiences, and then promote them with an eye toward ensuring that role models are available for all of our students. We need to expand our sometimes-narrow definition of an effective leader in order to make room for a more nuanced set of leadership traits.

3. **Rethinking the mentoring model**

We need to examine the small and large ways that mentoring happens in our schools. There are always opportunities for leaders to delegate work and place stakeholders in positions of leadership, whether it is tapping the strong faculty member who has mastered curriculum mapping in new and exciting ways to work with others who are struggling with the process, or naming as the new director of student life the outstanding team player who steps up constantly to build community outside the classroom. Whether it is the more subtle kind of mentoring that we practice or the more visible, we need to do a better job of recognizing the power we hold to shape careers and open new possibilities for upcoming leaders. We must tie this recognition directly to our goals of empowering young people to be change agents in the world based upon those they see as leaders at school.

4. **Spotlighting trustee education**

Trustees who come from corporate environments should already be familiar with research from the nonprofit group, Catalyst, that makes it clear that companies with the highest representation of women in their top management teams achieve better financial performance than companies with the lowest representation of women (2006). The financial bottom line is forcing corporations in the 21st century to make a solid commitment to inclusive hiring practices and to embrace diversity training as part and parcel of their globally minded business strategies. We must expect trustees, as the stewards of independent schools who ultimately hire, evaluate, and sometimes fire the school head, to bring such best practices to bear.

At the same time, boards need to look at their own pipeline for future trustees. Who are they choosing to join them and why? If a school's board is made up mainly of men, it's likely that they'll also gravitate toward male candidates for vacant spots on the board and, when the time comes, for head of school. Ideally, the makeup of any board and the list of future trustees in the pipeline should be 50 percent women.

Trustees have not only the ability but also the obligation to model the characteristics of inclusive leadership that they are learning in the corporate world. They must make their commitment public through crafting strategic plans, creating board structures, and drafting board agendas that promote a dynamic commitment to inclusivity, so that when the opportunities arise to search for heads of schools, they move beyond just paying lip service.

The challenges facing our schools to promote more women to senior leadership positions — including to the top position — and to encourage more women and men to reach out to and support the next generation of women leaders are not new nor beyond our grasp. But they require that we make an authentic commitment to changing the male-centric culture of leadership that dominates too many of our schools. There's work to be done, and it's time that we roll up our sleeves.

At the time this article was written, **Susan Feibelman** was upper school head at Packer Collegiate Institute (New York). She is currently in a doctoral program in education at the University of Pennsylvania. **Martha Haakmat** is the middle school head at the Brooklyn Friends School (New York). This article first appeared in the Fall 2010 issue of *Independent School*.

RESOURCES

Catalyst: Changing Workplaces. Changing Lives, June 2010, *www.catalyst.org*.

"Despite Media's Claims to the Contrary, Feminism's Work Ain't Done Yet," *Femme!, The Daily*, March 4, 2010.

Hilary Lips, "Women and Leadership: Delicate Balancing Act" Women's Media newsletter, April 2, 2009, *www.womensmedia.com/lead/88-women-and-leadership-delicate-balancing-act.html*.

The State of Independent School Leadership 2009 (Washington, DC: National Association of Independent Schools, 2010).

"Women in National Parliaments, " May 31, 2010 and June 12, 2010, *www.ipu.org/wmn-e/classif.htm*.

"Women Leaders: To Be Effective You Need to Understand Gender Role," Wharton@Work, The Wharton School, University of Pennsylvania, 2007, *http://executiveeducation.wharton.upenn.edu/ebuzz/0709/index.cfm*

Ultimately, our goal has been inclusion, not just compliance with regulation.

Through the Same Door

Universal Access and School Climate

::

BY TOM HASSAN

Over a decade ago, at the end of a Phillips Exeter Academy (New Hampshire) faculty meeting, a colleague calmly and courageously announced that she had recently been diagnosed with a rare degenerative muscle disease. We sat in stunned silence as we absorbed the news and thought about the implications of what our friend had just told us.

At that time, none of us could have known just how far-reaching and important the consequences of her announcement would become.

This teacher accepted the challenge of her disability, employing the same strong-willed determination with which she had tackled other crusades in her young life. She researched her disease — polymyositis — and became an expert on it even as her body started to deteriorate. As the *MayoClinic.com* site warns those afflicted with the rare disease: "You may find it difficult to get out of chairs, climb stairs, brush your hair, or work with your arms over your head."

For a number of years, this brave woman not only fought valiantly against the disease that would eventually take her life, but also became an outspoken advocate for those with limited mobility. Over the course of time, she transformed the thinking within our own school community. We went from striving for the conventional "handicapped access" to something she and others term "universal access."

In essence, the concept of Universal Access (UA) is to create a physical campus that is more accessible for everyone — from those who have permanent disabilities, to those with temporary disabilities, to those pushing baby carriers, to those experiencing increasing physical limitations as they age — so that literally everyone can enter through the same door. Gone are the gangly wooden ramps tacked on to grand entry stairs, replaced by gradual and subtle landscaping so that the physical needs of a wide range of individuals are easily accommodated. Over time, however, we also have come to realize that UA is not confined to landscaping or building alterations. It also involves a community mindset. To that end, we've set out to educate the community about disabilities through a variety of thoughtful speakers, school publications, campus clubs, and, of course, our own actions. Of equal importance to the physical alterations, we want to create community awareness about issues regarding disabilities and to foster a culture that embraces all individuals.

Ultimately, our goal has been inclusion, not just compliance with regulation.

Defining UA and getting our community to understand and support it took time, sadly paralleling the time of our colleague's steady physical demise. Each step of the way, though, she pushed us to think broadly about the concept and to look specifically at ways to make the campus easier for her and others to navigate.

Phillips Exeter Academy's earliest efforts in the area of handicap accessibility mirrored those of our sister schools. After the enactment of the Americans with Disabilities Act (ADA) in 1990, we looked for ways to comply with the new regulations. With a large campus footprint and numerous centuries-old structures in an historic district, it was particularly challenging for Exeter to meet the new ADA requirements. We were confused about which issues to tackle first. After sifting through the regulations, we realized that we needed experienced architects to help us move forward. We also required an action plan to guide us as the new ADA projects competed for construction dollars in Exeter's budgeting process.

Early on, we stumbled on a course of action that would serve us well throughout our efforts. One of the academy's teaching interns was partially dependent on a wheelchair for her mobility. We asked her directly what changes she felt would ease her navigation throughout campus. Boarding schools are concerned not only with the academic build-ings, but also with dormitories and faculty houses. We began to grapple with some very real questions: How would she navigate the icy pathways in the middle of a cold New Hampshire winter? How would she get around easily, whatever the weather, to a full day of classes, extracurricular commitments, and dormitory responsibilities?

Concurrently, we gathered a group of interested teachers, staff members, and stu-dents to give us ideas and feedback on making our facilities as accessible as possible. In 2001, we formalized the group, based on a request from our head of school and trustees, and asked the members to prepare a study of the status of the academy's compliance with ADA, and, more important, go beyond mere compliance. The group consisted of trustees, faculty, staff, and student representatives.

Through discussion and research, the group coalesced around the concept of Universal Design. The concept seeks to create design solutions that work for all users, "across a breadth of human diversity and across the lifespan." The following excerpt is taken from *www.AdaptiveEnvironments.org.*

> *Universal Design is a worldwide movement based on the concept that all products, environments, and communications should be designed to consider the needs of the widest possible array of users… (and) is based on the following premises:*
> - varying ability is not a special condition of the few but a common characteristic of being human, and we change physically and intellectually throughout our lives;
> - if a design works well for people with disabilities, it works better for everyone;
> - at any point in our lives, personal self-esteem, identity, and well-being are deeply affected by our ability to function in our physical surroundings with a sense of comfort, independence, and control; and
> - usability and aesthetics are mutually compatible.

The Exeter Universal Access Committee (UA Committee), as it would soon be known, eventually linked these universal design principles with the definition of Uni-versal Access. Universal Access — accessibility for all — is achieved through universal design principles.

At their October 2001 meeting, the school trustees adopted the following mission statement in support of Universal Access:

> *To fulfill our mission of embracing and respecting diversity, the Trustees endorse the goal of universal access to our campus facilities. We should continue to identify and implement ways of making our community more accessible. Of equal importance is fostering a culture which embraces all individuals. Our goal is inclusion, not just compliance with regulation.*

In implementing the goal of UA, the school has placed a priority on reviewing changes to our campus landscape, new building projects, and renovations of existing structures so that a wider range of individual needs can be accommodated. More specifically, the academy has committed itself to the following:

1. All new and renovated public buildings will be designed to be universally accessible. Examples include tearing down a wooden handicap ramp in front of a major academic building and putting in its place gradual landscaping of a natural ramp with plantings.

2. Recent and future landscaping efforts have or will ensure that people can more easily navigate the campus terrain. One recent example has been the removal of steep walking paths on a hillside, replacing them with gently sloping traversing paths.

3. As we renovate or build apartments in the dormitories or freestanding houses, the academy can choose to do one of the following:

   ▪ provide total accessibility for residential use, or

   ▪ provide visitor access (exterior access to first floor), or

   ▪ do little or nothing when accessibility needs have previously been met or when existing conditions limit access.

The goal is to have some flexibility when building or renovating faculty residences, recognizing that not all these residences need to be made universally accessible.

As we rolled out the concept of UA to the larger academy community, we looked for ways to make our mission clear. This helpful introduction, which appeared in a campus publication, is one such example:

> *Imagine the following scenario: You are making your way around our campus, whether going to class, your office, or the dining hall. Every time you encounter a change in level — a stair, curb, or other obstruction that is greater than ½ inch in height — you have to seek an alternate route. Try it for a day, or even just a few hours, and you would soon find yourself frustrated. Now imagine the following: you are pushing a stroller, traveling in a wheelchair, or struggling with an armful of heavy packages. You find a ramp instead of stairs, a powered door button to activate a door, an elevator to change levels. Now you can grasp the concept of Universal Access.*

The Phelps Academy Center, completed in 2006, is an example of a renovation that went well beyond the ADA standards and resulted in a building that fulfilled our mission to incorporate the tenets of UA into our structures. The challenge was to convert the former Thompson Science Building, a structure built in 1931, into a campus community center. The building, due to its age and construction, had many accessibility challenges, and we knew that we would have to incorporate plans for UA features in the early planning stages of the work.

When the new academy center opened, every public entrance was universally accessible. Each floor had several easy-to-read, "You are here" map signs, and the tiered seating in the third-floor Forum (a 300-person assembly hall) can be accessed from the lower and upper entrances. Additionally, the mailroom featured some student mailboxes placed at lower heights and provided with locks that were easier to operate than the conventional combination locks. These are just a few of the features that made the center a true crossroads for our entire community.

Over the years, we have spread our message of inclusion. Through our assembly program, which involves all of our students three times a week, we invite speakers to talk on a wide range of topics. The Universal Access Committee invites at least one speaker to talk about disability issues each year. Early on, we selected young people with whom our own students could identify, like Travis Roy, a former Boston University hockey player who was permanently paralyzed during his first collegiate hockey game. While we involve young disabled people to talk about living with their disability, we also include adults who offer perspectives about their careers who may or may not mention their own disability. Recently, a Broadway producer talked of his lifelong work, all from his wheelchair.

We also have encouraged student organizations that have a particular focus on disabilities. Exeter runs a successful Best Buddies chapter of an international organization that links abled and disabled youth in one-on-one friendships. Best Buddies offers a way for the students in our boarding school to connect with disabled youth from throughout the region. And, internally, we connect the local disabled youth with other academy students not involved in the friendship pairing when we invite our athletes to instruct the group in tennis, swimming, or dance lessons.

In all of Exeter's efforts, speakers, organizations, and facilities, we strive to deliver the same message: "No barriers." While we have made significant progress, we also recognize that each year brings a new group of students who must be educated and that our campus is in constant need of renovation. We are committed to making our school a place that people, whatever their ability, can easily navigate. We want to be a community that goes beyond mere compliance to foster a culture that embraces everyone.

I think back to that faculty meeting 10 years ago and I believe that, as we continue to address issues of Universal Access, we are honoring the wishes of our colleague and keeping her spirit and vision alive.

At the time this article was written, **Tom Hassan** was assistant principal at Phillips Exeter Academy (New Hampshire). He is now the principal at Phillips Exeter Academy. This article first appeared in the Winter 2009 issue of *Independent School*.

…we have the
opportunity to
redefine
learning
in a way that
avoids some of
the unfortunate
and limiting
assumptions
that the learning
disability and
learning difference
paradigms have
perpetuated.

From Disability and Difference to Diversity

A Copernican Revolution in Learning

::

BY PETER MCDONALD AND MICHAEL P. RIENDEAU

Disability or difference? This question — about how we label students who fall outside the learning "norm" — has been among the most provocative in educational discourse lately, especially among schools that have traditionally aligned their thinking and institutional missions with the interests of "learning disabled" students.

It is also a question that has been considered by every independent school, regardless of its historical orientation toward learning disabilities or the extraordinary achievements of its students. Despite the question's seriousness, we want to suggest that the debate is remarkably simple to settle. In fact, from our point of view, a thoughtful examination of the issue will lead us beyond these labels to a more significant question about our collective thinking about students.

When we talk about learning disabilities and learning differences, it is important to consider the assumptions about the world upon which these concepts rest. It is sometimes fashionable to call the sum total of these assumptions a "paradigm," and so we will consider here the paradigms of disability and difference. In reviewing these paradigms, three important considerations guide us: Where is disability/difference located? How is it defined or identified? And, once identified, what does it mean — what do we do with this information?

LOCUS OF DISABILITY/DIFFERENCE

Traditional thinking about learning disabilities is often described as issuing from the "medical model." That is, as a discipline, we have taken up the terminology and metaphors used within the field of medicine to described students' disabilities. In fact, mainstream thinking about learning disabilities has been so aligned with the medical perspective that many in the field now identify learning disabilities as medical conditions, and parents (and educational professionals) turn to pediatricians and neurologists for diagnosis and treatment. The picture of learning disabilities provided by the Individuals with Disabilities Education Act (IDEA), a federal law, guides us firmly in this direction by defining a specific learning disability as a:

> …disorder in one or more of the basic psychological processes involved in understanding or in using language, spoken or written, that may manifest itself in an imperfect ability to listen, think, speak, read, write, spell, or do mathematical calculations. This term includes such conditions as perceptual disabilities, brain injury, minimal brain dysfunction, dyslexia, and developmental aphasia. This term does not include children who have learning problems that are primarily the result of visual, hearing, or motor disabilities; mental retardation; or environmental, cultural, or economic disadvantage.

This language — language of the learning disability paradigm — makes evident the assumption that disabilities exist within individuals. By definition, psychological processes occur within individual minds (or brains). Disorders to those psychological processes, therefore, occur within individuals, and lest there be any misunderstanding, this so-called "exclusionary" definition notes additionally that if difficulties can be traced to "environmental, cultural, or economic disadvantage," then they should not be considered evidence of a learning disability.

The learning difference paradigm has a briefer history in the spotlight of American educational thinking and, perhaps because of this, a less well-defined and publicized agenda. The impetus for this perspective has come from two sources. First, caring and well-intentioned teachers and parents have used the term "difference" to try to preserve the self-esteem of students identified with learning "disabilities." Unfortunately, such efforts — at least in our experience with students — are usually unsuccessful. Even worse, such attempts can backfire when students feel that we are being disingenuous and euphemistic with them — and presuming that they are not sophisticated enough to realize it.

More productively, educators seeking to promote tolerance and reject discrimination have suggested a learning difference paradigm. Here, the more openly political motive is to describe students' abilities in terms of alternatives rather than in terms of deficits, and learning disabilities are redefined as learning differences. Nevertheless, most discussions from within this framework still imply that the "differences" in question can be located within individuals and are differences from the norm. In fact, it might be argued that without the notion of a norm, "different" (as it has been used in our field) becomes an ambiguous term at best.

DISABILITY AND DIFFERENCE DEFINED: THE NORM OBJECTIFIED

As suggested, both the traditional learning disability paradigm and the learning difference paradigm depend for their identification of disability/difference on the existence of an objectified norm. Students are identified as "disabled" or "different" based on the distance between their demonstrated abilities and the expectations that we have about "normal" abilities. What is statistically "normal" (i.e., occurs with greater frequency) becomes reified as a standard against which everything else should be compared. Both paradigms suggest that there is a point along a continuum of ability at which quantitative differences (differences in degree) become qualitative differences (differences in kind). In other words, there is a range of abilities within which normal learners find themselves; below that, one is "learning disabled" or has "learning differences." It is here that a distinction between the learning disability and the learning differences approaches is important: "You *are* learning disabled," in contrast to, "You *have* learning differences." Though some might argue that this distinction is again only one of semantics, it seems indicative of a more important shift in our thinking as educators. The difference paradigm continues to locate difference within an individual, but it allows (where the disability paradigm does not) that learning differences are characteristic of an individual's way of interacting with the world, not simply indicative of objectively defined deficiencies.

THE MEANING OF DISABILITY/DIFFERENCE: WHAT DO WE DO NOW?

The question of what it means to be learning disabled or to have learning differences can take several forms. For the present, let's look at what it might mean just in terms of educational approaches. Because both the disability and difference paradigms depend upon the notion of a norm to identify students, the goal of instruction (whatever form that takes) for identified students is typically this: to move toward the norm. It is here that distinctions between the two paradigms seem least significant in their practical implications for students. Whether we consider a student disabled, and therefore deficient in some essential ability, or different, and therefore unable to demonstrate an essential ability as most others do, our diagnostic reference to the norm leaves us little option but to ask students to work toward "normal" achievement. We may approach the "problem" with differing expectations or methodologies that issue from either the disability or difference paradigms, but our understanding of the situation from either perspective is similar: We see a problem.

From within the medical model, or disability paradigm, we might be likely to decide that some "problems" are insoluble — or at least not worth the effort to solve. In other words, our diagnosis of learning disability might lead us to conclude that some individuals will simply never develop certain abilities. This prognosis will likely then lead us to discussions of accommodations and modifications that will be necessary for individuals to experience success. Inevitably, such discussions leave individuals identified as learning disabled in a disadvantageous position. From this perspective, they are less able and more needy — and, ultimately, defined by their "deficiencies."

From within the difference paradigm, the expectation is that given the correct, "different" instructional approach, a student will succeed. The assumption — that every student can learn (and perhaps learn anything) — is clearly different than the assumption from within the disability paradigm. However, the goal of instruction (albeit modified instruction) remains the same: to approximate the achievement of a "normal" student. Again, despite the more hopeful agenda of the difference paradigm, students identified with "learning differences" are left in a disadvantageous position. Whether disabled or different, students identified within either model are not normal. And because both models objectify normalcy, making it simply another categorical marker (like animal, vegetable, or mineral), identified students become another class of people altogether. Put another way, a quantitative difference in performance becomes a qualitative difference: Learning disabled people or people with learning differences come to be considered a different sort of people than everybody else.

LEARNING DIVERSITY

We began noting that the question of "disability" versus "difference" has gained considerable currency lately. Given what we have described as important parallels between the learning disability and learning difference paradigms, we think that choosing sides in this debate almost doesn't matter when we consider outcomes for students. Given no other choice — and because we prefer to be hopeful — we would opt for the learning difference paradigm.

However, we do have another option: We can develop a new paradigm, one that might appropriately be called "learning diversity."

Taking up the reasoning and language of multiculturalism, we have the opportunity to redefine learning in a way that avoids some of the unfortunate and limiting assumptions that the learning disability and learning difference paradigms have perpetuated. The assumption around which we might structure such a new paradigm is deceptively simple: All students, all learners, are individuals. Reasoning forward from this, we must refuse to reference "norms" and look instead to individual students' skills, talents, interests, and predilections. The sequelae of such a shift in assumptions are many and complicated and are probably responsible for our reluctance to move forward in this direction.

Nearly every aspect of traditional education is made problematic when we begin with the notion that every individual is unique. That notion calls into question considerations as basic as elements of the curriculum and requirements for a diploma. It is no longer sufficient to ask the question. "What is it important for high school graduates to do and know?" Instead, we must ask the question for each student, repeatedly. Many of you are probably now asking yourselves, "Do they really mean that we should have no standards?" The answer is yes — we really believe that we should have no standards. Rather, we should have expectations, hopes, and dreams with and for our students.

What is required is a Copernican revolution in our thinking about learning — that is, a revolution that completely restructures our perception of the universe of teaching and learning. The obstacles to such a revolution are many, and we can already hear the common refrain, "But who is going to pay for this?" We are not Pollyannas; we do realize that the sort of changes that this point of view entails will be costly — not only monetarily, but also in other, perhaps more important, ways.

In fact, the risks in moving toward this new paradigm are legion. Chief among them is the possibility that we will lose what ground has been gained by the development of the learning disability paradigm — and this is some considerable ground. Because of the efforts of organizations like the Learning Disabilities Association of America and the many students, parents, and professionals that have taken up this cause, students have more rights and opportunities within our educational system than ever before. For this reason, we do not suggest that tonight we destroy our educational systems, laws, and practices — expecting that tomorrow a bright new phoenix will rise from the ashes. Instead, we suggest that we move — leaping when we can, but more often steadfastly lumbering — toward the vision of an educational paradigm that truly values individuals. One quiet but powerful way in which we can all do that is to begin to use critically the means available to us in the present system.

In practical terms, we think this means beginning to emphasize what students can do rather than what they cannot do. In taking this approach, we will be winking to each other and our students as we stare into the face of IDEA and educational reforms that take the form of high-stakes testing. In effect, we will need two languages: one for the courtroom and one for the classroom. Continuing to use what we have — for the good of students — while we work toward what we think is ideal seems to us both possible and positive. Letting our fear of losing what we have keep us from what we might make for ourselves in the future seems pessimistic.

We have suggested that what we need is a "revolution" in our thinking about learning — and about each other. We hope and believe that we are on the brink of such a revolution — and one that has historical precedents in this country. We would argue, as others have, that the thinking about learning disabilities has followed a path very similar to thinking about race, gender, and civil rights in our country. In each of these cases, the development in American thinking has followed a roughly analogous path. Members of the disenfranchised groups in each situation progress in status from unequal to "separate but equal" to fully equal. We are not suggesting that we have reached an enlightened state with respect to race and gender equality in practice — we clearly have a long way to go in these areas as well. What we have accomplished in race and gender relations that we have yet to accomplish within education is the presumption that we ought to be moving toward the practice of equality. In our thinking about learning as a nation, we are still at the point where we have yet to envision or expect equality.

The learning disability paradigm creates another class of people — deficient in some way — much as the Constitution designated some men equivalent to only 3/5ths of other men and left women altogether unconsidered. In moving through a learning difference paradigm — one that suggests that difference does not have to be deficiency — we think we parallel the passage of the 13th, 14th, 15th, and 19th amendments. But we cannot stop there — to do so would be to continue to accept "separate but equal" education for many of our students. We must look energetically forward to a learning diversity paradigm that demands that we consider each student not in terms of an idealized, objectified norm but in terms of his or her own abilities, hopes, and dreams.

Peter J. McDonald is head of Eagle Hill School (Massachusetts). **Michael P. Riendeau** is assistant head for academic affairs at Eagle Hill School. This article first appeared in the Fall 2003 issue of *Independent School*.

An essential part of the process is to **coordinate the support** within and outside of the school to assure the greatest academic success with the least amount of stress.

Inclusion in Exclusive Schools

A New Approach to Academic Support

::

BY LAURA VANTINE

Conor (not his real name) began his freshman year at a private high school outside of Boston with high hopes. Prior to enrolling, he had attended pre-K through sixth grade at a Montessori school.

According to his parents, Conor had no difficulty learning to spell or read. His admissions references described him as an optimistic and responsible person. He was also an accomplished soccer player and hoped to write for the school paper. In short, he seemed like a good fit for the school.

But Conor's first quarter comments indicated that he was starting to struggle. He had difficulty remembering math facts, and his performance on tests was inconsistent. His teachers commented, "Conor is motivated, participates in class discussion, and works well in small groups." But they also saw a "tendency to rush, resulting in careless errors." His English teacher wrote, "Although Conor has great ideas, he has trouble expressing them in writing." At his teachers' suggestion, Conor's parents decided to have him tested to find out if he had a learning difference that was affecting his grades.

The testing revealed Conor's superior overall cognitive ability, but also showed difficulty integrating discrete skills. Slower processing speed combined with attention and executive function weaknesses made it even more difficult to meet academic demands. Given the results of the assessment, Conor was diagnosed with a learning disability that qualified him for special accommodations, which the school then provided. A simple story, right? Well, not exactly.

Until recently, most independent schools weren't set up to offer students like Conor special accommodations. Indeed, most independent schools have worked hard to enroll a homogenous group of students with both the motivation and ability to succeed in the schools without special accommodations. This doesn't mean that they haven't admitted students with learning differences; they have just done their best to help such students through small class sizes, low student/teacher ratios, and dedicated teachers willing to provide individualized instruction as needed. And, for the most part, this has worked well for students.

But the growing number of students being tested for learning disabilities — not to mention the Americans with Disability Act (ADA) that requires schools to make reasonable accommodations for those students who qualify — has led to increased demand for academic accommodations and services. As a result, formal learning centers in competitive independent schools have become a fast growing phenomenon. The schools developing such programs are not necessarily geared towards students with learning disabilities (LD) or Attention Deficit Hyperactivity Disorder (ADHD), nor do they actively seek to recruit students with learning differences. Yet, it turns out that as many as 10 to 20 percent of their student bodies now include those with diagnosed learning issues. The challenge for schools is to figure out how to maintain their academic integrity and still meet the needs of this population.

My own involvement with academic support services in independent schools began in 1995, when I was hired to be the director of the learning center at a school in central Massachusetts. The purpose of the school's learning center was ostensibly to assist students with learning issues as well as those who required additional support beyond regular instruction in order to be successful in the classroom. However, what this support was supposed to look like in practice — and my role in making it happen — was distinctly unclear.

The headmaster told me to keep a bowl of candy in my room to attract kids. The school counselor gave me a stack of WISC tests left on the floor of her closet from the previous counselor. Many people mistook me for a student; others ignored me. Admissions tour guides avoided me, rushing past on their way to show off the new computer lab. I felt like the mad aunt, kept tucked out of the way in a closet. Stories abound of learning specialists working in library basements, under bell towers or other out-of-the-way locations. Ten years ago, learning specialists were hired to provide study skills support or to take care of those kids who needed extended time. But the landscape of academic support and the role of the learning specialist in independent schools have changed dramatically over the past decade.

Schools are facing a number of trends that make the development of a coherent program especially important, if challenging. For one, the schools' increasing commitment to financial aid and diversity initiatives means that they are enrolling a broader range of learners. In addition, the cultural anxiety about college admissions is pushing more and more students to seek private tutoring off campus, either to keep up or to get ahead. The pressure of high-stakes testing is also leading more and more families to get their children tested for learning differences. One of the greatest changes schools are seeing is the number of students now being offered extra time for such tests. For the most part, these students don't have severe learning difficulties but rather lesser — although still real — learning differences that affect their performance in school and on tests.

Given this new landscape, how should schools best respond? I believe the answer is three-pronged. First, schools must establish clear policies and procedures for students with learning differences and view these policies and procedures as important — not with ambivalence. Second, schools need to help students in need access appropriate direct-service support — whatever it may be — either within the school or with an outside specialist, and make sure that such support is coordinated with the regular academic program.

An essential part of the process is to coordinate the support within and outside of the school to assure the greatest academic success with the least amount of stress. Third, and perhaps most important, teachers need support and training in instructional practices that can better meet the needs of diverse learners. By incorporating these three steps into their support services, schools can do a much better job of "taking care of their own" and may alleviate the need for students to seek support off campus, and possibly reduce the number of students being referred for testing.

THE FOUR C'S OF A GOOD ACADEMIC SUPPORT PROGRAM

Unlike finding an English teacher or athletic director, hiring a learning specialist and developing an academic support program is not a neutral action. The decision to acknowledge the need for academic support is intrinsically connected to a school's mission. The essential elements of a thoughtful academic support program begin with what I call the Four C's: clarity, communication, collaboration, and coordination.

Schools must explicitly name the issue, or assess current reality, determine goals for the program, and allocate personnel and resources in support of these goals. Schools need to adopt a common language and shared understanding of the expectations for academic support. Collaboration between learning specialists, program coordinators, and other support people must be intentional and consistent. The learning specialist should be included on the admissions committee, administrative team, student life committee, and department heads groups.

After assessing the number of students who have been tested or require academic support, policies for students with learning disabilities as they relate to the College Board and classroom accommodations need to be clearly stated and shared with faculty and parents. Given the sensitive nature of the issues, documentation management should be carefully considered as well. This may include setting up a database to keep track of communications about testing and accommodations. Such elements require a shared vision. Once they are in place, the real work of academic support can begin.

GOING PUBLIC ABOUT PRIVATE TUTORING — STUDENT SUPPORT

For some students, small class sizes, low student/teacher ratios, and flexible teachers willing to provide individualized instruction can still take the place of formal support services. But for many students, private tutoring has become the solution of choice. Google "Tutoring" and "Boston," for instance, and you will get 1.5 million hits. Narrowing the search to "Private Tutoring" and "Boston" yields 44,700. Recent research has found that the extent of private tutoring among private school students nationally has increased significantly. In one survey, approximately one-third of the students received some kind of private tutoring. About half of the respondents had tutoring for standardized test prep, either for entrance to private school (SSAT or ISEE) or for college entrance exams (SAT or ACT). The other half received subject-specific tutoring, most often for math, science, or writing.

Reasons for seeking private tutors vary from student to student, but what matters here is that families are turning to tutors, and they are doing so, in most cases, without the school's knowledge. Most schools are aware of the increase in tutoring, but they don't have a good handle on how many of their families hire private tutors or how much time is being spent with these tutors — nor do they have a clear sense of the quality of the tutoring.

Collaboration Among Learning Specialists

The role of the learning specialist is greater than the sum of its parts. Recognizing that learning specialists needed a cohort, a group of educators gathered at Hotchkiss School (Connecticut) in 1999 to discuss the issues unique to supporting students with LD and ADHD in independent schools. Soon after, The North East Association of Learning Specialists (NEALS) was born.

We returned to Hotchkiss in the fall of 2006 with 120 members in our network. The increasing interest speaks not only to the fact that more schools recognize the need for academic support, but also to the increasing demand for services and support.

The primary goal of NEALS is to increase collaboration and communication among learning specialists in independent schools for the purpose of improving the support that we provide to our students. A more far-reaching goal is to educate the larger community of educators, including classroom teachers, college counselors, admissions officers, health care providers, and administrators about student support. In particular, NEALS hopes to raise awareness of "cognitive diversity" among our student bodies and to expand our internal programs to address issues such as special educational law, parent assumptions and expectations, standardized testing procedures, adolescent development, ADHD, and brain research. NEALS hopes to bring academic support out of the closet and publicize what each school provides — with the hope that we can develop programs that enrich our schools as well as support our students.

Given the stigma often associated with tutoring, students tend to be quiet about the kind of tutoring they are getting outside of school. As one student put it, "No one's going to say 'I don't get it' in a school like this." But when private tutoring becomes a clandestine operation, there is a problem. According to one private tutor in suburban Boston, "Some parents do not want their child's teacher to know he or she is being tutored outside of school because they are afraid that the teacher will question how much of the work is being done by the tutor." Other parents may not want their child's teacher to know that their child is struggling. Schools need to address such fears head on. Why? Because allowing so much tutoring to be clandestine creates a disconnect between private tutors and classroom teachers that can undermine curricular expectations and instructional goals, cause students greater stress than needed, and often mask learning difficulties that could otherwise be addressed in school.

Recognizing that private tutoring is the current coin of the realm, I initiated a plan at Noble and Greenough School (Massachusetts) that we call the Independent Tutoring Network. Its goal is to improve communication and collaboration between private tutors and teachers, as well as to alleviate students' already overscheduled evenings and weekends. Previously, families found tutors through word-of-mouth or from a list of names kept on file in our academic office. What happened next was mostly between the families and the tutor. We wanted to streamline the process to be able to connect families with tutors who would best meet their child's needs. The network comprises a select group of professionals with a wide range of expertise and includes subject tutors, tutors who specialize in standardized test prep, and educational specialists who are trained to work with students who have learning differences. But the greatest value of this new openness is that the school can now coordinate services with the tutors, setting goals, facilitating communication between tutors and teachers, and establishing benchmarks to determine how those goals are met. Equally important, the transparent system helps to destigmatize support services so that students who need help can get it without feeling that they are alone.

INTERNAL SUPPORT

Students need direct support for a variety of reasons, and individual tutoring is one solution. But, in my experience, I have found that successful academic support programs are integrated into the academic program, rather than something peripheral. If we return to the student with whom we started this article, Conor, we can see how such integration works.

Conor's school had created an academic skills center to support students with learning differences. His parents shared his full neuropsychological assessment report with the director of the center. The director, in turn, read the report and wrote a Learning Profile — essentially a summary of the results, including Conor's strengths and areas of difficulty, with recommendations for accommodations and strategies. Then the director met with Conor's teachers, parents, and the psychologist who administered the assessment to discuss the findings and determine an appropriate support plan for Conor.

The new support team agreed that Conor needed weekly one-on-one tutorial assistance to help with organization and time management, along with learning strategies for planning and self-monitoring. In addition to regularly scheduled meetings with a learning specialist in the center, Conor would receive, among other accommodations, extended time on his tests, quizzes, and in-class writing assignments. The team would follow Conor's progress through bimonthly grade-level meetings, as well as quarterly grades and comments.

On the surface, this may seem a straightforward process. But, to do it well, someone has to manage it — from Conor's first referral, through the testing process, to the communication of the results and the coordination of his ongoing support, including requesting accommodations for college entrance exams.

Connor's school has a full-time coordinator of support services, as well as learning specialists on campus to help him and many other students develop the strategies they need to be successful. Direct support includes not only strategy instruction, but also helps students develop self-awareness, self-acceptance, and the opportunity to take ownership of their learning styles to be able to advocate for themselves.

TEACHER SUPPORT

For independent school teachers, the language of learning differences and accommodations can cause considerable confusion and frustration. With that in mind, we wanted to find a way to translate testing and accommodations into instructional practice. Last fall, I collaborated with a U.S. history teacher in a class that included four students who had diagnosed learning differences and established Learning Profiles. The nature of their learning differences varied, but they each called for similar accommodations, including making sure that the teacher provided a copy of the class notes or an outline of the lecture.

I spent two periods a week in the class and, working with both the teacher and the students, identified note-taking as the primary skill that students needed to develop. Student feedback gathered through questionnaires and informal interviews suggested that many students struggled to record all of the information presented in class discussion.

After I modeled note-taking by projecting my own notes of the discussion onto a screen, students took turns serving as the class note-taker. The practice proved successful on several fronts. Students with weak auditory processing skills were able to refer to the notes throughout the period, ensuring that they did not miss information. Because students experimented with the format of notes — adding graphic images, highlighting, and listing information — the level of engagement in class discussions increased.

In addition, the teacher was more available to guide the discussion because she was no longer busy trying to get all her main points on the board. Although students were still required to take their own notes, they could draw upon the collective information throughout the class period. Such collaborations in the classroom are concrete examples of how we can bridge the chasm between direct service to students with learning differences and instructional practices in the classroom.

Independent schools have the leeway, by the nature of their private status, to create their own internal policy for supporting students who need accommodations. As Rosemary Bowler, a principal and public school teacher, and Carolyn Oliver, associate director of planning at Landmark College, put it in their book, *Learning to Learn*, "The extent to which they do so and the quality and results of their programs range from grudging acceptance of the law to wholehearted endorsement of the *value of unlocking the potential of all students*" (my italics). To destigmatize our collective understanding of learning differences, and to promote the advantages of cognitive diversity, the nature of academic support needs to shift to an integrated system that helps and enriches the entire school.

Laura Vantine has worked as a learning specialist, academic support program director, and consultant in independent schools. Her primary area of interest is what factors affect the achievement of students with learning differences in independent schools. Currently, she is the coordinator of academic support at The Winsor School (Massachusetts). This article first appeared in the Summer 2008 issue of *Independent School*.

If conversations
are both honest
and respectful, we
can deepen our
understanding of both
self and others.

Let's Talk About It!
Conversations with Students about Diversity

::

BY JUDITH GASTON FISHER

For some 20 years, while working at various independent schools, I have observed a new but undefined curriculum emerging — one that has focused on educating children to tolerate, accept, appreciate, and learn from others different from themselves. We file such initiatives under the catchall category of diversity and recognize both the need and the desirability of building institutions and communities in which different backgrounds, races, and cultures are fully represented and valued.

But I've also observed at many of these schools that such initiatives have not been as successful as their creators intended. Often, they have been trial-and-error endeavors, the outcomes of which have not been measured, and the results of which have therefore been uncertain. None of that has been due to a lack of commitment or belief in the importance of diversity work, nor is it from an absence of academic study and research. As I see it, the problem in teaching our children to develop positive attitudes toward culture, race, and ethnicity has not been in the "what" or the "why," but largely in the "how." How exactly do we help students navigate the inclusive classroom and community?

Call it multicultural education, diversity, or cultural sensitivity training, each initiative I've been involved with has comprised important concepts of race, culture, religion, and socioeconomic status. But where was a school to start in developing an elementary school child's sensitivity and understanding regarding these topics?

Often the process of program development began with roundtable discussions among administrators in which questions predominated. Should teachers be educated first? What about parents? Should we mail informational fliers to them? Should teachers conduct curriculum nights? Should parents be required to attend school-supported race and equity workshops? And what about the children? Were there any "best practices" we could adopt? Should it be a separate curriculum or integrated into academic subject areas or the character education program?

At Community School (Missouri), where I work, educating the faculty of pre-kindergarten-through-sixth-grade students became the first line of attack. Seminars and in-service training focused on identifying, addressing, and role-playing stereotypes. The entire staff watched movies (e.g., *Brown Eyes, Blue Eyes*), read books (e.g., *Race Manners*), and discussed their meaning and application to our community. Teachers attended multicultural conferences and summer workshops. And various committees were formed: the committee on holidays and celebrations; one uniting the board, teachers, and parents; and one for designing international potlucks and gatherings.

Even so, it was still not clear how all this translated into the daily interactions between teacher and students.

Last September, I found myself leaving the world of administration to re-enter the classroom. Classified as a learning specialist, I now sought to face squarely the issues that I had addressed in a more indirect fashion, usually from the safe remove of a committee member engaged in interminable planning sessions. I was now alone with students, in my own classroom behind closed doors, facing the necessity of developing a realistic approach to a persistent challenge. How would I apply the tools and techniques of education to increase appreciation of cultural and racial diversity and to address the powerful cluster of harmful attitudes and practices we commonly associate with stereotyping and racism?

It was time, I believed, to roll up my sleeves and jump in feet first, to practice what I preached. I sought to go beyond class meetings and literature studies where issues were caged in the safety of fictional characters. Instead, I desired to hit these issues head-on, using reliable data and real-life stories as vehicles for discussion. I admit to second thoughts when I considered engaging students in sensitive racial discussions. I feared parent and administrative reaction. I feared perceiving the influence of stereotypes where none existed. I feared my lack of expertise. But a persistent and honest desire to raise awareness drove me forward, a desire to uncover the veil of fear surrounding the issue of race.

A small group of sixth graders became my target group. My initial materials were stories from current newspapers and journals, as well as the perspectives presented in Bruce Jacobs' *Race Manners*, a book previously studied and discussed by the faculty. We blended literature and social studies material: Paul Fleischman's *Seedfolks*, Lois Lowry's *The Giver*, and Mildred Taylor's *The Land* complemented the students' study of the Civil War and ancient cultures. The material gave psychological depth and emotional resonance to issues that provided an important key to understanding the foundations of societies and the conflicts that can wrench them apart. I often asked students to extrapolate to the current state of racial affairs in the United States. A connection could be made from the past to the present to the future. It was a beginning.

That first day when I sat down with my class — not exactly a cross-section of America, but diverse in its own distinctive way (i.e., white, African American, Jewish, and Christian) — I was scared. I had sought advice from several teachers, had spent considerable time planning my introduction, and had chosen the particular themes I wanted to discuss. Still, I was hesitant.

Attempting to be confident and to project an air of assurance, I began by having the students design guidelines for these "important discussions." We defined *respect*, *honesty*, and *confidentiality*. We even implemented a sort of fail-safe measure. Anyone could invoke the "ouch" rule — that is, just say "ouch" whenever anyone used a word or broached a topic that made others fearful or have hurt feelings.

And then I threw out the question: "If you were getting on a bus by yourself, and the only open seats were next to a black man wearing baggy, low slung jeans, or a Hispanic, or an Asian, what seat would you choose?"

There was dead silence, eyes darting sideways, heads down trying to hide in the pages of a notebook. "What is the first thought that jumped into your head?" I asked, my gaze moving from one student to another. Finally, a hand shot up. "Well, I have a Mexican gardener, so I am comfortable around Hispanics." That comment seemed to open the door for further exploration.

"I am really afraid of anyone speaking another language," offered a reticent young man. "It makes me nervous."

"I think it's the baggy pants that bothers me. When I'm in the mall, seeing someone dressed like that makes me uncomfortable. But I remember last year there was a black — I mean, an African-American — sixth grader here who wore baggy pants and a large earring. His pants were always neat and clean. And boy, was he ever a good football player," commented another.

"What race usually dresses like that?" I asked.

"Blacks, or African Americans. What term should we use anyway?" questioned the boy who had spoken about the baggy pants. "I never know what is correct so I just don't use anything!"

And so the conversation that ensued attempted to explore and discuss racial terminology, stereotypes and racism, accepted preconceptions, and "you have a problem" indicators. As the students left, I felt a mixture of success and pride as I looked forward to what our next day together might bring.

Weeks later, I had become accustomed to hearing, "Hey, Mrs. Fisher, is this a 'Talk Day'? All right!" — a frequent question tossed out as these sixth graders entered the door. Talk Day was a term coined by the students to indicate class time devoted to the exploration of these issues of race and identity. Topics of discussion were as varied as my students. We learned about identifying real fear and fear that bubbles up just because of skin color or dress. We studied statistics regarding the separation and differential treatment of minorities in our own community. Who was more likely to get pulled over by traffic police? We talked about affirmative action and the apparent resegregation of our public schools. Topics from the news media had a way of making it onto our agenda: charges against three members of the Duke University lacrosse team and reports of genocide in the Darfur region of Sudan.

While I believed that my students were beginning to understand past and present-day stereotypes, I needed more than just excitement to confirm that Talk Day was making a difference. I began to watch and note the students' mannerisms: Rachel[1], herself Jewish, was confident and verbal and ready to argue a wide range of issues; Hunter, who was white, was a sensitive boy whose head often remained resting on an arm as he saved his stories and comments until the end of class; Yolanda, the lone black girl, whose eyes gave not a glimpse of anger, acceptance, or even surprise at various accounts we considered that vividly portrayed acts of racial and social injustice against African Americans. And then there was Tom, the jokester whose indiscreet, often rash, comments betrayed a privileged and perhaps somewhat pampered life; Bob, a nonstop talker who could scarcely contain his enthusiasm for each topic; and, finally, Jim, the quiet thinker.

One non-Talk Day, I was surprised at the following conversation. Slipping into my mother's distinctive, presumably Ozark, dialect, I instructed, "Let's clean up, y'all." My

---

[1] All names of the students have been changed for confidentiality.

vocabulary included curiosities such as *anti gogglin*, *dad gummit*, and *picayune*, all phrases I assumed were indicative of my parent's southwest Missouri roots.

"Mrs. Fisher. Use proper English! You sound like a Texan," concluded Bob as he shut down his laptop.

"Hey, that's a stereotype… isn't it?" remarked Yolanda trying to apply what had earlier been discussed in class. She eyed me cautiously waiting for my remark.

"Is it?" I countered.

"Well, Bob implied that all Texans speak like you just did. That is a stereotype." The conversation among the children continued as they filed out the classroom for their next subject.

As the year drew to a close, the students completed a written survey regarding Talk Day. Did I find that authentic discussions based on factual information promoted a personal awareness of stereotypes and racial issues? Definitely. Each student enjoyed Talk Days, identified personal stereotypes and those used by others, and became aware of actions stemming from stereotypes. Yolanda wrote, "[Understanding stereotypes] makes me move forward and get to really know other people better, instead of being put off by 'weird' dress or behavior. Who knows, they could turn out to be my best friend."

One of the deepest lessons I believe my students have learned has to do with the power of conversation. My students were able to talk about difficult and sometimes uncomfortable realities. Inequalities built around race, religion, gender, and other distinctions are often pervasive, but they are also typically obscure, and students can benefit from seeking to take their measure. These steps can help:

- Talk with students; don't lecture them. Help them find their voice.
- Work across the curriculum. Diversity is a big topic that can reach across various subject areas and tie them together in powerful ways.
- Connect outside the classroom. The relevance of race, ethnicity, and gender can be witnessed daily, whether the perspective is global, local, or personal.

If conversations are both honest and respectful, we can deepen our understanding of both self and others. But if the toughest or most-sensitive topics are "off-limits" or given shallow treatment, students will have little faith in the power of open inquiry and clear thinking to chip away at our most intractable problems. I haven't created global harmony, but my students' eyes have been opened.

Judith Gaston Fisher is a teaching specialist at Community School (Missouri). This article first appeared in the Fall 2007 issue of *Independent School*.

Increased awareness, increased connectedness, and increased capacity to help or hurt others, of course, bring increased responsibilities.

Going Glocal
Adaptive Education for Local and Global Citizenship

::

BY CHRIS HARTH

Many independent schools have come to understand their obligations to their neighbors, but in this age of growing connectedness—locally, nationally, and globally—who exactly are our neighbors?

Calling for an embrace of what he describes as "cosmopolitanism," Kwame Anthony Appiah, professor of philosophy at Princeton University, argues persuasively that ongoing technological changes in recent years have rendered strangers in distant lands into neighbors — as real to us as those in our local communities. While we remain physically distant from "others," such distances are regularly bridged with rapid transit or instantaneous communication. For better or worse, what happens in one country increasingly ripples across the planet and affects people in other countries. Such interconnectedness and interdependence are now found in a host of essential fields — especially in areas related to economics, the environment, and human health — with important moral implications for all residents of our shared planet.

Given this new human landscape, educators have little choice but to consider both the meaning and effects of such changing conditions. Indeed, the ethical and educational implications could hardly be more important.

Ubuntu

One useful ethical cornerstone in such an interconnected, "glocal" world is the notion of ubuntu, a Bantu term that Archbishop Desmond Tutu and others translate roughly as "I am because we are" and that involves defining ourselves in our interactions with others. Much like Buddhist principles of first doing no harm and then doing as much good as possible, ubuntu emphasizes the connectedness we share and how much we help or hurt ourselves as we help or hurt others.

As Nelson Mandela has noted, even if one wants to improve his or her own lot in life, this should be done in a way that does not make it harder for someone else to do the same thing; rather, we should seek to capitalize on those positive-sum opportunities that can uplift all people or, at the very least, will not lower some in the process.

THE EMERGENT GLOBAL IMPERATIVE

Technological advances in communications, transportation, and information processing have deepened and broadened connections on multiple levels, local through global, thickening the webs of interactivity that bind us to each other economically, politically, militarily, socially, culturally, environmentally, and ethically. As with most complex systems, changes in one domain or part of the world affect what happens in others, with small changes often magnified because of the interconnectedness of the system and because of the power of positive feedback loops to reinforce emergent patterns of thought and behavior. Malcolm Gladwell highlighted some of this in his best seller, *The Tipping Point*, and other researchers have made it crystal clear. More than ever before, our local actions can generate expanding waves of effects, some of which are unintended and unpredictable. At the same time, regional, national, and global waves wash up on local shores and must be reconciled and applied in local contexts.

These two-way causal flows — local interactions generating global trends and global trends being adapted for local contexts — capture the essence of the term, "glocalization," which was coined by British sociologist Roland Robertson (who credits the Japanese word dochakuka as his inspiration). Robertson defines "glocalization" as "the simultaneity — the co-presence — of both universalizing and particularizing tendencies." In *The World Is Flat*, Thomas Friedman also used this term, defining it as the process by which a "culture easily absorbs foreign ideas and best practices and melds those with its own traditions." In Friedman's case, however, he captures only the global-to-local dynamic, while missing the other side of the equation.

Beyond characterizing the emergent nature of our operating environment, such mutually constitutive relations between local and global levels also influence our identities — a complicated, evolving notion of who we think we are. Consider, for instance, something as simple as how we respond to the question, "Where are you from?" Most of us tend to identify with multiple places and sustain multiple levels of loyalty to them, which are sometimes overlapping and sometimes conflicting. We are simultaneously citizens of a locality, a state or province, a country, and the planet we all share. In this sense, we are all "glocal" citizens.

Increased awareness, increased connectedness, and increased capacity to help or hurt others, of course, bring increased responsibilities. While we may have a greater obligation to those who are close to us than to those who are distant, the dividing lines between these two groups are now blurred. Many problems in our world — extensive poverty, pandemics, economic or political instability, environmental degradation, fanatical ideologies, or terrorism, to name but a few — easily spill over borders and generate transnational challenges that cannot be ignored nor effectively redressed unilaterally. Instead, multiple actors — especially those with the greatest at stake and the capacity to create positive change — must address such borderless challenges.

In this sense, citizens of the United States have a particularly large role to play, as do independent schools and their leaders. As the nation with the greatest capacity to catalyze and sustain change, the United States is uniquely positioned on the proverbial peak of the international landscape. While unlikely to last forever, this position brings with it important responsibilities, not the least of which involve educating our young citizens as effectively as possible. In a global context, this means preparing them for the myriad opportunities and challenges that they will face in their adult lives and helping them to grasp the ongoing changes in our world; teaching them to be flexible and adaptive, reflective and imaginative, forward-looking and growth-oriented; and instilling in them a healthy respect for themselves and others, given how often they will need to work with others to solve common problems or realize shared objectives.

A similarly adaptive orientation would serve educational leaders well as they strive to keep up with the quickening pace of change. Such adaptive leadership will help them look ahead, assess changing contexts (local through global), and craft suitable strategies, policies, and practices that can best prepare themselves, their students and faculty members, and their institutions for the future. Given the inherent autonomy, relative flexibility, and greater potential to enact efficaciously purposeful change, independent schools have a particularly important role to play — both for their own communities and as potential models for other schools that do not have the same capacity to adjust as readily.

Regardless of institution type and the local challenges associated with adaptation to the changing landscape, all educational leaders must recognize that, as the world spins, our contexts, connections, and communities continue to evolve. The world into which our students will enter is not the same world in which today's adults grew up. What was once necessary and sufficient educational preparation may no longer be either. This is not to say that independent schools need to completely reinvent themselves. Much of what independent schools have offered students for decades — educating for both mind and heart, the self and others — still holds sway. But it does mean that they need to be ready and willing to adapt to the sea changes in our evolving contexts and communities.

THE GLOCAL SCHOOLHOUSE

With this emergent "glocal" reality as the backdrop, what type of education do our young citizens need in order to develop identities and connections to multiple communities? How can we prepare them for this type of interconnectedness and dynamism? More specifically, what knowledge, skills, and perspectives will best enable them to thrive as glocal citizens?

As a starting point, all students should have a base level of knowledge in key subject areas, including mathematics, the sciences, the arts, the humanities, and social studies. As author E.D. Hirsch, Jr. and others have argued, this essential background information enables people to be "culturally literate" and, therefore, to interact more effectively with others who share such knowledge. However, given intensifying global interactivity and the expanding context for learning and living, we need to update our definitions of "core knowledge" to include essential elements from non-Western cultures, which currently include roughly 85 percent of the world's population. While knowledge of Western heritage remains necessary, it grows less sufficient daily.

Increasingly, all students should have awareness of, and appreciation for, cultures from around the world — near and far. Moreover, they need to understand their global and local contexts and the various levels in between. Toward these ends, they should study world art, literature, and religions, as well as world history, geography, economics, and politics — which, of course, include local, national, and regional facets. Multidisciplinary, issue-oriented classes — especially those with real-world, service-learning, and other experiential opportunities — offer one promising vehicle for engaging students, but multiple means can effect such ends.

While core knowledge is indispensable, it is but one of three essential components of glocal literacy and competence. No less important are the various skill sets that can empower young citizens to thrive in multiple contexts and communities. We live in a technology-rich era with an abundance of accessible information. Facts, theories, and other bits of information can be retrieved via any computer or phone connected to the Internet. While digital divides still prevent all people from having equal access to such

Practicing Glocal Citizenship

Local and global learning opportunities can and should be combined to generate transformational educational outcomes. Local subjects can be explored with international guests; global topics can be collaboratively studied with local partners; and international partners can work together to serve local communities. As part of a larger effort to help connect neighbors, exchange views, broaden perspectives, and prepare glocal citizens, students at St. Andrew's Episcopal School (Mississippi) have role-played with students from six other schools in the area in a geopolitical simulation with author Harm de Blij, competed in statewide events such as Model United Nations and the International Economic Summit, and coordinated with other schools to visit local international exhibits and museums.

Student travel progresses from the local and state levels in the lower school, through regional and national travel in the middle school, to international travel in the upper school. Parent-student trips to Mexico and Italy are now offered in grades 5-8 and more than a dozen international trips and exchanges to five continents

offered for grades 9-12, with a growing emphasis on service, sustainability, and the developing world.

In addition to offering student and faculty grants at St. Andrew's to support such layered travel, faculty participate in professional development on local, state, regional, national, and international levels. St. Andrew's students and faculty also have been piloting new models of reciprocal service — with teams of students from St. Andrew's and the Hermann Gmeiner International College in Ghana performing joint service-learning projects in both Mississippi and Ghana.

Even more potentially transformative is a new three-tiered exchange program with Carnoustie High School in Scotland. One team hosts and performs joint community service in one locality, followed by reversed roles of hosting/visiting and more joint local service. The program concludes with a trip to a third place, unfamiliar to both sets of participants, where they can again live and work side-by-side, experience something new together, and learn about themselves and "others" as they contribute positively to multiple communities.

information, we often find ourselves now wrestling with too much information, trying to discern what is reliable and relevant for a given question and whittling away less germane sources.

Increasingly, students need to learn how to ask the right questions and how to sift through various sources of information to find workable answers. They also need to be able to identify and research important issues, to analyze and share the information they process, and to collaborate with people from other parts of the world to solve our shared problems and realize our shared opportunities. In this respect, the premium on cross-cultural communication skills and foreign language proficiency continues to grow, as does the value of technological competence and computer skills.

At the same time, we cannot afford to slight more traditional concerns such as reading and writing. Nor are quantitative and scientific skills any less important in our current era. The growing challenge with developing age-appropriate skills,[1] as with suitable background knowledge, is to integrate emergent concerns with key concepts, building

---

[1] For a widely cited and useful framework for thinking about what knowledge and skills might be most appropriate for our current age, along with specific suggestions as to how we might best promote them, see The Partnership for 21st Century Skills at *www.21stcenturyskills.org/*.

on the necessary base to generate a higher and more appropriate level of sufficiency —
in terms of both knowledge and skills — for our ever-changing contexts.

More important than skills and knowledge are perspectives and attitudes. These
help shape our vision, define our character, and influence how we live our lives. They
also affect the questions we ask, the knowledge we pursue, the skills we develop, and
how we put these qualities and information together to do good work. Given their role
as underlying drivers, perspectives and attitudes are pivotal for education and citizenship. Specifically, we need to cultivate glocal perspectives and attitudes in our students,
including an awareness of our growing interconnectedness, an appreciation of cultures
from all over the world, and a willingness to consider different viewpoints and opinions.

As glocal citizens, our students should recognize both similarities and differences,
avoiding prejudice and bigotry as they try to learn about themselves and others. Top
priorities also include an inquisitive spirit and a lifelong love of learning, as well as an
understanding of complexity and an appreciation for nuance. In a shifting terrain with
multiple actors, inchoate identities, and evolving ends and means, our citizens must be
intellectually engaged and agile; open-minded and pragmatic with their selection of
appropriate tools and techniques; and ready, willing, and able to adapt to changing
conditions.

As part of their attitudinal repertoire, our young citizens must develop an ethical
compass that enables them to see beyond themselves, to recognize their connections and
obligations to others, and to chart a responsible course of action that will serve them,
their families, and their communities — including their schools, neighborhoods, towns
and cities, counties, states, regions, countries, and shared planet, (See Ubuntu sidebar.)
Balancing and fulfilling these numerous and sometimes conflicting demands is one of
the challenges associated with glocal citizenship.

Difficulty, however, does not obviate responsibility. We do not often get to choose
whether we are citizens of our towns, state, nation, or planet. We are all of these, and
more, simultaneously. To this end, it is vital that young citizens not only have the req-
uisite knowledge and skills, but also actually put their knowledge and skills into action
while still in school. Doing so helps them build the self-confidence they need to believe
that such steps are feasible and can make a difference. (See sidebar, "Practicing Glocal
Citizenship.") In this respect, glocal research, collaboration, service, and internships can
be wonderful complements to classroom learning. They can serve as powerful developmental tools that reinforce the need for and viability of the hallmark of glocal citizenship: concerted and constructive action on multiple levels, local through global.

Ultimately, what matters most is that we prepare our students for their increasingly connected futures and provide the tools they will need to succeed and lead in multiple communities and a rapidly changing world.

THE WORLD TO COME

The vast majority of humanity currently lives as what Harm de Blij, author of *The Power of Place* calls "locals" in the developing world. Current population projections indicate that another two billion people may inhabit the planet with us in the next 40 years, almost all of whom also will live in the developing world, mostly in urban areas. In the same timeframe, projections have the population of the United States increasing by another third, with half of us as people of color. Without question, the challenges ahead will be great. Those individuals, groups, and institutions with wealth, power, and access must work with their neighbors to integrate the less enfranchised and to provide opportunities for them to improve their circumstances — or else the socioeconomic, environmental, and political challenges we face are only likely to grow.

Much like the collaborative, forward-looking leadership needed on the international stage, educational leaders need to recognize these changing circumstances, appreciate local constraints and opportunities, and work with others to identify and actualize strategic steps forward. With a view toward maximizing multiplier effects and positive feedback loops, successful leaders rally others to important causes, encourage them to think anew, empower them to grow, and bring them together as an adaptive community

In the context of a school, this translates into a thriving learning, teaching, and serving community. The more students and faculty can work together in a lifelong pursuit of knowledge, virtue, and excellence — Aristotle's notion of areté — and in the service of others, the more meaningful and constructive the educational experience and the more valuable the associated civic preparedness. Ideally, educational leaders model such behavior with and for faculty, faculty model it with and for students, and then students have the opportunity to put it all into practice, at an early age and in authentic settings. If they do this, the knowledge, skills, and values that they learn will serve them and others well.

Chris Harth currently serves as both president of the Global Studies Foundation, an educational nonprofit, and co-chair of the Assessment Community for the National Council for the Social Studies, as well as the director of global studies and world languages at St. Andrew's Episcopal School (Mississippi). This article first appeared in the Fall 2010 issue of *Independent School*.

REFERENCES

Benedict Anderson, *Imagined Communities: Reflections on the Origin and Spread of Nationalism*, Revised Edition (London: Verso, 1991).

Kwame Anthony Appiah, *Cosmopolitanism: Ethics in a World of Strangers* (New York: W. W. Norton, 2006).

Per Bak, *How Nature Works: The Science of Self-Organized Criticality* (New York: Copernicus, 1996).

James A. Banks, *Educating Citizens in a Multicultural Society*, 2nd Edition (New York: Teachers College Press, 2007).

Albert-Laszlo Barabasi, *Linked: How Everything Is Connected to Everything Else and What It Means* (Cambridge, MA: Perseus Publishing, 2002).

Mark, Buchanan, *Ubiquity: The Science of History … or Why the World Is Simpler Than We Think* (London: Weidenfeld and Nicolson, 2000).

Nicholas A. Christakis and James H. Fowler, *Connected: The Surprising Power of Social Networks and How They Shape Our Lives* (New York: Little, Brown and Company, 2009).

Harm de Blij, *The Power of Place: Geography, Destiny, and Globalization's Rough Landscape* (New York: Oxford University Press, 2009).

Carol S. Dweck, *Mindset: The New Psychology of Success* (New York: Random House, 2007).

Thomas L. Friedman, *The World Is Flat: A Brief History of the Twenty-First Century* (New York: Farrar, Straus, and Giroux, 2005).

Malcolm Gladwell, *The Tipping Point: How Little Things Can Make a Big Difference* (New York: Little, Brown and Company, 2000).

Ronald Heiftiz, Alexander Grashow, and Marty Linsky, *The Practice of Adaptive Leadership: Tools and Tactics for Changing Your Organization and the World* (Cambridge, MA: Harvard Business Press, 2009).

E.D. Hirsch, Jr., *Cultural Literacy: What Every American Needs to Know* (New York: Houghton Mifflin, 1987).

John H. Holland, *Hidden Order: How Adaptation Builds Complexity* (Reading, MA: Helix Books/Addison-Wesley, 1995).

Ryszard Kapuscinski, *The Other* (New York: Verso, 2008).

Merry M. Merryfield and Angene Wilson, *Social Studies and the World: Teaching Global Perspectives* (Silver Spring, MD: National Council for the Social Studies, 2005).

Martha C. Nussbaum, *Cultivating Humanity: A Classical Defense of Reform in Liberal Education* (Cambridge, MA: Harvard University Press, 1997).

Daniel H. Pink, *A Whole New Mind: Why Right-Brainers Will Rule the Future* (New York: Riverhead Books, 2005).

Roland Robertson, "Comments on the 'Global Triad' and 'Glocalization,'" in *Globalization and Indigenous Culture*, ed. Nobutaka Tnoue, (Institute for Japanese Culture and Classics, Kokugakuin University, 1997), available online at *www2.k0kugakuin.ac.jp/ijcc/wp/global/15robertson.html*.

Saskia Sassen, "The Repositioning of Citizenship: Emergent Subjects and Spaces for Politics," *Berkeley Journal of Sociology* (2002): Vol. 46.

Harold Sprout and Margaret Sprout, *The Ecological Perspective on Human Affairs* (Princeton, NJ: Princeton University Press, 1965).

Tony Wagner, *The Global Achievement Gap* (New York: Basic Books, 2008).

The Inclusive School
A Selection of Writing on Diversity Issues in Independent Schools

…the ideas you are indoctrinated with from early childhood through eight or nine years old are the ideas that will **permeate your being** and influence you for the rest of your life.

Bridging the Culture Gap
Diversity and International Relations

BY SUSAN CHENARD

Given the technological advancements in transportation and communications, no nation can isolate itself from others. Like it or not, we are interdependent.

And, like it or not, ours is a multicultural world. When our children grow up they will be called upon to make decisions in the interest of human progress that will demand extensive knowledge of many cultures. As educators, we are called upon to instill cultural knowledge now, eliminate misconceptions, and model appropriate behavior by accommodating ethnic diversity and promoting mutual coexistence.

As I reflected upon my own insular educational experience in the United States in public and private schools compared to the multicultural educational experiences of expatriate children in Persian Gulf countries and in Egypt where I have served as an educator, I was drawn by a recent statement by Robin Cook, the British Foreign Secretary, in *The Egyptian Gazette*. Calling for greater understanding with Islamic culture, he encouraged high-level dialogues between European Union and the Organization of Islamic Conference. "We must work together to improve our understanding of each other, to break down stereotypes and erase mistrust," he said. "Osama bin Laden is no more representative of Islam than the [Unibomber or Oklahoma City bombers] are of the values of the West." Cook develops his point clearly, but it all boils down to the need for all of us to understand cultural diversity. My own experiences confirm this need. Educators across the disciplines, in the U.S. and abroad, must embrace ethnic diversity in all its richness and prepare students to break down barriers of ignorance.

What follows are some of my observations of education in the United States, a Persian Gulf country (which I prefer not to name), and Egypt where I currently teach.

STARTING OUT IN AN INSULAR AMERICA

My Western cultural experience is based upon my childhood in New Britain, Connecticut, where my days at private religious elementary schools and in a public secondary school led me to view the world from a culturally limited perspective. In the 1960s and 1970s, New Britain was the home of Fortune 500 industrial giants such as Stanley Tool and was known as the "hardware city of the world." These industrial giants supported the integration of immigrants from Europe, Korea, and Latin America. My private, elementary school classmates were ethnically Irish, Scottish, Italian, Lebanese, African-American, German, and Slavic (from Poland and Lithuania). Some of these children were first-generation Americans. No one had any difficulty speaking English, although some of them spoke a second language at home.

What we held in common was our Roman Catholic beliefs — and they served to insulate us from other religious and ethical views. As Catholics, for instance, we were trained to believe that our faith was the one and only. At the same time, we were instructed to respect and tolerate others as children of God who held different beliefs and opinions. But given the fact that our Catholic culture was the dominant one, it was hard not to view others of different religions "warily."

As educators know, the ideas you are indoctrinated with from early childhood through eight or nine years old are the ideas that will permeate your being and influence you for the rest of your life. Good news and bad news underlies that truth. The bad news is it is difficult (but not impossible) to create better understanding among adults of vastly different cultures. The good news is that we have a real opportunity with children. By introducing young children to basic knowledge of cultural diversity, we can pave the way for future generations to avoid conflicts and coexist in peace.

In the 1970s, American public high schools were short on revenues because of the migration of industries to points south of New England. Without the tax revenues from the industrial giants, our two-high-school city was forced to consolidate into one massive high school. Children from all over town were bused to the new single high school. Although not by thoughtful planning, the new high school became a religiously, ethnically, and racially diverse group of about 3,000 students.

As a college-bound, advanced-placement student, my experience in a large, public, ethnically diverse population had both advantages and disadvantages. On the positive side, I indirectly gained knowledge of other ethnic groups within the community, which led me to question some of my own views and to explore religious and ethical differences. The enormous melting pot helped me to clarify exactly what I believed and previously took for granted. That could not have happened in my previous school because I had been surrounded by people who thought the same way that I did. Although challenging at times, my experiences in a multicultural high school helped me grow personally and gave me a much stronger sense of identity. Key to this growth was learning that my views had been culturally and ethnically biased.

At the same time, the cultural diversity did create tension in the system, and violent outbreaks occurred at times. Most of the violence seemed to be racially and economically motivated. From my limited white, middle-class perspective, I at first believed that poor and underprivileged black and Hispanic students had deliberately joined forces to adversely alter the educational policies of the majority white administration and student body.

It was an era when antidiscrimination laws were being newly enforced, and our city was encouraging welfare recipients to move in to boost its financial support from the federal government. It was a highly politically charged environment. Students led numerous demonstrations for minority rights.

Looking back on this scenario, with insight from an article by Mark Nathan Cohen, a professor of anthropology at the State University of New York, "Culture, Not Race, Explains Human Diversity" (*The Chronicle of Higher Education*, October 1998), I would now conclude that a gross misunderstanding of cultural diversity was a large part of the problem. White middle-class educators and administrators in the 1970s were blinded by their own ethnocentric value systems and unable to understand the behavior of minorities in context. They were quick to judge what other people were doing based on their own biased, stereotypical perceptions of race and their ignorance of cultural diversity. All this at a time when our educational community's critical challenge was to open up a dialogue between diverse minority and ethnic groups and to promote knowledge and understanding of the needs of all people from different economic, racial, and ethnic backgrounds.

CONFRONTING TRIBAL VALUES

In June of 1989, I accepted a teaching position in the Persian Gulf. As an educator, I was immediately struck by the differences between the modern industrial society's approach and values and those of an insular, developing, and traditional society. The schools were both religiously and culturally intolerant. Children were trained to believe that their culture was superior to all others and that Islam was the only religion in the world. Within the Gulf school system, even the knowledge of other religions was banned. Children learned about other cultures and religions from watching cable television programs, which unfortunately only enhanced stereotypical views of Westerners as rich, promiscuous, and immoral. This distorted Hollywood image led some local people to hate all Westerners.

In school, misinformed local children sometimes singled out expatriate children as targets of harassment. Of course, that harassment was not from or supported by everyone. Generally speaking, it is natural in a traditional society where social classifications are accepted that outsiders are not appreciated or tolerated. I recall a second grade expatriate girl's experience when one of her classmates stood up in class and shouted that her parents were dirty and they would all burn in hell. Fortunately, the Syrian homeroom teacher quickly responded by punishing the naughty girl and trying to comfort the expatriate girl.

When I retold the story in the expatriate community, I discovered that others had similar experiences and, in even greater frequency, in isolated rural areas. It seemed that the frequency and severity of negative social encounters were directly related to the local people's level of education and exposure to different cultures. In urban areas with a larger population of educated individuals, I found a greater willingness to accept other cultures.

Of course, it is difficult to ignore the political context for such cases, especially given all that has gone on in the world between Arabs and Westerners. Arab politicians certainly suffer a great deal of frustration as they battle diplomatically in the international community to protect the rights of Muslims around the world who are being challenged by Western biases toward Arabs and Muslims. The case in Bosnia most vividly comes to mind.

One of the greatest challenges for the Gulf country is to find a means of instilling knowledge and replacing the old insular and markedly ignorant tribal values of people's grandparents with moderate and tolerant Islamic ethics and values. Moderate Islamic approaches will eliminate ignorance and instill knowledge that will successfully lead the country into a strong and peaceful position in the international community. It is interesting to note that the Koran teaches that we were made into nations and tribes so that we may know each other (49:13). This "knowing" or knowledge is what helps us to avoid conflict.

EMBRACING MULTICULTURAL TOLERANCE

By contrast, in Egypt, a semi-modern developing Arab country with an economy that highly depends on international tourism, I experienced a great willingness among Egyptians to tolerate and accommodate Western culture and diverse religious values. Historically in Egypt, Muslims and Coptic Christians have lived together in harmony for generations. Their children are educated together, and the dependence of the Egyptian economy on promoting tourism has affected the Egyptian educational system. Egyptian educators reinforce the importance of harmonious coexistence of Muslims and Coptics as being of primary importance to the social stability of the nation. The Egyptian people are first Egyptians and second Muslims and Christians. This attitude is similar to what I know in the States.

In schools, the children use textbooks that directly promote cultural tolerance and respect for ethnic diversity. In my first two years in Cairo, I was affiliated with Egyptian private language schools, and two years later I moved to the secular American school system. The differences between the two systems — from a moral and ethical perspective — is instructive.

Of course, it was a major transition to move from a traditional, religiously intolerant school system to a private, semi-modem, religiously tolerant, international Egyptian language school. In Egypt, Arabic and English were taught "equally" in the curriculum, and French was presented as a second language. Both Christian and Muslim students were accepted. I was fascinated to observe Egyptian children who had been educated in the Gulf make the transition into the Egyptian educational system. These Gulf-educated children were amazed when they realized that both Muslims and Christians were together in the same school. The only time the Christian and Muslim children were apart was when they were sent to different classrooms to study religion.

The private Egyptian language schools acknowledged both Muslim and Christian holidays. The schools wanted to make it very clear that Muslims could tolerate and peacefully coexist with Christians. At this point, I was correctly learning that Islam, in fact, does tolerate other religions, and it does teach that nations should not despise each other. Each child's religious, moral, and ethical values were preserved and honored, yet all students were integrated to study non-religious curricular subjects. Negative incidents in Egypt against other cultures were related to isolated, ignorant groups who were unable to appreciate or tolerate differences in other cultures' values and lifestyles.

Upon moving to Cairo American College (CAC), a modern, international, secular school system, I observed teachers and administrators for the most part attempting to treat students from diverse backgrounds equally, with respect and tolerance. CAC wants to set the moral tone of multicultural tolerance, and that tone, at least officially, dominates the environment. That's not to say that the potential for ethnocentricity doesn't exist. American cultural values predominate. Children from non-American countries, for better or worse, quickly change their way of dressing and speaking to match the styles and manners of the American children and professionals.

Within such a multicultural community, there are also cliques of children whose parents all work at the same company and cliques of those from the same home country. Many of the children who attend our school have never lived in their "home" country or the country of their parents and are considered "global nomads." They form another clique in our school.

One of the challenges of the school is to help children who have never lived outside their own country understand their new host country. The things these children say, the way they dress, and some of their behavior, which they previously took for granted, may be offensive to people in their host country. The children need to learn how to positively deal with the frustration of making changes to avoid conflicts in the community. Leaving family and friends behind and having to make new friends is difficult enough, but now they need to change their way of thinking and behaving. It's a challenge for them.

Many programs are offered with the intention of helping new students make friends and participate socially in activities that highlight their own distinct talents and abilities. The fact that CAC offers such a large variety of activities does make it possible for students to find their own niche. In addition, CAC's institution within the curriculum of the Egypt Culture program has been highly successful in positively introducing students to Egyptian Coptic and Islamic values and Egypt's rich heritage and natural beauties.

As an international school, CAC students do experience a certain degree of ethnically and racially motivated harassment from their classmates and faculty and administrators. What's important is how the school deals with these situations when they occur — violating parties are sometimes expelled from school — and how the school infuses the curriculum with lessons of tolerance, acceptance, and understanding, promoting cultural diversity.

CAC has a multifaceted program that reaches students, parents, and new faculty quickly and efficiently. New-student orientation programs the first week of school provide initial awareness of cultural issues, and an Egypt Culture program is offered to students within the curriculum. The Community Service Offices provides parents with open discussion forums within the school during orientation and throughout the year. Brochures are also distributed to inform parents and family members of programs of the parent teacher association, community centers, and religious institutions. Faculty and administrators are also reached via orientation programs that promote tolerance of ethnic diversity. In addition, the school's teachers association takes an active role in promoting activities that encourage tolerance and respect for local customs and traditions.

What I've learned from my experiences in the United States, the Persian Gulf, and Egypt is that the commonly shared fundamental source of tension and negative social interaction is ignorance of, and the consequent lack of appreciation for, cultural diversity. I've come to believe that, as educators, we have a moral duty to instill knowledge of cultural diversity, eliminate misconceptions, and model tolerance of all diverse religious and ethnic backgrounds to our students. Educators across disciplines must train students to recognize the importance of understanding cultural relativism and to get beyond the blinders that foster racism.

As American independent schools strive for a greater diversity, they can take a lesson from the international schools where educators must be consciously aware of the ignorant racially or ethnically motivated remarks made by individual students and of the self-selective grouping of students in class as they relate to religious and ethnic diversity. This applies to all other forms of diversity as well. Groups can be designed by instructors to include a variety of students. By modeling respect and tolerance for a wide array of outlooks and opinions, educators can help students learn that diversity enriches all of our lives.

Advanced technology and communication systems have broken down the barriers that allowed for insular educational policies. Whether a school is domestic or international, there is a critical global need for the knowledge of cultural diversity. Schools must set a moral tone of tolerance for cultural diversity and cooperate among themselves to find solutions to problems that arise as a result of diverse opinions.

The safety and prosperity of our future generations depend on that knowledge.

At the time this article was written, **Susan Chenard** taught at the Cairo American College in Egypt. She is currently a professor of English at Gateway Community College in New Haven, Connecticut. This article first appeared in the Winter 1999 issue of *Independent School*.